ADOBE® PREMIERE® 6

Digital Video Editing

AGAINST THE CLOCK
PERFORMANCE SUPPORT & TRAINING SYSTEMS

Prentice
Hall

Upper Saddle River, NJ 07458

Library of Congress Cataloging-in-Publication Data

Adobe Premiere 6.0: Digital Video Editing/Against The Clock.
    p.   cm. -- (Against The Clock series)
ISBN 0-13-094261-8
1.Motion pictures — Editing — Data Processing. 2. Digital Video.
3. Adobe Premiere. I. Against The Clock (Firm) II. Series.

T3899 .A37 2002
778.5'235'0285 — dc21

2001036243

Editor-in-Chief: Stephen Helba
Director of Production and Manufacturing: Bruce Johnson
Executive Editor: Elizabeth Sugg
Managing Editor-Editorial: Judy Casillo
Editorial Assistant: Anita Rhodes
Managing Editor-Production: Mary Carnis
Production Editor: Denise Brown
Composition: Against the Clock, Inc.
Design Director: Cheryl Asherman
Senior Design Coordinator: Miguel Ortiz
Cover Design: LaFortezza Design Group, Inc.
Icon Design: James Braun
Prepress: Photoengraving, Inc.
Printer/Binder: Press of Ohio

Pearson Education LTD.
Pearson Education Australia PTY, Limited
Pearson Education Singapore, Pte. Ltd
Pearson Education North Asia Ltd
Pearson Education Canada, Ltd.
Pearson Educación de Mexico, S.A. de C.V.
Pearson Education -- Japan
Pearson Education Malaysia, Pte. Ltd
Pearson Education, Upper Saddle River, New Jersey

10 9 8 7 6 5 4 3 2 1

ISBN 0-13-094261-8

Contents

Purpose

The Against The Clock series has been developed specifically for those involved in the field of computer arts and now — animation, video and multimedia production. Many of our readers are already involved in the industry in advertising and printing, television production, multimedia and Web design. Others are just now preparing for a career within these professions.

This series will provide you with the necessary skills to work in these fast-paced, exciting and rapidly expanding fields. While many people feel that they can simply purchase a computer and the appropriate software and begin designing and producing quality presentations, the real world of high-quality printed and Web communications requires a far more serious commitment.

The Series

The applications presented in the Against The Clock series stand out as the programs of choice in professional computer arts environments.

We've used a modular design for the Against The Clock series, allowing you to mix and match the drawing, imaging, multimedia and page-layout applications that exactly suit your specific needs.

Titles available in the Against The Clock series include:

Macintosh: Basic Operations
Windows: Basic Operations
Adobe Illustrator: Introduction and Advanced Digital Illustration
Macromedia FreeHand: Digital Illustration
Adobe InDesign: Introduction and Advanced Electronic Mechanicals
Adobe PageMaker: Introduction and Advanced Electronic Mechanicals
QuarkXPress: Introduction and Advanced Electronic Mechanicals
Microsoft Publisher: Creating Electronic Mechanicals
Microsoft PowerPoint: Presentation Graphics with Impact
Microsoft FrontPage: Designing for the Web
MetaCreations Painter: A Digital Approach to Natural Art Media
Adobe Photoshop: Introduction and Advanced Digital Images
Adobe Premiere: Digital Video Editing
Macromedia Director: Creating Powerful Multimedia
Macromedia Flash: Animating for the Web
Macromedia Dreamweaver: Creating Web Pages
File Preparation: The Responsible Electronic Page
Preflight: An Introduction to File Analysis and Repair
TrapWise and PressWise: Digital Trapping and Imposition

We've designed our courses to be "cross-platform." While many sites use Macintosh computers, there is an increasing number of graphic arts service providers using Intel-based systems running Windows (or WindowsNT). The books in this series are applicable to either of these systems.

All of the applications that we cover in the Against The Clock series are similar in operation and appearance, whether you're working on a Macintosh or a Windows system. When a particular function does differ from machine to machine, we present both.

There are a number of standard icons that you will see in the sidebars. Each has a standard meaning. Pay close attention to the sidebar notes as you will find valuable comments that will help you throughout this course and in your everyday use of your computer. The standard icons are:

The **Pencil** icon indicates a comment from an experienced operator or instructor. Whenever you see the pencil icon, you'll find corresponding sidebar text that augments or builds upon the subject being discussed at the time.

The **Bomb** or **Pitfalls** icon indicates a potential problem or difficulty. For instance, a certain technique might lead to pages that prove difficult to output. In other cases, there might be something that a program cannot easily accomplish, so we might present a workaround.

The **Pointing Finger** icon indicates a hands-on activity — whether a short exercise or a complete project. Note that sometimes this icon will direct you to the back of the book to complete a project.

The **Key** icon is used to point out that there is a keyboard equivalent to a menu or dialog-box option. Key commands are often faster than using the mouse to select a menu option. Experienced operators often mix the use of keyboard equivalents and menu/ dialog box selections to arrive at their optimum speed.

If you are a Windows user, be sure to refer to the corresponding text or images whenever you see this **Windows** icon. Although there isn't a great deal of difference between using these applications on a Macintosh and using them on a Windows-based PC, there are certain instances where there's enough of a difference for us to comment.

For the Reader

On the CD-ROM, you will find a complete set of Against The Clock (ATC) fonts, as well as a collection of data files you will use to construct the various exercises and projects.

The ATC fonts are solely for use while you are working with the Against The Clock materials. These fonts will be used throughout both the exercises and projects, and are provided in both Macintosh and Windows formats.

A variety of resource files have been included. These files, necessary to complete both the exercises and projects, are also provided in Macintosh and Windows formats. These files may be found on the CD-ROM within the RF-Premiere folder.

For the Instructor

The Instructor's CD-ROM includes various testing and presentation materials in addition to the files that are supplied with this book.

- **Overhead Presentation Materials** are provided and follow along with the book. These presentations are prepared using Microsoft PowerPoint, and are provided in both native PowerPoint format and Acrobat Portable Document Format (PDF).

- **Extra Projects** are provided along with the data files required for completion. These projects may be used to extend the training session, or they may be used to test the reader's progress.

- **Test Questions and Answers** are included on the Instructor's CD-ROM. These questions may be modified and/or reorganized.

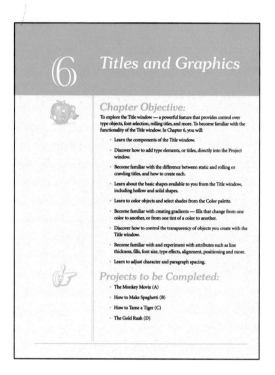

Chapter openers *provide
the reader with specific objectives.*

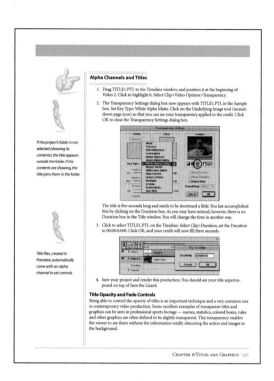

Sidebars *and* **hands-on
activities** *supplement concepts
presented in the material.*

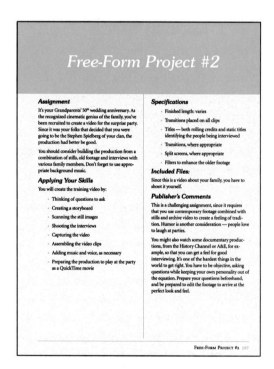

Free-Form projects *allow you to use
your imagination and your new skills
to satisfy a client's needs.*

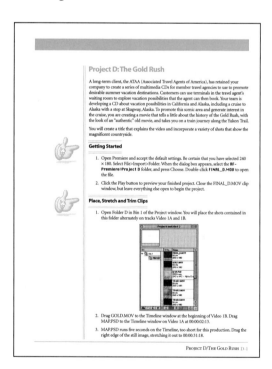

Step-by-step projects *result in
finished artwork — with an emphasis
on proper file-construction methods.*

In addition to explanatory text and illustrations, Against The Clock books have been constructed with two primary building blocks: exercises and projects. Projects always result in a finished piece of work — digital imagery built from the ground up, utilizing images and video from the library supplied on your CD-ROM.

This book, *Adobe Premiere 6: Digital Video Editing*, uses step-by-step projects on which you will work during your learning sessions. There are also free-form projects immediately preceding the two reviews. You will find images of the step-by-step projects you will complete displayed on the inside front and back covers of the book. Here's a brief overview of each:

Project A: The Monkey Movie

In your first project, you will produce a basic video about monkey play, which will later become part of a zoo fund-raising campaign. This basic production will allow the client to review the basic components before approving the more expensive enhancements other team members will add. This project will help you to create a real-world video production. You will import a number of short video clips and build a basic project. You will learn how to add transitions and generate a QuickTime movie. Every great career starts with mastering the basics.

Project B: How to Make Spaghetti

You are working on a multimedia cookbook for new cooks. This interactive cookbook will include a series of videos illustrating some of the finer techniques in preparing tasty dishes. In this project, you will import 15 short video clips and build a production. You will add transitions, credits and music. You will also create titles that explain the key points of the video. When complete, your movie will teach the viewer how to make spaghetti.

Project C: How to Tame a Tiger

By the time you reach Project C, you will have learned about many of the tools needed to create special effects for more advanced productions. This project will take off in a different direction. You will import seven video clips and build a humorous production that will be part of a Web site teaching children about safety issues. In this project, you will create one component of that Web site: a story about not teasing animals, and comprised of video clips shot in two different locations at different times, . By skillfully interweaving the video clips, you will tell a story with a beginning, a middle and a surprise ending. You will add transitions, rolling credits and music to your clips. You will also work with staggered credits that appear on the screen at different times. When you are finished, your movie will teach the viewer "How to Tame a Tiger."

Project D: The Gold Rush

You are creating a series of multimedia CDs for travel agencies to use to promote summer vacation destinations. This particular CD will be about vacation possibilities in California and Alaska, including a cruise to Alaska with a stopover at the port of Skagway, Alaska. To promote this stopover and generate interest in the cruise, you are producing an "authentic" oldtime movie about the history of the Gold Rush and a train journey along the Yukon Trail. You will create a title that explains the video and incorporate a variety of shots that show the magnificent countryside. You will create a production that features advanced editing techniques.

Acknowledgments

I would like to give special thanks to the writers, illustrators, editors and others who have worked long and hard to complete the Against The Clock series.

Thanks to the dedicated teaching professionals whose comments and expertise contributed to the success of these products, including Michelle Ratliff of Santa Fe Community College and Doris Anton of Wichita Area Technical College.

Thanks to Dean Bagley and Michael Barnett for their technical, editorial and production expertise.

Thanks to Terry Sisk Graybill, senior editor and final link in the chain of production, for her tremendous help in making sure we all said what we meant to say.

A big thanks to Judy Casillo, developmental editor, and Denise Brown, production editor, for their guidance, patience and attention to detail.

— Ellenn Behoriam, May 2001

Our History

Against The Clock (ATC) was founded in 1990 as a part of Lanman Systems Group, one of the nation's leading systems integration and training firms. The company specialized in developing custom training materials for such clients as L.L. Bean, *The New England Journal of Medicine*, the Smithsonian, the National Education Association, *Air & Space Magazine*, Publishers Clearing House, the National Wildlife Society, Home Shopping Network and many others. The integration firm was among the most highly respected in the graphic arts industry.

To a great degree, the success of Lanman Systems Group can be attributed to the thousands of pages of course materials developed at the company's demanding client sites. Throughout the rapid growth of Lanman Systems Group, founder and general manager Ellenn Behoriam developed the expertise necessary to manage technical experts, content providers, writers, editors, illustrators, designers, layout artists, proofreaders and the rest of the chain of professionals required to develop structured and highly effective training materials.

Following the sale of the Lanman Companies to World Color, one of the nation's largest commercial printers, Ellenn embarked on a project to develop a new library of hands-on training materials engineered specifically for the professional graphic artist. A large part of this effort is finding and working with talented professional artists, authors and educators from around the country.

The result is the ATC training library.

About the Author

Debbie Rose Myers is an energetic instructor at the Art Institute of Fort Lauderdale, where she has taught for 20 years. She is a state-certified art instructor who has provided in-service training with Adobe Premiere, PageMaker, Photoshop, Illustrator and QuarkXPress for educators from around the United States.

Debbie has developed and taught courses in multimedia, covering such areas as nonlinear editing and designing for multimedia and Web display. Debbie has also originated advanced design courses covering all aspects of the college's desktop publishing and computer graphics curriculum, including vector-based and raster-based drawing as well as scanning and image-processing.

In recent years, Debbie has won inclusion in three national, juried museum shows. She also won Best in Show at her recent M.F.A. graduate art show. Her work can be viewed as part of the permanent collection at the Lowe Art Museum, in Coral Gables, Florida.

Debbie's life, outside anything that relates to computers, includes embracing all things science fiction, shopping and most importantly, her husband Glenn.

Getting Started

Platform

With only few exceptions — books targeted at teaching specific operating systems — the entire Against The Clock series is designed to work for both Macintosh and Windows learners. This book will serve you equally well, however you're a Macintosh user, or a Windows user working with Windows 95, NT, 98, Millennium or Windows 2000.

We should note, however, that there are a number of differences between how Premiere works on a Macintosh and how it works on a Windows machine. Almost all of these variances are essentially cosmetic: some things look different, while working in exactly the same fashion.

Naming Conventions

In the early days of the PC, the Windows operating system placed several restrictions on what you could call your files. All file names consisted of two parts: a name, which could contain no more than eight alphanumeric characters; and a three character suffix. The suffix defined the nature of the file. Applications generally ended with the .exe (for executable) suffix, while documents used suffixes like .doc (document), .txt (text file), .wav (wave, a sound format), .htm (HTML documents) as well as many others. The Macintosh operating system never imposed this limitation. Nor did it use extensions or suffixes to identify files to the operating system.

For at least the past five years, Windows systems no longer restrict you to eight characters for the name; you can use 256 characters. Every application appends a three-character suffix to its files. You might not see these extensions, however. By default, the Windows operating system hides extensions for "known" file types. These known file types include just about every file you're going to use in this book.

To configure your system so that file extensions are visible, click the Start button (in the lower-left part of your screen), and select Settings>Folder Options from the pop-up menu. Select the View tab, and uncheck the "Hide file extensions for known file types."

While viewing file extensions isn't required in order to use the book, changing the setting will ensure that what you see on your monitor matches the screen shots and illustrations used in the discussions and exercises. If you're on a Macintosh, we still recommend using the suffixes.

Key Commands

There are two keys generally used as *modifier* keys — they do nothing when pressed unless they are pressed in conjunction with another key. Their purpose is to alter the normal functions of the other key with which they are pressed.

The Command (Macintosh) or Control (Windows) key is generally used when taking control of the computer. When combined with the "S" key, it functions to save your work. When combined with "O," it opens a file; with a "P," it prints the file.

Another special function key is the Option (Macintosh) and Alt (for alternate) (Windows) key. It, too, is a modifier key, and you must hold it down along with whatever other key (or keys) is required for a specific function. The Option and Alt keys are often used in conjunction with other keys to access typographic characters having an ASCII number higher than 128. Under Windows, they are used in conjunction with the numeric keypad.

The Macintosh and Windows access context-sensitive menus in similar but different ways. On the Macintosh, holding down the Control (not the Command) key while clicking the mouse button will bring up context-sensitive menus. Under Windows, this is accomplished by clicking the right mouse button (right-clicking). We generically call accessing the context menu "context-clicking."

The CD-ROM and Initial Setup Considerations

Before you begin using your Against The Clock course book, you must set up your system to have access to the various files and tools to complete your lessons.

Resource Files

This course comes complete with a collection of resource files. These files are an integral part of the learning experience — they're used throughout the book to help you construct increasingly complex elements. Having these building blocks available to you for practice and study sessions will ensure that you will be able to experience the exercises and complete the project assignments smoothly, spending a minimum of time looking for the various required components.

In the Resource Files folders, we've created sets of data. Locate the **RF-Premiere**, folder and drag the icon onto your hard disk drive. If you have limited disk space, you may want to copy only the files for one or two lessons at a time.

Creating a Project Folder

Throughout the exercises and projects you'll be required to save your work. Since the CD-ROM is "read-only," you cannot write information to it. Create a "work in progress" folder on your hard disk and use it to store your work. Create the folder at the highest level of your system, where it will always be easy to find. Name this folder "Work in Progress".

System Requirements

On the Macintosh, you will need a Power PC 604 processor or above, running the 9.04 operating system or later; 32 MB of application memory (128 MB recommended); 135 MB of available hard-disk space (40 MB for installation); a monitor with a resolution of at least 800 × 600 or greater, a CD-ROM drive, and Apple QuickTime 4.1.2 or later.

On a Windows operating system, you'll need a Pentium-class processor or equivalent, running Windows 98/2000, Windows ME, or Windows NT 4.0 (with Server Pack 6); 64 MB application memory (128 MB recommended); 135 MB of available hard-disk space (40 MB for installation); a monitor with a resolution of at least 800 × 600 pixels, a CD-ROM drive, and Apple QuickTime 4.1.2.

Prerequisites

This book assumes that you have a basic understanding of how to use your system.

You should know how to use your mouse to point and click, and how to drag items around the screen. You should know how to resize a window, and how to arrange windows on your desktop to maximize your available space. You should know how to access pull-down menus, and how checkboxes and radio buttons work. Lastly, you should know how to create, open and save files.

If you're familiar with these fundamental skills, then you know all that's necessary to utilize the Against The Clock courseware library.

Notes:

Introduction

Success is often just an idea away.
— Frank Tyger

Adobe Premiere, one of the most popular nonlinear video editing programs on the market, lets you apply many professional editing tools and techniques to rough video footage, audio clips and still images. It's a rare occasion when you don't have to edit your productions — usually you need to combine and trim footage. Often you need to remove extra material to make a story fit in a specific time limit. Sometimes you find that a particular shot, such as a close-up, tells the story more effectively than the one originally planned.

As an example, one morning we were preparing to shoot a commercial for a class we were taking in video production. We planned to shoot a commercial about a little boy and his various attempts to get to the bank to make a deposit. For talent we used a classmate who looked like a little boy, along with an eclectic selection of bicycles, skateboards and pogo sticks.

There was only one problem — Bob, our star, was, let's say, grace-challenged. He couldn't stand on the skateboard, much less ride it into the picture. Every time we tried to get a shot, Bob would shoot by, flailing his arms wildly and yelling at the top of his lungs. After about the tenth take, we were becoming panic stricken, that is until inspiration struck.

We decided to shoot the commercial with Bob falling and screaming, and then edit it down to the best of the silly stuff. In one of our favorite clips, Bob tried to hop on a pogo stick and ride it into the shot. Through the camera's eye, you saw Bob for about two hops, then just the empty pogo stick bouncing in by itself. Needless to say it was very funny.

We juxtaposed all of the outrageous shots so that it looked planned. In class, everyone howled as the commercial was played, and we were thrilled with both the results of the production and the enthusiastic response from our "studio audience."

What made the production work was the editing, also called the "postproduction." Video production generally takes place in three stages: preproduction, production and postproduction. Preproduction centers on the creative process. In this stage you first decide what and where to shoot. You bring in actors to speak the written words of your script. You select music and special props. You create the storyboards to illustrate the essentials— camera angles, key visual elements, sequence of shots and more.

Once you have completed the planning, you are ready for actual production. Now you move to the video studio or perhaps go out to a location you have chosen. You carry cameras, lights and tripods. You shoot from the preset shot list.

When all of the shooting is complete, you move into the postproduction phase. This is where Adobe Premiere comes in. Premiere features an easy-to-learn interface coupled with a full spectrum of special-effects tools. This program is a must for anyone who wants to edit video within a relatively sane budget.

Most productions today are completed using nonlinear editing systems. The term *nonlinear* refers to the process of shooting out of order, then using a computer to reassemble the video. Premiere makes this easy. With nonlinear editing, you transfer all of your videotapes to a computer and then edit the video and audio portions. You can copy, cut and paste the various shots much as you would work with words, sentences and paragraphs in a word-processing program. The computer plays an important role in nonlinear editing systems. It acts as an interface between creative decisions and their implementation.

How are these productions used? Well, first the obvious — commercials and openings for television programs. But nonlinear editing can be used for so much more: multimedia, Web pages, games, film and training productions.

This book will give you a solid understanding of the nonlinear production process. You will have an opportunity to create a variety of interesting and amusing projects. As you work through the exercises, you will learn about and practice many of the dramatic effects that Premiere can produce.

Premiere 6 provides the solid, proven platform that you need to gather, manage and assemble a wide range of video, audio and still footage. With dramatically enhanced audio-editing tools, robust and direct support for capturing digital video, an improved interface and many other upgraded functions. Premiere stands alone as the leading video-editing application.

But keep in mind that not even the most elaborate digital-editing system can improve the original footage or make the creative decisions for you. The better the original material is, the easier and more efficient your postproduction activities will be. Thinking about postproduction, even in the shooting stage, helps to make the editing chores relatively easy and effective. Always consider postproduction an essential part of the creative process.

You are about to enter a remarkable world, a world where you can alter reality to tell a story the way that it should be told. Welcome to the world of nonlinear editing!

> *To get anywhere, strike out for somewhere, or you'll get nowhere.*
> — Martha Lupton

1 *Basic Principles*

Chapter Objective:

To become familiar with the basic principles of video editing and the Premiere application. In Chapter 1, you will:

- Become familiar with the role of the Preferences file, and learn how to delete the existing set of preferences to set your system for Premiere and this book.

- Discover how to apply custom settings to ensure the most effective working environment.

- Explore the authoring environment, or workspace, where most of your editing and videography work will take place.

- Learn how to build a small production, using video clips supplied on the CD-ROM that came with the book.

- Discover how to preview your productions.

Projects to be Completed:

- The Monkey Movie (A)

- How to Make Spaghetti (B)

- How to Tame a Tiger (C)

- The Gold Rush (D)

Basic Principles

Many of the films you see today were edited at least in part using Adobe Premiere. Premiere is an application that enables the user to capture video into the computer. Once the video is there, the user can edit it, assign special effects and enhance it to create a unique project. When the editing is complete, the project can be compressed into a QuickTime movie. The final movie can then be used in a number of different ways: as a multimedia training tape, as a video scrapbook or as part of a Web site.

Like most computer programs, Premiere is easy to learn but tricky to master. It has many hidden goodies to unearth. As you find and use them, this book will help you to unleash the program's full potential. Each chapter builds on the previous one, as you learn the program through the exercises and projects.

In this chapter, you will start the program, customize your settings, take an initial look at the dialog boxes, menus and windows and create your first video production.

Customizing Your Work Environment

Before you begin the exercises and projects in this book, it's a good idea to locate and delete the Premiere Preferences (Prefs) file. This will cause Premiere to create a new Prefs file that you customize to your needs. Once you replace this file, your assignments will closely resemble those illustrated in this book.

Deleting the Preferences Files

If you are using Adobe Premiere for the first time following its installation, removing the Preferences file may not be necessary. The program creates a new one during installation. To be on the safe side, though, let's walk through the procedure of removing the Prefs file.

Delete the Preferences File — Macintosh

1. Be certain that Premiere is not running. If you are unsure and want to double-check, click and hold down your mouse button on the Finder icon (located in the upper-right corner of your screen). You should only see the Finder (and perhaps Launcher). No other programs should be listed. If you do not see any other programs listed, you may proceed to step 3.

2. If any other programs are running, quit them. Although this is not critical, it is best to quit all programs before deleting Preferences files.

3. Locate and double-click the **System** folder. Locate and open the **Preferences** folder.

4. In the Preferences folder, you will find a list of the preferences files that have been created for many programs on your computer. Locate the **Adobe Premiere 6.0 Prefs** file.

5. Click and hold down the mouse button. (Do not double-click because this will launch the program and you will have to quit.) Drag the Prefs icon to the Trash.

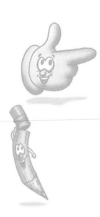

If you're using this book in a classroom or network environment, don't perform the recommended changes to your working environment until you check with your instructor or network administrator. It's possible that the computer has been set up so that you cannot follow these procedures.

Throughout this book, we will use the following abbreviations for measurements, as needed:

p = pica(s)

px = pixel(s)

in = inch(es)

ft = foot (feet)

pt = point(s)

° = degree(s)

% = percentage

6. Close all open windows. (Click the Close button on the upper-left side of the open window. Holding the Option key while closing one window will close all open windows at once, unless they need changes saved.) Choose Special>Empty Trash. This will permanently remove the old file. While you may now launch Premiere, it might be a better idea to wait until the next exercise. In it, we'll make a number of settings to configure your work area appropriately.

Delete the Preferences File — Windows

1. Right-click on My Computer to display an information window. Select Find to display the Find: All Files dialog box. The dialog box appears.

2. In the Named window, type "*.prf". Click the Find Now button. The computer searches for the Premiere 6.0 Preferences file. It is possible that other files will be listed in the window — ignore them. For now we are only interested in the Premiere preferences file.

3. Drag the **Prem60.prf** file to the Recycle Bin. You will be asked if you wish to send the file to the Recycle Bin. Click the Yes button.

4. Right-click on the Recycle Bin, and select Empty Recycle Bin. When asked, "Are you sure you want to empty the trash," click Yes.

Windows users, once the Prem60.prf file appears in the Find dialog box, you can right-click the file name and select Delete from the pop-up menu. Macintosh users, use Control-click to access the contextual (pop-up) menu.

Assigning Custom Settings

Many of Premiere's settings can be customized. When you first launch the application, it's important to work through many of the major dialog boxes and windows, assigning settings for use on a particular project. (We'll discuss these settings in more detail in later chapters.)

In one such dialog box, for example — the Load Project Settings dialog box, which is the first that Premiere presents — you assign custom settings for each project you create. Since the settings for a full-screen television production (640 px × 480 px) are quite different from those for a production created for the Internet (160 px × 120 px), you will want to set this dialog box carefully.

In the following exercise, we will set up Premiere for the projects created throughout this book. You may well find these settings also useful for your work after you finish working through this book.

Make the Initial Settings

1. Double-click on the Premiere icon. You'll see the Load Project Settings dialog box.

2. If you're using a Macintosh, select Multimedia as the starting setup from the Available Presets window. Windows users, select Multimedia QuickTime as the starting setup from the Available Presets window.

Premiere is very picky about where files are when you open them. For example you can't open files directly from the CD-ROM. They must be moved to the hard drive before they can be used. We suggest you move the contents of the entire RF-Premiere folder to your desktop. Next, create a folder at the desktop level of your computer and name it "Work in Progress". This is where you will save the exercises and projects that you create during the course of this book.

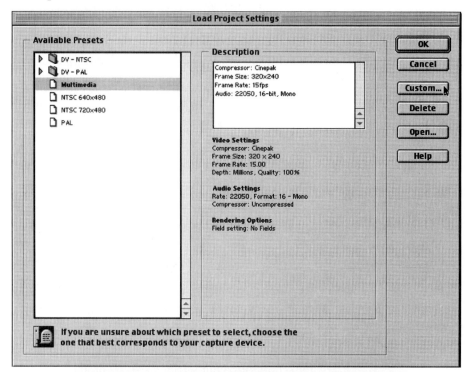

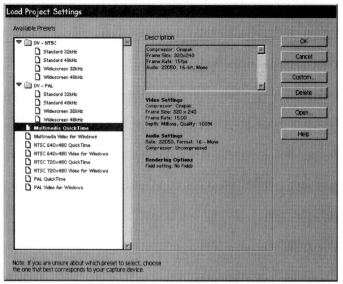

3. If you're using a Macintosh, click the Custom button, and select:
   Top drag-down menu: General, Editing Mode: QuickTime, Timebase: 29.97, Time Display: 30 fps Drop-frame Timecode.

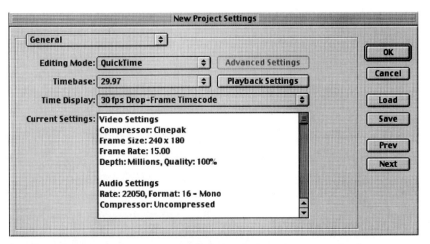

If you're using a Windows system, click the Custom button and select:
Top drag-down menu: General, Editing Mode: Video for Windows, Timebase: 29.97,
Time Display: 30 fps Drop-frame Timecode.

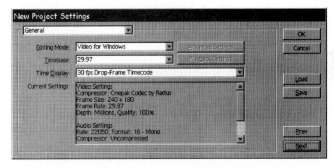

4. Click the Next button on the right. Now create the Video window settings.

Macintosh Users
Make the following settings:
Top drag-down menu: Video, Compressor: Cinepak, Depth: Millions, Frame Size H:
240 and V: 180, 4:3 Aspect: checked, Frame Rate: 15, Pixel Aspect Ratio: Square Pixels
(1.0), Quality: 100% High, Data Rate Limit Data Rate to 1000 K/sec: unchecked,
Recompress: Always and unchecked.

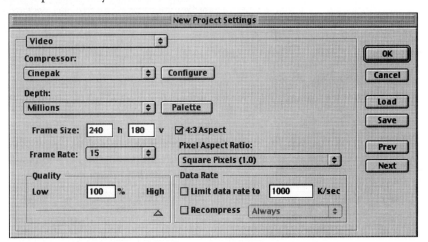

Windows Users
Make the following settings:
Top drag-down menu: Video, Compressor: Cinepak, Depth: Millions, Frame Size H: 240 and V: 180, 4:3 Aspect: checked, Frame Rate: 15, Pixel Aspect Ratio: Square Pixels (1.0), Quality: 100% High, Data Rate Limit Data Rate to 1000 K/sec: unchecked, Recompress: Always and unchecked.

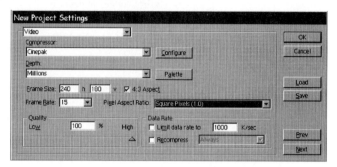

5. Click the Next button (on the right). Now create the Audio window settings.

Macintosh Users
Make the following settings:
Top drag-down menu: Audio, Rate: 22050 Hz, Format: 16 Bit - Mono, Compressor: Uncompressed, Interleave: 1 Second, Processing Options — Enhance Rate Conversion: Best, Use Logarithmic Audio Fades: unchecked, Create Audio Preview Files If There Are: 5 or More Active Audio Tracks and 1 or More Audio Filters Applied.

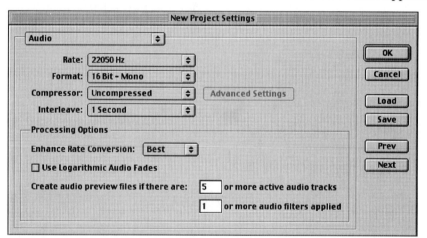

Windows Users
Make the following settings:
Top drag-down menu: Audio, Rate: 22050 Hz, Format: 16 Bit - Mono, Compressor: Uncompressed, Interleave: 1 Second, Processing Options — Enhance Rate Conversion: Off, Use Logarithmic Audio Fades: unchecked, Create Audio Preview Files If There Are: 5 or More Active Audio Tracks and 1 or More Audio Filters Applied.

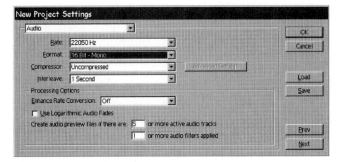

6. Click OK. Premiere will complete the start-up process.

7. In the Monitor window, select Dual view (the icon at the far left). The window expands.

8. Leave the file open for the next exercise.

Getting to Know Premiere

Premiere is a complex program with many different windows, palettes, dialog boxes and more, all of which enable you to create video productions. You've explored a few in the process of customizing your setup. Now it's time to explore the working environment and get to know the major windows and dialog boxes.

The Premiere Authoring Environment

Once you've selected File>New Project and adjusted all the settings, an untitled project document is created. The three windows that appear — Project, Monitor and Timeline — are the windows that you will use the most in creating your movies. There are many other functions, windows and palettes that you will be able to access, but these are the primary windows you will use most frequently.

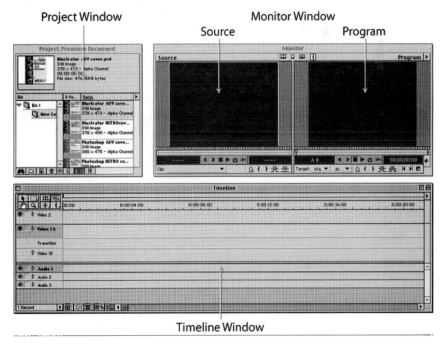

Project Window   Monitor Window
                        Source   Program

Timeline Window

- **Project window.** This is the main holding area for all of your video clips, graphics, sounds, titles and other assets. It is where your assets are stored before you add them to a project. The Project window can also contain clips and other assets that are never actually used in the final rendering.

- **Monitor window.** This useful window is divided into two different windows called "views." The Source view (on the left) allows you to preview individual video clips. The Program view (on the right) displays whole segments of a video project as it is created.

- **Timeline window.** This very important area of Premiere displays a visual diagram or schematic of the entire video project you are composing.

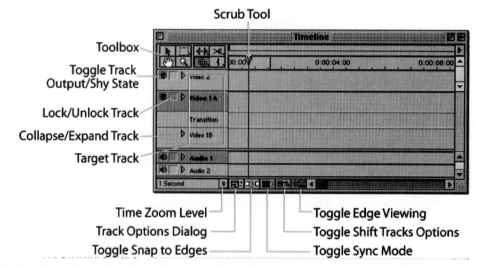

The Toolbox of the Timeline offers a number of very important tools that allow you to select, edit and modify the frames. Several of the tool icons have small triangles that denote that there are more tools available. Click-hold the mouse on these icons to show the optional tools.

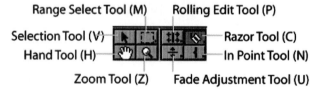

Each of the palettes in Premiere can be undocked or pulled away from the other palettes. This allows you to keep frequently used palettes available while tucking away those used less often.

Thumbnail view gives the most detailed information about your video clips.

Many palettes have additional options or settings available. The Options menu is found under the small black triangle at the top right of the palette.

The Window menu is the source for obtaining your other controlling palettes that allow you to apply their unique effects to the selected frames.

- **Navigator palette**. This palette allows you to zoom in, zoom out and, in general, move all around the Timeline window quickly to get a better view of one particular area of your video.

- **History palette**. This palette tracks your production as you create it and allows you to step back in time to correct problems.

- **Commands palette**. This palette allows you to customize the most frequently used commands. You can create a procedure and assign a keyboard shortcut to it. You might, for example, designate the F10 key as a shortcut for Select All.

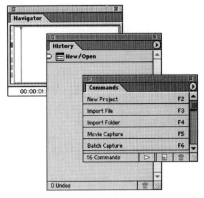

- **Info palette**. This palette displays information about a selected clip or transition. If you drag a clip in the Timeline, you can watch the starting and ending time change in the Info palette. The information displayed in the palette will change depending on conditions such as the media type and the current window.

- **Effect Controls palette**. This palette allows you to set motion controls on a video clip and preview the results.

- **Transitions, Video Effects and Audio Effects palettes**. The Transitions palette serves as the holding area for all of Premiere's transitions, such as wipes and dissolves. All effects/filters are stored in the Audio or Video Effects palette. Effects are grouped by type: for example, all video effects that create a blur are listed in a Blurs folder in the Video Effects palette. You can hide effects that you don't use and create new folders containing special groups of commonly used or rarely used effects. The Audio Effects palette offers a variety of special effects that can be applied to audio clips.

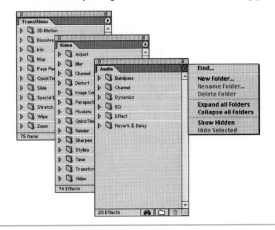

Customizing the Premiere Interface

Each window in Premiere can be customized to suit your needs. For example, as you bring a video clip into Premiere, that clip appears in a Project window or Bin along with its file name, file type and duration. You can customize how information is displayed in these windows, and you can apply different display options to each individual window. Clips can be previewed from inside the Project window.

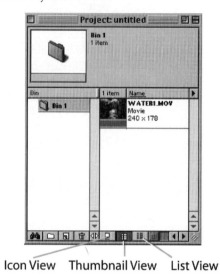

Icon View   Thumbnail View   List View

One way that you could customize the Project window for a specific project would be to select the most appropriate view. You would select (click on) the Icon View, Thumbnail View or List View buttons at the bottom of the window. (All of the images in this book were created using Thumbnail View.) The amount of detail provided about your file changes, depending on which view is selected.

You can also customize the Timeline display, including how it represents clips when you view or edit them in the Timeline. Some video editors find it easier to work with clips when they are represented more visually on the Timeline.

To customize the Timeline window, you would choose Timeline Window Options from the Timeline Options menu under the black triangle at the far-right side of the Timeline window. In the Icon Size section, you would select the size of the preview icon you want in the Timeline. Most editors prefer to use the middle icon. In the Track Format section, you would select one of the four options:

- The first option displays sample frames along the duration of a clip. This makes it easier to find a frame, but slows display and does not include the file name. For the purposes of most of the exercises in this book, we have chosen the first option.

- The second option displays the clip's poster and ending frames as well as the name of the file.

- The third option displays the poster frame and the file name.

- The fourth option displays the file name only. This option displays the fastest and is the default setting for Premiere.

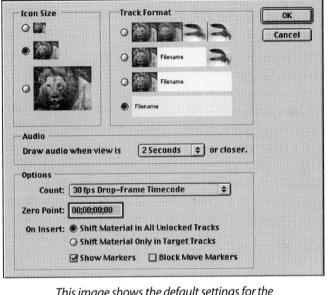

This image shows the default settings for the
Timeline Window Options. It's what we use throughout the book.

Every project has only one Project window. If you close this window, you close the project file.

Your First Production

Before we move on to actually creating your first movie, we should take a moment and talk about the workflow of video production. *Workflow* is simply a technical term for the steps that go into creating something — whether it's a woodworking project or the production of *Titanic*. You have to do certain items in a certain order to ensure that you're working efficiently, and don't leave anything out. While certain tasks can be happening at the same time (like someone working on putting the audio tracks together while another person searches the archives for existing footage), certain processes are milestones, or critical processes. Think of going grocery shopping — you can't do that until you've picked up your wallet or purse with the money or credit card you plan to use. If you rearrange the steps, you'll end up unable to shop when you get there.

You'll want to keep these key considerations in mind:

A project is a file that contains all the information necessary to replay your masterpieces. Among the many things it tracks are clip information, duration, stills, special effects, titles, audio and more.

- All projects start at the end or final result of what you're trying to achieve. A storyboard — a tool we'll work with at length later in this chapter — is the starting point for all Premiere projects.

- All projects contain a collection of components or assets, often referred to as "source materials." These assets include raw video footage, titles and sounds. Pieces of raw video footage are called "clips." Individual clips are assembled into final visual streams using transitions.

- A *project* is a single Premiere file that describes, manages and creates a video program. It stores references to all clips in that file as well as information about how you arranged them. It also includes details of any transitions or effects you applied. You can add, remove and organize clips in bins within the project. All of the clips that you import into your project — whether video, still images, sequences or audio — are listed in the Project window. As is the case with most other Premiere interface elements, you can modify the window's settings to accommodate your personal style and the requirements of the project on which you're working.

• After you've collected your assets and imported them into your project, you'll use the Timeline window to organize your clips sequentially, make changes to their duration and location, add transitions, superimpose clips, apply effects, modify opacity and create motion.

• Once you've completed all of your editing, you render the content of the Timeline so that it can previewed and ultimately output. Among the formats available are Web-compliant streaming formats and standard videotape. Since Premiere is a popular and widely used tool among professional moviemakers, your ability to manage your creations all the way to the big screen is limited only by the hardware and post-production tools that are available to you.

Exercise Set-up

Now it's time to import some video footage and start a production. First, let's take a moment to talk about what you will do. In this exercise you will import four video clips and build a production. This is a two-step process. First you will import the clips into the Project window. Think of the Project window as the holding area for your video and other related files. Your video footage waits for you to decide how best to complete a project. Once the video clips appear in the Project window, you will drag them onto the Timeline window to build a project.

Import Video Clips

1. From the File menu, select Import>File.

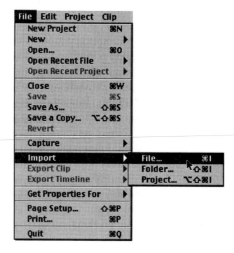

Video and audio clips aren't actually embedded in a Premiere project — the program simply keeps track of which files were used, how they were edited and where they're located on your hard drive.

2. A dialog box appears. From the **RF-Premiere>Water** folder, select the **WATER1.MOV** file and click Open. The file is imported and displays in the Project window. Switch to Thumbnail View.

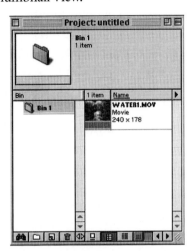

3. Now you will import three additional clips. Again, from the File menu, select Import>File. Double-click (or click once, then click Open) the **WATER2.MOV** file from the **RF-Premiere>Water** folder. Repeat this step and import **WATER3.MOV** and **WATER4.MOV**. You should now have four video clips displayed in the Project window.

If you've ever used Photoshop to create layered images, and then saved them out as .tif files, you know exactly what we mean by rendering. While you're putting together your Premiere movies, all the different objects (sounds, video footage, stills, etc.) are stored on their own discrete tracks on the Timeline. When you're done rendering, everything is mixed together in a single stream.

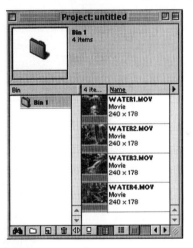

4. Leave this file open for the next exercise.

Previewing Video Clips

Premiere offers you a number of ways to preview the clips you just imported. One of the easiest is through the Source view of the Monitor window. The Source view enables you to preview individual video clips and obtain information about their running times.

You can also preview video clips directly on the Timeline. Throughout this book you will see the terms "rendering" and "scrubbing."

Rendering is the process whereby all the individual components of your production are merged or flattened into one streaming masterpiece, which you can preview on your monitor and ultimately write onto disk, tape or television.

Scrubbing refers to manually moving the playhead, advancing through clips one frame at a time in either direction. The technique is very helpful when you need to identify and mark events precisely. Scrubbing has no effect on the production, whereas rendering applies all of your edits to the final output.

Preview Video Clips

In the following exercise, you'll have the opportunity to preview the water files you've seen listed above.

1. Let's view the WATER1.MOV clip. In the open Project window, select the thumbnail image WATER1.MOV, and drag it to the Source view in the Monitor window.

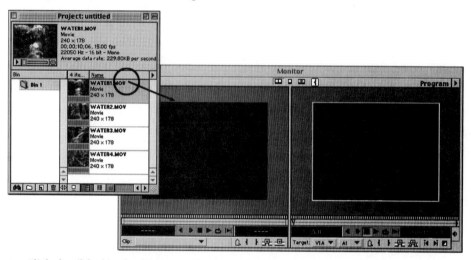

You can drag this clip from either the Project window or the Source view. It makes no difference.

2. Click the (black) Play arrow at the bottom of the Source view window to see a preview. The clip now plays. Stop the playback by pressing the black square next to the Play arrow. Restart the playback by pressing the Play button again. Try pressing the Spacebar to stop and restart the playback.

3. Any or all of your movies can be moved to the Source view to be viewed before you include them in your production. Drag WATER2.MOV into the Source view to select it. In the Clip menu of the Source window, click on the arrow next to WATER2.MOV to display a list of available clips. You can see that both listings are now available for playback by clicking the black Play button.

4. Leave the file open for the next exercise.

Assembling the New Movie

Once you have imported your raw video footage and previewed it to determine what you have, it's time to actually assemble and render the production. The concept of video editing is actually quite simple: you place individual video clips on the Timeline. The Timeline is the visual representation of the actual production in process. You can "see" how the production will look as it is developed.

The Timeline has both a Video 1A and Video 1B track. These two tracks are stacked with a Transition track between them. This arrangement allows you to place videos that overlap to create transitions. (You will learn how to do this in the next chapter.)

As you create the production, keep in mind that everything placed on the Timeline can be reordered. You can change your mind at any point in the production process. You can place clips in new positions at any time, or delete or duplicate them. The entire production process is actually quite fluid.

Once a production is underway, you can also add more effects, such as transitions like wipes and dissolves. You might also enhance your production by including special-effect filters. You can even give your movie an old-time silent-film look by colorizing it with one of Premiere's many color effects.

Assemble and Render the Movie

It's time to assemble the actual production. Begin by looking at the Timeline window. You will place clips on Video 1A and Video 1B at the left of the Timeline window.

1. In the open file, notice the Clip menu at the bottom of the Source view. Click the down arrow next to WATER2.MOV and note that WATER1.MOV is available there as well.

2. Drag WATER1.MOV to the beginning of Video 1A. The clip expands to fill some of the space on the Timeline. Notice that audio is shown as well on the Audio 1 track. Premiere separates the components of your production. (This will help you later when you add extra sound effects and voice-overs.)

Rendering your project does not save your production. It is held in memory until the next time you save. You should always save your projects before rendering.

PPJ is the extension that Premiere uses to identify native files. This extension is automatically appended to files on the PC (even though you might not see it), while on the Macintosh it's not mandatory nor is it automatically added onto a file name when you save your files. We do, however, strongly recommend that you stick to this naming convention — especially if you're working in a cross-platform environment, or if you expect that someone working on a Windows machine may need to access your project files.

Although we're not going to work with audio in any detailed way until Chapter 7, you will occasionally see audio tracks appear on the Timeline. These are attached to the video footage and when it's imported, so are the accompanying sounds.

3. Drag the clip WATER2.MOV onto Video 1A, directly behind WATER1.MOV. Premiere makes certain that you know which files you have placed on the Timeline. As you may have noticed, the file name appears as each is dragged into position.

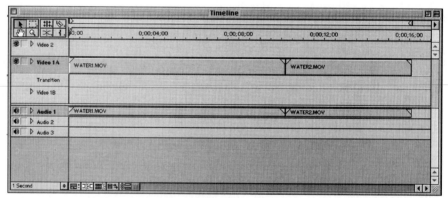

4. Click the Timeline to make it active. Press the Spacebar. Your production will start to play in the Program view of the Monitor window. You can stop the playback by pressing the Spacebar again. Now, drag both WATER3.MOV and WATER4.MOV onto Video 1A, following the other video clips. It is possible that some of the other Premiere windows are blocking your view. If so, close or collapse these windows. Press the Spacebar and take a moment to enjoy your production.

5. Leave the file open for the next exercise.

If you don't see the three-letter extensions (called suffixes) when viewing files on your Windows machine, select Start>Settings> Folder Options. On the View tab there's a checkbox that's labeled "Hide extensions for known file types." Make sure this option is unchecked, and you'll be able to see the extensions for Premiere (and all the other applications on your system).

Reviewing the Production

Now that you've assembled a movie and rendered it, you may want to review the production, frame by frame. The perfect tool for this purpose is the Scrub tool. The Scrub tool allows you to check edits or effects in real time. There are actually two components to consider. The first is the Edit Line tool, which actually serves two functions, and the second is the Scrub tool, which serves only one purpose — scrubbing your project. Scrubbing doesn't get your project cleaner — it lets you see what's going on.

Edit Line Tool   Scrub Tool

- **Edit Line tool**. This tool activates the Scrub tool. When you click at the top of the Timeline, the Edit Line tool is activated. It either allows you to scrub the production or acts as a marker for editing excess video.

- **Scrub tool**. This tool allows you to check edits or effects in real time. For example, to preview a transition, you render-scrub the section of the Timeline containing the transition. You render-scrub by holding down the Option/Alt key while dragging the Scrub tool. This action causes a (slower) real-time render, but is very impractical for anything over a couple of seconds. With render-scrubbing, you can see the transition's effect quickly, without waiting for Premiere to build an entire preview file.

Preview the Production with the Scrub Tool

1. In the open file, review your production frame by frame using the Scrub tool. Click on the arrow-shaped tool — the Selection tool. Move it over the Scrub tool at the top of the Edit Line. When you hold down the mouse button with your cursor over the shuttle, a small black triangle appears superimposed on the shuttle. This small black triangle is the Scrub tool.

2. Move the Scrub tool to the left and right on the Timeline. Your project plays.

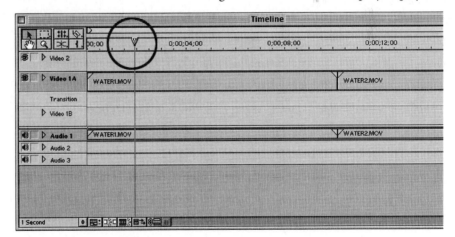

3. Save and close the file.

Creative Planning

Much of what you need to know about the technical aspects of video-production editing begins with Premiere, but it does not end there. In fact, great videographers need to be creative while paying close attention to the technical aspects of their work.

Practice Creative Visualization

1. Take a look around the room. What do you see? What do you *really* see? Computers? Chairs? The lighting? Are there other people in the room? Perhaps your pet? Try the experiment below.

2. Close your eyes and count to three. Now open your eyes and look around the room, but this time look at the room in color. What do you see? Are things any different now? Chances are that you see things a little differently. Most people don't pay much attention to their surroundings. This is where the creative individual comes into the picture. The creative person doesn't just exist in an environment: he or she uses the environment to tell a story.

3. Look around your room again. This time try to find the most unusual and creative camera angle you can locate. It could be looking through the legs of your chairs, at floor level. Or perhaps your perfect shot is taken from the ceiling looking down at your colleagues at work. How about a shot looking through the lightswitch plate back at others from the inside out?

We've supplied a PDF file on the RF-Premiere CD-ROM that contains blank storyboards. Print out a few to use for this exercise — and you're free to use the file for any project you might work on in the future.

You see, it's all about telling a story in the most creative way possible. We usually sit in a room without paying too much attention to what's around us, yet everywhere you look there are interesting camera shots. If you can learn to identify these shots, you will be well on your way to becoming a great video director.

Storyboarding

One technique frequently used by videographers to plan their video productions is storyboarding. A *storyboard* is a series of sketches of the key visualization points of an event along with audio information. It often includes camera angles, camera movement and key phrases from the script. A storyboard can range from a series of rough sketches to a finely illustrated set of panels worthy of hanging on a wall. The important thing to remember is that storyboards form the basis — indeed the very foundation — of all the production work you'll ever do. Without a good storyboard, your best ideas can become muddled and lose their continuity when executed in Premiere.

The following storyboards were created by Dan Rossi, Darren J. Brent and Dy'Andrea Travis. They are students at the Art Institute of Ft. Lauderdale and created these storyboards as part of their course in Adobe Premiere.

Storyboards often list dialog and possible music under each panel. This helps the director connect the script with the visuals. It's not important that the drawings be perfect or life-like; it's only important that the person looking at the storyboard understands the intent of the shots. It helps identify the duties and requirements of the team members as the production gets underway.

Exercise Set-up

The best way to learn about storyboarding is to practice creating one. In this exercise you're going to produce a storyboard detailing your morning wake-up routine.

Your storyboard should contain roughly eight panels, although you can use a few more if you feel they're important to telling the story. Add instructions for dialog or music if you feel their inclusion will enhance or strengthen the story.

Create a Storyboard on How You Get Up in the Morning

1. Create a storyboard that details your wake-up routine. It should include about eight panels. Let your sense of humor have free reign.

2. Think about and use unusual angles from which to film (view) the scenes. How about just outside your window, looking in? Or perhaps the camera could be placed above the ceiling paddle fan, looking down at the person sleeping in bed. The camera would show how the fan turns under the shot of the camera.

3. To help you get some storyboard ideas, we've included some examples created by students at the Art Institute of Fort Lauderdale. They are fresh and original ways of solving this assignment.

Dan Rossi — Storyboards

Storyboarding is also used in cartooning, Web site development, animation, stage production, seminar or presentation preparation and other situations where artists needs to organize their work before putting it together. It's like having a set of plans at hand before you start building a house. You know where you want the rooms, but without the plans, all you have is undifferentiated concrete, bricks, wood, hammers, nails and saws. A well done storyboard provides directors, actors, camera operators and other personnel with a simplified visual overview of the entire production.

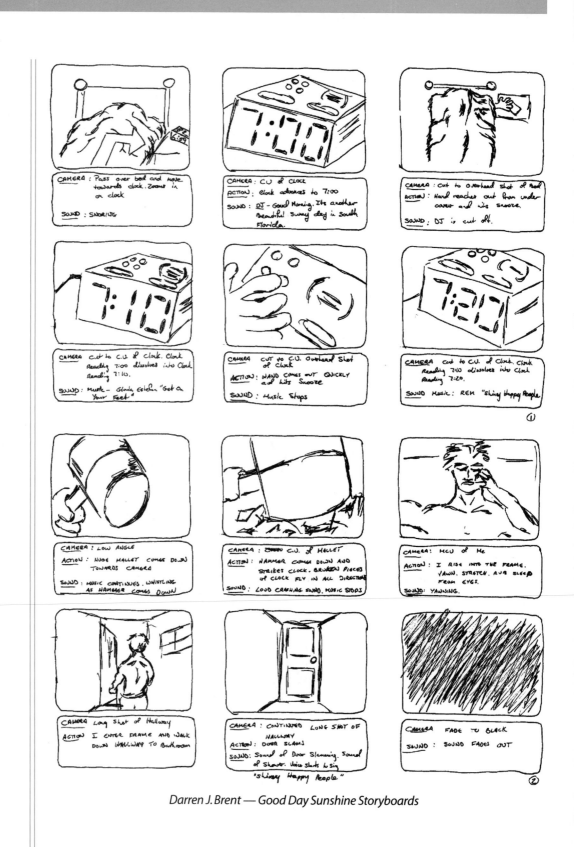

Darren J. Brent — Good Day Sunshine Storyboards

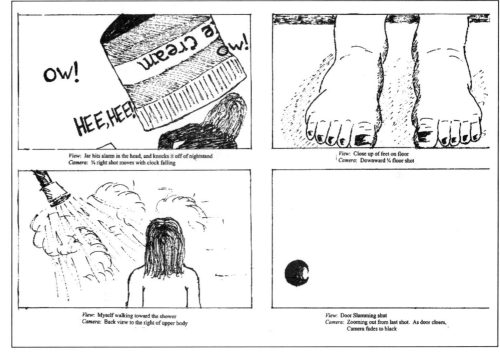

D'Andrea Travis — How I Get up in the Morning Storyboards

Storyboards

Blank storyboard files are provided in PDF format on the resource CD.

4. What are we trying to say here? The act of waking up in the morning is not inherently a very exciting event, but it can be made funny and interesting with the right treatment. Very few people enjoy getting out of bed while it is still dark, but it is something to which we can all relate. As you find ways to tell this story in a humorous and engaging fashion, you will be starting to think in a new and imaginative way.

Summary

In Chapter 1, you've become familiar with Premiere's main windows, dialog boxes and palettes. You've set up Premier to work with the projects and exercises throughout this book. You have learned how to import and preview rough video clips from which you created a simple movie. You have gained proficiency in reviewing movies using the Scrub tool, as well as building and rendering a final movie. You've also explored the key skills of storyboarding and creative visualization.

2 *Production Essentials*

Chapter Objective:

To explore the basic functions of Premiere by working through a simple production. To learn about essential production skills and organization. In Chapter 2, you will:

- Learn about gathering video and audio clips.

- Become familiar with aspect ratio — the relationship between the width and height of the footage — and how to ensure consistency when importing clips into a new production.

- Discover how to import multiple clips at one time, an effective way to save time when preparing for production.

- Learn to place simple transitions — special effects that occur when one clip replaces another.

- Discover how to preview transitions using the Scrub tool.

- Learn to trim clips by altering In and Out points.

- Become familiar with the importance of proper file and folder organization, a critical skill when dealing with the complex components that make up many video productions.

Projects to be Completed:

- The Monkey Movie (A)

- How to Make Spaghetti (B)

- How to Tame a Tiger (C)

- The Gold Rush (D)

Production Essentials

Developing a storyboard, gathering your assets and editing them into a cohesive and well-balanced production requires a great many skills and talents — far more than can possibly be taught in a single book. Premiere itself can be a daunting application — there are many different tools and techniques that you need to know in order to effectively and efficiently produce quality video.

One way to get a handle on how the basic tools and functions operate, is to work on a simple movie that uses many, but not all, of Premiere's tools. Once you've had a chance to get a general idea of how the program works, we can move on to a more detailed discussion of some of your many options, such as special effects, transitions, audio mixing, animation, graphics and titles.

Gathering Assets

Once you've made a storyboard of your concept, done the planning and shot (or bought) the required footage, the next logical step is importing those assets into a Premiere file. Simply importing them isn't the end of the process, however — it's only one stop on the journey to a finished production.

Workflow Considerations

In this chapter, we're going to look more closely at several critical processes: efficiently importing multiple clips, trimming clips to isolate the exact footage we need and applying simple transitions.

Because projects often contain dozens — even hundreds — of discrete assets, it's important to keep everything organized. The issue of proper organization and folder structure is important even for basic productions, and becomes increasingly critical as the complexity of your productions increase. We'll discuss organizational strategies at the end of the chapter.

An example of keeping organized can be seen when you import a Premiere project (as opposed to importing a rendered movie) — the program creates a new bin to contain the project's elements. The name of the bin is the same as the file from which it was created.

Aspect Ratio of Imported Clips

Aspect ratio is the proportion of the width to the height of movie. Motion picture and television industry standards determine this ratio to be three units vertically by four units across the horizontal axis. Commonly referred to as "four-three", or "4:3", this standard is essential and required for motion pictures, commercial video and television production. On the other hand, you're free to use different aspect ratios for other applications, such as projects destined for the Web, CD-ROM or network applications. Depending on what you intend to do with the production, your finished movie might be tall and thin or short and wide. You're only limited by your imagination and the requirements of the assignment.

Raw footage brought into Premiere often needs to be trimmed. Trimming clips gives us the ability to isolate specific footage and determine its duration, regardless of the length of the original imported clip.

A rendered Premiere movie isn't any different than a single piece of footage — it's treated the same way as any other clip when imported into the current project. That means that when you import a rendered clip, the assets that were used to create it aren't imported into the current project.

Import Multiple Video Clips

1. If it's not already open, launch Premiere. When the first dialog box appears, click the Custom button, and then the Next button. In the New Project Setting window, click the Next button to go through the different settings windows. Apply the following settings. Set Editing Mode: QuickTime/Video for Windows, Timebase: 29.97, Frame Size:
240 × 180, Time Display: 30 fps Drop-frame Timecode. When finished, click OK to close this window. Click OK in the next window to accept the settings and close.

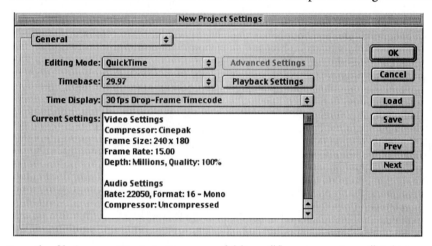

The current project determines the size of any imported assets; Premiere automatically stretches or squeezes any imported assets to conform to the project's settings. This can lead to unwanted distortion of clips and stills. To avoid the problem, make sure that any items intended for a Premier project are correctly proportioned. Stills can be sized in a program like Adobe Photoshop, Macromedia Flash or Adobe Illustrator, animations in Flash or Adobe's LiveMotion, interactive content in Macromedia Director and others. Premiere supports dozens of file formats — just make sure they fit correctly.

2. Save the file in your **Work in Progress** folder as "flower_movie.ppj". Select File>Import>File. In the dialog box, select **FLOWER1.MOV** from the **RF- Premiere>Flowers** folder, and click Open. The file transfers to the Project window.

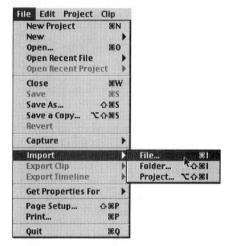

3. Now that we've imported one of the clips required for the movie, you will import five additional clips in one step. Select File>Import>File. Click on **FLOWER2.MOV**. Hold down the Shift/Control key and select **FLOWER3.MOV, FLOWER4.MOV, FLOWER5.MOV** and **FLOWER6.MOV**.

Depending on how you have your machine configured, you might see the file names in all caps, lower case or sentence case. Remember, the file names are what matters — not whether they're in lower or upper case.

What you see on your monitor will better match the illustrations in this book if you change the settings in the Timeline Window Options dialog box to the third option under Track Format. Select Timeline Window Options from the Timeline window Options menu (under the black triangle at the top right of the Timeline). Making this change will give you a small picture preview at the beginning of your video clip.

4. They all become highlighted. Click the Open button. The clips transfer to the Project window.

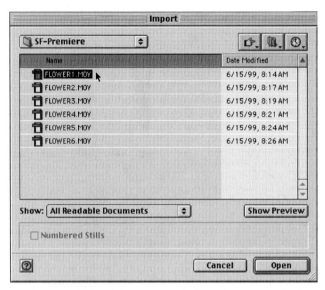

Five clips were imported at once, and all six clips are now in the window

5. Preview the first file, FLOWER1.MOV, before it is placed on the Timeline. In the Project window, select the FLOWER1.MOV icon and drag it to the Source view in the Monitor window. Play the clip by clicking the Play arrow at the bottom of the Source view.

6. Save the file, but keep it open for the next exercise.

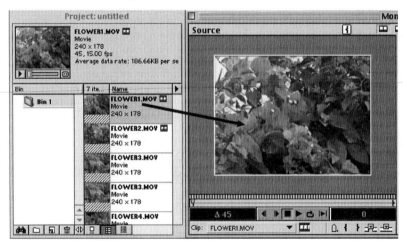

Transitions

A transition occurs when you change from one clip (or scene) to another. You see transitions every day — on television, in movies and on the Web. It might be sudden: one moment you're looking at one piece of footage and the next moment you're looking at another. You used this transition in the last chapter — it's called a "cut." Another example of this is when the scene you're watching fades until the screen is black, and another scene appears.

Placing Transitions

You add a transition by dragging it onto the Transition track of the Timeline, between two video clips. You can only apply transitions to clips that are on the Video 1A and Video 1B tracks. Video 2 (and sequential numbers above this) are used for superimposed tracks — something we'll learn about later in the book.

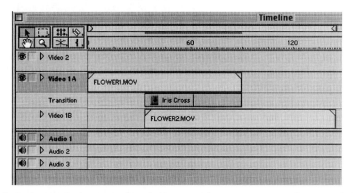

A "cut" is the simplest and most common transition. It occurs when one clip simply takes the place of another.

You can also click the Default Transition button in the Monitor window. By default, Premiere uses Cross Dissolve — second in popularity only to the common cut (see the sidebar). If you use another transition frequently, you can make it the default.

Replacing a transition is easy — you just drop your replacement transition on top of the original. When you replace a transition, Premiere retains the duration and alignment of the previous transition. Premiere uses either default settings from the new transition or any Master settings you've defined in the Transitions palette.

Use Transitions

1. In the open file, drag FLOWER1.MOV to the beginning of Video 1A (at the left of the Timeline window). You can grab this clip from either the Project window or the Source view, if you have been previewing your files. The clip expands on the Timeline.

2. Drag the clip FLOWER2.MOV to Video 1B, so that it is under and just to the right of FLOWER1.MOV. They should slightly overlap. Since Premiere displays the clips as they are dragged into position, you know which files you have placed on the Timeline.

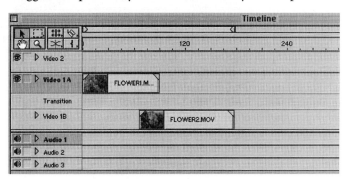

Pressing the Spacebar starts and stops playback.

3. Open the Wipe folder in the Transitions palette. Drag the Barn Doors transition from the Transitions palette to the Transition track. It should snap into position in the space where the two movies overlap.

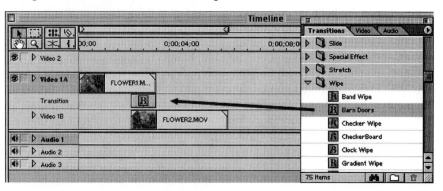

4. Want to see what this new special effect looks like? You could try to scrub through the Timeline window, as we did in the last chapter, but you will discover that Premiere won't allow you to see the effect unless you hold down Option/Alt while scrubbing. To see the entire production in real time, you have to render it first.

5. Be certain that the Timeline window is active or highlighted. Press Return/Enter. Premiere asks you to save your production. (You must complete this to see your transitions taking effect. Of course, it's a good idea to save often.)

6. Save your project as "FLOWERS.PPJ" to your **Work in Progress** folder. The project now plays with all of your transitions in place.

7. Let's add the rest of the clips. Drag the clip FLOWER3.MOV onto Video 1A, above and just to the right of FLOWER2.MOV. Again, they should slightly overlap.

8. Drag a different transition of your choice to the Transition track. It should snap into position in the space where the two movies overlap. Continue to add the other flower video clips to the Timeline. Select different transitions, and place them in the space where the flower clips overlap.

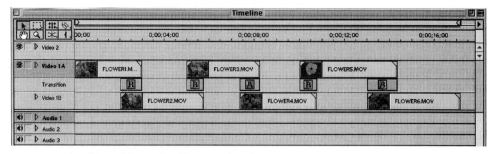

9. Save the file and leave the file open for the next exercise.

Previewing Transitions

As you add transitions and other effects, you'll want to be able to view them and see how they're working. You can preview all or part of the video program as you edit. You have already previewed individual clips in the Monitor view. You can also display previews in the Source view.

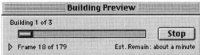

While rendering, you'll see this window often while Premiere builds the preview, which may take some time. Be patient.

Previewing is relatively fast on a production that simply cuts between clips. Applying other transitions, effects or superimposition settings, however, adds processing time to a preview. Premiere offers two methods to preview your project: scrubbing the Timeline and previewing in real time. The method you choose depends on whether you want a quick preview, a preview at a precise frame rate or a compromise between the two. Your choice may also be affected by how large a segment you want to preview. Let's take a look at these two methods.

Scrubbing the Timeline

The easiest way to preview a portion of your production is with the Scrub tool, which enables you to check edits or effects in real time. With scrubbing, you can see the transition's effect quickly, without waiting for Premiere to build the entire preview file.

Clicking the Play button in the Monitor window does not automatically update your file and show you the transitions you have selected. Instead, Premiere has two different ways of solving this problem. The first is to use the Scrub tool.

Use the Scrub Tool

1. In the open file, with the Timeline window active, press the Spacebar. Your production starts to play in the Program view of the Monitor window.

2. Hold down the Option/Alt key. Slowly drag your cursor onto the ruler, just below the yellow Work Area bar. The pointer turns into an arrow.

3. Move the Scrub tool to the left and right on the Timeline with the Option/Alt key still selected. Your project now plays with the transitions.

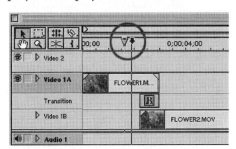

4. Leave the file open for the next exercise.

Previewing in Real Time

Scrubbing the Timeline is a great technique for previewing, but if the production is longer than a few seconds, this operation can be tiring. Premiere provides another way to look at your production — previewing all or part of your production.

When you look at the top of the Timeline window, you should see a small yellow bar with a small gray triangle on either end. This is the Work Area bar. At the moment, it extends to the end of your project. This bar serves a very useful purpose — it enables you to preview specific areas of your production. Whatever is contained inside the yellow bar plays during a render. If the marker stretches out over the entire production, a full render will occur. If you move the marker to cover a smaller area of the production, only that part of the project will be updated for you.

Why use the Work Area bar? If you are working on a two-minute project, you usually complete the first minute before moving further into the production. The Work Area bar lets you bypass the first minute by pulling the marker over to just the area you wish to watch. This way you won't have to watch the same minute, over and over, when you really want to focus on the later part of the production. It will save you a lot of time in the long run.

Preview the Production

1. In the open file, make certain that the Timeline window is active (i.e., click on the Timeline bar to activate it). Press the Return/Enter key. A progress box displays as the preview builds. Your production plays again.

2. Drag the triangle from the right side of the Work Area bar to the left (toward the center of the production). Pull the triangle on the left side of the bar to the right (also toward the center of the production). Press the Return/Enter key.

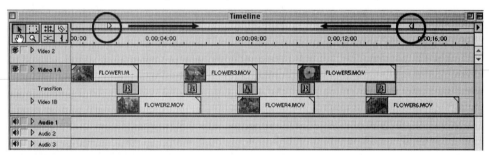

The Work Area bar lets you bypass the beginning of the project and move directly to just the area you wish to watch. This enables you to view a smaller segment of the production with visible transitions.

3. Return the Work Area bar to the original positions at the beginning and end of the entire production.

4. Press the Return/Enter key again. The progress box displays as the preview builds. This time the entire production plays from start to finish, with all of your transitions.

5. Save your production again. Leave this file open for the next exercise.

Trimming

It is common to capture too much footage when you are working with video, whether accidentally or intentionally (to permit edits after capturing). If this happens, you need to trim the excess. Premiere is a very flexible program, so it offers a number of ways to make a trim. The one you choose will depend on your personal working preferences and the nature of your project.

Some techniques involve working in a window before the clip is placed in the Timeline. Others involve working with a clip already placed on the Timeline, either by working on the clip directly on the Timeline or by bringing up an individual Clip window. Regardless of your choice, you have the control; your clip is trimmed and the production continues in its usual fashion after the trim is complete.

Making Trims with In and Out Points

Cutting off that extra footage begins with setting and manipulating In and Out points, which mark where you want the clip to begin (In point) and end (Out point). Your choice of most appropriate technique for setting In and Out points and completing the trim depends on how technically precise you need the production to be.

Suppose you wanted to trim exactly one full second of bad video at the end of the production and 0.5 seconds at the beginning. If, for example, you are setting up a soap opera scene with a required cutaway on a precise word, you must set exact In and Out points because timing is the essence of the shot. You might choose the first technique for making a trim — working with the clip in the Source view of the Monitor window.

Pressing Option/Alt and clicking the cursor in the yellow Work Bar automatically expands the bar to the ends of the production.

You would first move the shuttle in the Set Location area to the exact place where you want the first trim to occur. The shuttle is the small slider just above where you can see a series of zeros. (Those numbers are the production's timecodes, which will be discussed later.) The area containing the slider or shuttle is the Set Location area. Notice that the clip already has In and Out points (brackets) in the Set Location area. (When those brackets have been set or moved, inside the area they mark off is a yellow bar indicating the active area of the Set Location area.)

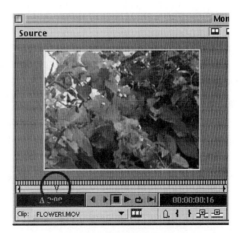

Just because the production plays after rendering does not mean that the file has been saved. You must make a conscious effort to save every few minutes.

Once the shuttle is placed where you want the trim to occur, you would click the Mark In or Mark Out bracket at the bottom right of the Source view. When you click the Mark In bracket, it sets the new starting point and trims off the rest of the footage. Clicking the Mark Out bracket has the same effect, creating the new ending point. Once a mark/bracket is set, you can move it around by putting your cursor over it and dragging it to the exact point you want. You can move it backward or forward to adjust and refine the trim. Your final step, in this technique, is to drag the clip from the Source view to the Timeline. Once you place it, you will find that it is already trimmed. (One variation on this technique is to move the shuttle to the moment you want by typing the time in the Timecode area on the right of the Source window (instead of dragging the shuttle.)

The above technique, or using the Program view in the same fashion, is particularly helpful if you need to be precise, since you can set the points *numerically.*

A second approach to making trims works well if you prefer setting points more *visually* and using your mouse. If your footage doesn't require a technically precise edit — perhaps it's a shot of flowers wafting in the wind — exact numerical accuracy won't be essential. In this case, you'll probably be most comfortable editing with the Edge Trim tool in the Timeline. The cursor automatically changes to the Edge Trim tool when you move the Selection tool near the edge of a clip in the Timeline. Where the cursor touches the front or back edge of the clip, a small red bracket with an arrow appears. By pulling that marker in, you shorten the clip from that end. As you shorten the clip, you are making the trim.

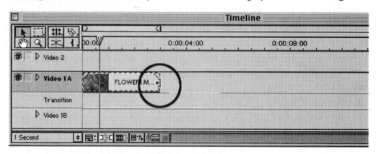

The Edge Trim tool is particularly helpful for making rough cuts (less technically precise work), but it can also be used more precisely if you set the Timeline to display individual frames. You can set the Timeline to display at this individual-frame level by zooming in with the Zoom tool or by selecting the 1 Frame option from the drag-down menu in the bottom-left corner of the Timeline. Working with the Timeline set this way is particularly helpful for producing animations, since it can be important to work on them one frame at a time.

A fourth technique also involves working with a clip already placed on the Timeline. This time, however, you double-click the clip on the Timeline, thus opening the Clip window for that piece of footage. When you set the In and Out brackets, an Apply button appears at the bottom of the window. When you click this button, the clip shortens in both the Clip window and on the Timeline.

So the choice is yours — you can edit before the clip is placed on the Timeline or once it's already there, with a numerical approach or a more visual approach; whatever you prefer. You may also find yourself choosing different approaches for different types of productions.

Trim a Clip

1. In the open file, double-click on FLOWER5.MOV in the Timeline window. This causes it to appear in a unique Clip window.

2. Click the Play button. Notice the excess footage at the back end of the clip.

3. Slowly drag the button to the left. The Set Location button scrubs through the FLOWER5.MOV clip so that you can look at it frame by frame.

4. At 3:20 on the timecode, observe that the shot changes to the red hibiscus. This is the section that we will trim off.

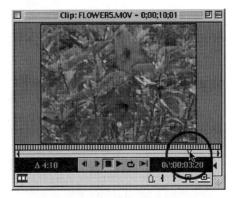

5. Click the Frameback arrow (the black, left-pointing arrow) until the clock turns back to 3:18. The red hibiscus disappears.

6. Click the Mark Out bracket. (You can also press "O" on the keyboard.) A small bracket appears in the upper-right corner of the window.

7. Notice that an Apply button appears at the bottom of the Clip window. Click Apply. Your clip shortens in the Timeline window to accommodate this new trim.

8. A gap has been created on the Timeline by this trim. Shift your previously selected transition and FLOWER6.MOV to the left so that they again overlap FLOWER5.MOV.

9. Save and render the file to see these new changes.

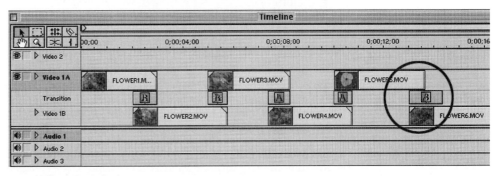

10. Close Premiere.

File and Folder Organization

Every computer program has its eccentricities, and Premiere is no exception. As you have worked on this chapter's assignments, Premiere has been hard at work behind the scenes, keeping track of your clips, transitions and more. Premiere does this by creating the Adobe Premiere Preview Files folder

Preview Files Folder

The Preview Files folder contains all the data related to your production. If it's unavailable, Premiere re-renders the entire project.

Even if it flies in the face of your creative spirit, keeping track of little details is critically important. Remember when we mentioned that the best videographers need to be both technically adept as well as creative? File and folder organization is one of the critical junctures of the two disciplines.

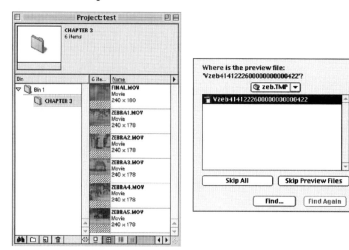

Project File

Finally, there is the named project file, which in this chapter is FLOWERS.PPJ. This is a small file containing data related to the overall project. It includes information about your video clips (which are in a separate folder), but does not include rendered versions of the project. All of the additional information related to your transitions or filters is in the Adobe Premiere Preview Files folder.

What does this mean? It means you have to keep careful track of where everything is while you are creating a production. You have to set up the appropriate folders and make certain that you put all components in them from the very beginning of your work. If you're missing a file, or Premiere simply can't find it, the program will prompt you to browse to where the file is stored. If there are multiple files that the program needs, and they're in one folder, all you have to do is double-click the first one in the list; Premiere will find the balance of the content that's in that folder.

Summary

In Chapter 2, you learned how to improve productivity by importing multiple clips, folders of assets and components of existing projects. We discussed transitions — beginning with the most basic cuts, dissolves and fades. You learned how to apply transitions on the Timeline. Lastly, you learned the importance of proper organization — a critical consideration when building complex projects.

3 *Using Filters for Special Effects*

Chapter Objective:

To learn to use filters. To become familiar with how filters work, and what effects you can achieve with them. In Chapter 3, you will:

- Learn the basic definition of a Premiere filter.

- Explore applications of filters.

- Become familiar with and practice using the Video Effects palette which contains more than 70 predefined effects.

- Observe the difference between native and After Effects filters, and learn how to recognize them in the Video Effects palette.

- Discover how to work with the Effect Controls palette— which control the attributes and variables for each specific filter.

- Learn to use keyframes.

- Learn to combine filters to achieve custom special effects.

- Discover how to use the Razor tool to edit clips while applying effects.

- Learn how to create QuickTime movies and cross-platform productions.

Projects to be Completed:

- The Monkey Movie (A)

- How to Make Spaghetti (B)

- How to Tame a Tiger (C)

- The Gold Rush (D)

Using Filters for Special Effects

Special effects are the foundation of many of today's hit movies — it almost seems as if a movie without special effects is somehow lacking. While that conclusion may be questionable, there's no question that you need a facility with special effects in your arsenal of video skills. Premiere helps you with this skill by providing an extensive collection of filters that can be dragged from the Video Effects palette onto any clip on the Timeline.

Suppose you want to create the effect of an old, black-and-white silent movie. Premiere accomplishes this for you with a filter called "Black & White." It strips your video clip of its color. You might then apply Film Noise, another filter that would give the clip an old-time look, this time by adding some graininess. The best part of using filters like these is that they do not in any way touch the original video footage. This means that you can experiment until you find the right look for your production without harming your original footage.

Once a production is underway, you begin adding special effects to any or all of your clips. You do this by using the Video Effects palette in conjunction with the Effect Controls palette. The Video Effects palette holds the different types of effects, and the Effect Controls palette controls the adjustment or look of the effect over time. If you don't like an effect, you can easily delete it. You can even apply the same effect multiple times to the same clip with different settings.

The Video Effects Palette

The process of selecting filters begins in the Video Effects palette, which offers a selection of 74 different filters or effects. These effects may be added to any clips you have placed on the Timeline. Effects are grouped in folders, which can be expanded or contracted as you make your selections. Unused filters stay tucked away until you need them. Two types of filters appear in the window. The first type are native filters — built into Premiere. They can be identified by the "V" in the icon. The second type is plug-ins — After Effects plug-ins from the Adobe application of the same name. Their icon is a small electrical plug.

Be aware that rendering special effects filters can add considerable time to the rendering process — not itself the fastest process in the world. Some filters require much processing horsepower and can hold your system up for a while.

Note that we have resized the palette so that we could show two columns of icons — yours probably shows only one column.

The Video Effects palette provides a number of productivity enhancements. One such enhancement is the small set of binoculars at the bottom of the palette, which lets you search through the effects for the one you want. In this example, we clicked the icon and typed the name of the Crystallize filter in the Find field.

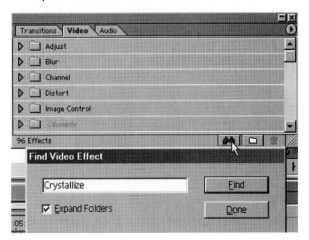

The Effect Controls Palette

When you apply an effect to a clip, the effect is listed in the Effect Controls palette. You can use this palette, therefore, to manage your effects. The palette contains information about every effect applied to clips in your video production. If you have applied multiple effects to a clip, the Effect Controls palette lists them all, in order from top to bottom in this list. You can reorder the effects in this list to change which effects are rendered first.

Each effect also shows on the Timeline along with a set of triangles that represent the keyframes for the effects.

A *keyframe* is a marker that tells Premiere when to begin applying an effect and at what intensity. Filters have different settings, which you can control and change at specific points on the Timeline through keyframes. There are no limits to the number of keyframes you can apply to a clip.

Let's say, for example, that you're dissolving or crystallizing a clip. You would like the process to start slowly, then increase in speed, so that your clip begins free of the effect, but the effect then speeds up and intensifies toward the end. Keyframes enable you to accomplish this. They delay effects, speed them up and adjust other effect-specific values on the Timeline.

The keyboard shortcut to import a folder is Command/Control-Shift-I.

Similarly, if you wanted the full effect of the filter to show at the beginning of the clip, slowly resolving to the finished, unfiltered footage, you would use keyframes to accomplish your goal. You would need to set two keyframes — the first with heavy crystallization and the second with light crystallization. That second keyframe would be placed partway into the clip. Because Premiere automatically updates the distortion (impact of the effect) between keyframes, the crystallization would gradually decrease between the first and second keyframes, and would end after the second keyframe.

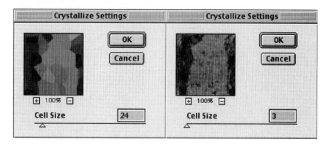

Get Started

1. If it is not already open, launch Premiere and accept the standard settings. Open **RF-Premiere>Zebra>zebra_final.mov**. It opens as a separate window. Play the movie by clicking the Play button at the bottom of the Clip window. Once you've seen the finished piece, close the window.

Import Video Clips in a Folder

1. Select File>Import>Folder. A dialog box appears. Select **RF-Premiere>Zebra**, and click Choose/Select. The folder, with all its contents inside it, will transfer to the Project window.

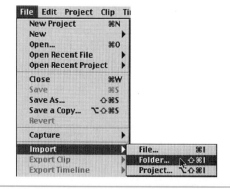

You can also select the clip and click the Play button at the top of the Project window.

2. You now have a Zebra folder in Bin 1. Double-click the folder icon to open it, revealing six clips inside. You can instead click on the triangle in the Bin window to reveal the clips folder.

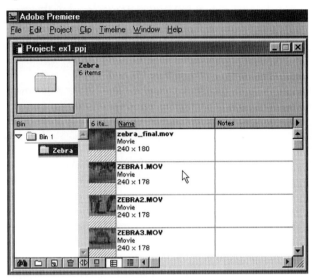

3. Leave this file open for the next exercise.

Apply a Special Effect

1. Drag ZEBRA1.MOV to Video 1A on the Timeline. Drag ZEBRA2.MOV to the Timeline window, and place it on Video 1B so that it slightly overlaps ZEBRA1.MOV. The yellow Work Area bar automatically extends to the end of the video clips.

2. Select a transition of your choice, and place it in the Transition track between ZEBRA1.MOV and ZEBRA2.MOV.

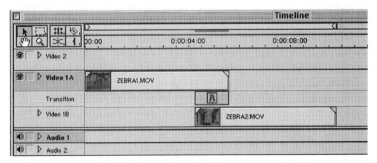

3. Click on ZEBRA1.MOV. The "walking ants" shows that the file is selected. Make sure the Video Effects palette is open. (If it is not, select it from the Window menu.)

The peach-colored line that shows above your newly placed transition in the Timeline window lets you know that a transition is in place but not yet rendered. Once rendered, the line changes to aqua blue.

4. Open the Blur folder, and drag the Camera Blur icon onto ZEBRA1.MOV. The Effect Controls palette indicates that the filter has been placed. Expand the Video 1A track by clicking on the triangle to the left of Video 1A. Keyframes are automatically added at the beginning and end of the clip.

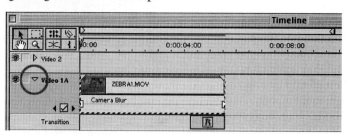

Clicking the triangle to the left of Video 1A, Video 1B, etc., expands the track downward and reveals any keyframes applied to the clip(s) on that track.

5. Click on the first keyframe in the Timeline, and then click the Enable Keyframing box in the Effect Controls palette. A small clock appears. Set the Percent slider bar to 100.

Keyframing Enabled Box

6. On the Timeline, click the right-side keyframe of ZEBRA1.MOV. In the Effect Controls palette, set the Percent bar to zero (0).

7. Press Return/Enter. Save your file as "FILTERS.PPJ" to your **Work in Progress** folder. The movie now renders, and you see the results of using the Camera Blur effect.

Combine Filters

1. In the Video Effects palette, close the Blur folder and open the Image Control folder. Drag the Black & White filter icon onto ZEBRA2.MOV. Expand the Video 1B track by clicking on the triangle. The track expands, showing the keyframes at the beginning and end of the clip.

2. Drag the Tint filter icon onto ZEBRA2.MOV. Click the Enable Keyframing box in the Effect Controls palette. Click on the first keyframe for ZEBRA2.MOV.

   In the Tint Settings dialog box, click on the Map Black to box. The Color Picker dialog box appears. Set it to Red: 172, Green: 26, Blue: 0, and click OK.

The green line that shows above your newly placed effect in the Timeline window lets you know that an effect is now in use.

Click on the Map White to box. Set the Color Picker to Red: 255, Green: 121, Blue: 87, and click OK.

Set the Amount to Tint bar to 28.

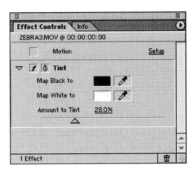

3. Click on the second keyframe for ZEBRA2.MOV. (Notice the colors in the Tint box default back to black and white).

In the Tint Settings dialog box, click on the Map Black to box. In the Color Picker, set Red: 0, Green: 16, Blue: 245, and click OK.

Click on the Map White to box. Set the Color Picker to Red: 200, Green: 212, Blue: 255. Set the Amount to Tint bar to 28, and click OK.

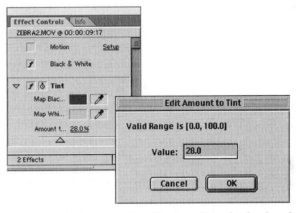

4. Press Enter/Return to render your file. The two clips play back to back with a transition. The second clip changes from a sepia color to a shade of blue.

5. Drag ZEBRA3.MOV to Video 1A, ZEBRA4.MOV to Video 1B and ZEBRA5.MOV to Video 1A. Overlap them slightly. Select three more transitions, and drag them to the Transition track between the two clips.

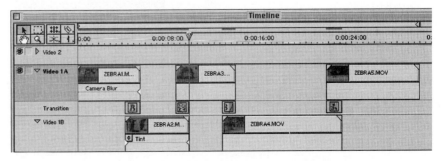

Using filters does not alter your original video footage. You can add as many special effects as you wish to the same clip. You can even apply different filters to the same clip and use it at different times in the same production.

6. Now you'll add filters to the three other video clips. This time, however, we'll try something a little different.

   If it is not already open, expand the Video 1A track by clicking on the small gray triangle at the left of the track. As it expands, you can see the keyframes at the beginning and end of the clip.

   In the Video Effects palette, open the Pixelate folder, and drag the Crystallize icon onto ZEBRA3.MOV on the Timeline. In the dialog box, set the Cell Size slider bar to 40, and click OK. In the Effect Controls palette, click on the Enable Keyframing box. A clock appears.

7. Click on the second keyframe for ZEBRA3.MOV. From the Effect Controls palette, set the Crystallize Cell Size slider bar to 3.

8. Make sure the Work Area bar is extended to the end of the production. Render the project by pressing Return/Enter. It will take several moments for Premiere to render these new changes. This time the entire production plays from start to finish with all the new filters in place.

   As you watch the clip play and see the Crystallize filter, you may notice that the filter doesn't allow you to see the actual video. What you would prefer is for the filter to work on part of the clip and leave the rest untouched. This problem can be easily solved.

9. Select ZEBRA3.MOV on the Timeline. Pull the right Keyframe icon about halfway to the left, until the timecode on the Program side of the Monitor window reads approximately 00:00:12:00.

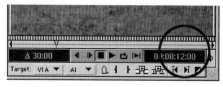

The more transitions and filters you use, the more time it takes to render the production. Moral of the story — have patience and lots of RAM!

10. Press Return/Enter. This time the entire production plays from start to finish, with the Crystallize filter affecting only the beginning of ZEBRA3.MOV. It now looks like shapes are morphing into the zebra.

11. Next you'll apply filters to ZEBRA4.MOV and ZEBRA5.MOV. On the Timeline, click on ZEBRA4.MOV.

Open the Adjust folder, and drag the Extract icon onto ZEBRA4.MOV. Click Setup in the Effect Controls palette. Set the left Input Range slider to 91, and leave the right slider set to 192. Check Invert, then click OK.

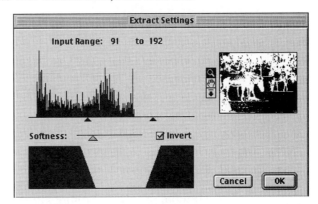

12. Save and then render your file. Observe the changes as the movie plays.

13. Click on ZEBRA5.MOV. Open the Stylize folder, and drag Replicate onto ZEBRA5.MOV. Click Setup in the Effect Controls palette. In the Replicate dialog box, set the slider to 3, and click OK.

Macintosh   Windows

14. The Work Area bar should extend the length of your production. If it doesn't, move the right handle to the end of the footage. Save and render the file.

15. Save the project but leave it open for the next exercise.

Splitting a Clip

You can split a clip in the Timeline by using the Razor tool. Splitting a clip creates new and separate parts of the original clip. This process can be useful when you want to use different effects at the same time. For example, you might want a jogger to run at two different speeds.

When you split a clip, Premiere creates a new slice or section of the clip and any clips to which it is linked. Premiere allows you to split any clip into two or more parts. Each part becomes independent and can have unique filters applied. Premiere splits only the audio or video portion of linked clips.

One important tip: always be sure to reselect the Selection tool when you are finished using the Razor tool. This is very important, since if you don't click back to the Selection tool, you will continue to cut your clip into smaller and smaller pieces.

The Find button at the bottom of the Video Effects palette will locate any effect. Click on the folder icon, and type in the name of the filter. When finished, click Done.

Note: if you want to change effect settings over time, you don't need to split the clip; you can apply keyframes to it instead.

Use the Razor Tool

Now let's use the Razor tool to allow us to see the zebras, first from a distance and then from a much closer vantage point.

1. We'll begin by removing the Replicate filter that was applied to ZEBRA5.MOV. In the open file, click on ZEBRA5.MOV. The clip shows that it is selected. In the Effect Controls palette, select the Replicate effect. Click the Trash button at the bottom of the palette. When prompted, click Yes to delete the effect. Look at the Timeline, and note that ZEBRA5.MOV no longer has the green line above it. The filter has been removed.

2. Position your cursor on the Timeline at 00:00:26:00, and click. (Use the Info palette to see the exact location of the pointer.) Your position marker will jump to the new position. Select the Razor tool (on the left side of the Timeline).

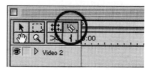

3. Position the Razor tool on the ZEBRA5.MOV clip so that it lines up with the Edit Line, and click. The clip splits in two. You will see two portions (or segments) of ZEBRA5.MOV on the Timeline, side by side.

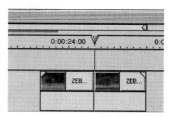

4. Now select the Selection tool (press "V"). Remember: if you don't first click back to the Selection tool, you will continue to chop your clip into ever-smaller pieces.

Now that you have two distinct sections of ZEBRA5.MOV, you can apply two different effects. We're going to leave the first half of the clip alone and apply the Crop filter to the second half.

5. Open the Transform folder, and drag the Crop icon onto the second half of the ZEBRA5.MOV clip. Click Setup in the Effect Controls palette. Set all four sliders (Top, Bottom, Left and Right) to 20%, and click OK.

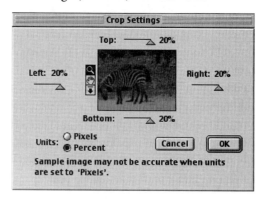

To access the Razor tool, press "C". To access the Selection tool, press "V".

It's important to reselect the Selection tool after using the Razor tool. If you don't, you'll cut up the clips into ever smaller and smaller segments.

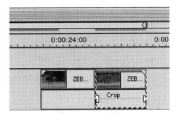

6. Save your file, then press Return/Enter to render your file. Observe your latest changes.

Exporting as a QuickTime Movie

The last process we're going to apply to this effect-enriched movie is to save it out as a QuickTime movie. This is an important production skill that you'll be using throughout the book. If you're in doubt about how to do it, you can always refer back to this chapter. From this point forward, if we say "export a QuickTime movie," we'll be referring to this process.

Export as a QuickTime Movie

1. In the open file, select File>Export Timeline>Movie.

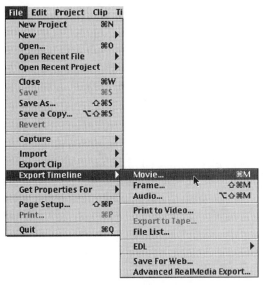

Name the project "FINAL.MOV". Click the Settings button. Uncheck the Export Audio box, since there is no audio in this project. Click Next.

2. Set Frame Size H: 240, V: 180, Compressor: Video, Frame Rate: 15, Quality: 80% (which will help reduce the size of the file).

You may need to change the Compressor setting if you want the produciton to be cross-platform. If the project will run on both Windows and Macintosh systems, set compressor to Cinepak.

3. Click the Next button. This will display the Audio Settings area, which we will skip for now since there is no audio in this production. Click OK to return to the main (General) area of the Export dialog box.

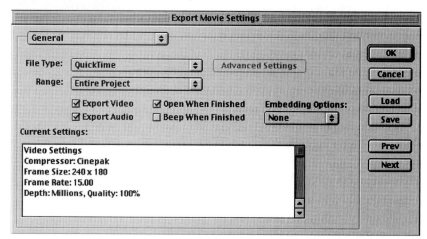

Cinepak takes longer to render, but it's the only way to create a truly cross-platform project.

4. Double-check where your file is about to be saved. Save it to your **Work in Progress** folder. It will take several minutes to fully complete the rendering process. Now your production is a self-contained piece. If you wish, you can delete all of the other files related to this production, since you no longer require them.

5. Play the movie to make sure everything went as planned.

6. Close the file and close Premiere.

Summary

In Chapter 3 you learned to use multiple filters on a single clip to create many varieties of special effects. You also learned to split a clip in order to add special effects to parts of the clip. You began the chapter by becoming familiar with how to import multiple clips efficiently in a single folder. You learned how to apply and remove special effect filters to and from a clip by applying and removing keyframes. You also learned how to create QuickTime movies and cross-platform productions.

4 Transitions

Chapter Objective:

To work extensively with transitions — a critical component of any professional video production. To become more familiar with transitions — previewing, customizing and applying them to achieve special effects. In Chapter 4, you will:

- Learn more about the Transitions palette and how to use its options.

- Explore some of the more than 70 transitions that come with the application.

- Discover how to animate the icons in the Transitions palette, so that you can preview any transition before applying it.

- Learn to customize the Transitions palette so that it better suits the way you work.

- Become familiar with categories of transitions, from the most basic cuts to dissolves, fads, wipes and blends.

- Discover methods of customizing transitions, both in the Transitions palette and on the Timeline.

- Observe and practice using transitions to create popular effects, such as picture-in-picture and split screen effects.

- Learn how to export single frames as individual still files, and how to use transitions to introduce those stills back into your productions.

Projects to be Completed:

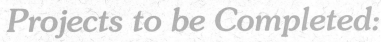

- The Monkey Movie (A)

- How to Make Spaghetti (B)

- How to Tame a Tiger (C)

- The Gold Rush (D)

Transitions

As we discussed earlier, a transition occurs when one clip replaces another — the scene changes from the fireside to the ski slopes, for example, or from the fisherman drinking a beer to the shark lurking beneath the hull of his boat. Transitions are at the heart of all production and video editing.

Premiere comes with some 75 transitions already built into the Transitions palette. Each of them can be customized in a variety of ways, providing you with an almost unlimited array of choices.

The Transitions Palette

Transitions can be over-used; in most cases, subtle is better. If you place too much emphasis on your transitions, the importance of the clips can be diminished. Remember: it's the footage that contains the content of your production.

Transitions are accessed from the Transitions palette. They're organized within folders, by kind, with an icon and/or description representing each.

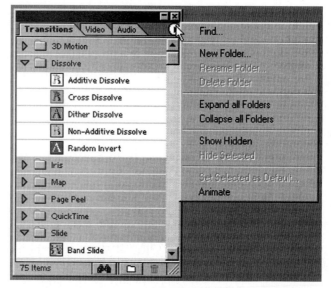

Premiere ships with more than 75 transitions. Under the black triangle in the top-right corner of the palette is the Transitions palette Options menu.

Cross Dissolve is the default transition when Premiere is first installed. You can select any transition in the Transitions palette and use the Set Selected as Default command to change this new transition to the default.

One useful function available on the Transitions palette Options menu is Animate. If you select Animate, the icons show a preview of that transition (to the extent that you can really see a transition in a 12-pixel square).

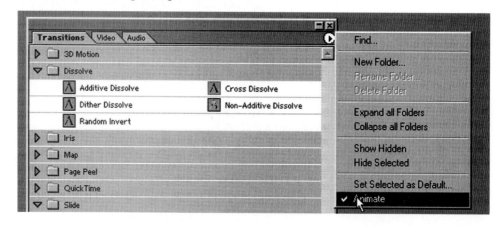

Customizing the Transitions Palette

The Transitions palette offers a number of special features to help you speed up your work. Let's examine several of the special properties in its Options menu.

To add a folder to the palette, select New Folder from the Options menu. Once you create a new folder, you can populate it by dragging transitions into it from other folders.

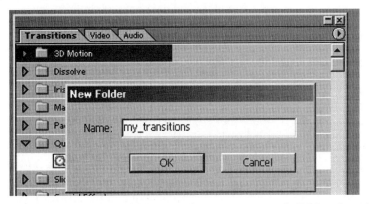

Clicking the triangle to the left of a folder reveals its contents, and clicking the triangle again collapses the folder. To view all the contents of every folder, choose Expand All Folders from the Options menu.

Another measure you might want to take is to hide transactions, to reduce clutter and make it easier to move around in the palette. If you're using a Macintosh, use Shift-click to select non-contiguous transitions. Control-click is the Windows equivalent. You can use this method to select transitions in separate folders.

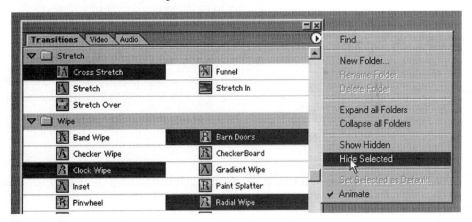

Types of Transitions

Before computer editing, transitions were made by splicing two pieces of film together. Premiere's digital techniques not only mirror conventional methods, but also provide transitions that are very difficult — or impossible — to achieve using manual techniques.

Premiere provides an extensive assortment of transitions, and many more are available both free and commercially. Built-in transitions include:

- **Cut.** This is the simplest form of transition — one clip is replaced with another in a single frame.
- **Dissolve.** With this transition, the clip that's playing slowly dissolves, and the new clip dissolves into the scene, replacing the first one.

- **Blur.** This transition is similar to a dissolve, except that one clip loses focus while the next clip sharpens.

- **Blend.** With this transition, the incoming clip is seen on top of the current clip, increasing in intensity until the previous clip disappears.

- **Wipe.** This transition enables the incoming clip to "wipe" or erase across the screen, displacing the previous clip. You can control where the wipe begins: at the top, bottom, sides or corners.

Editing Transitions

You can customize any transition. The exact adjustment settings depend on several factors, including the type of transition. There are two ways for you to edit a transition. Understanding the difference between the two is quite important, and can have a major (and, at times, unexpected) impact on your productions.

- **Editing a single instance.** If you double-click a transition that's already in place on the Timeline, you're making changes to that one instance only. The original transition (the one in the Transitions palette) remains untouched, as are other uses of the same transition elsewhere on the Timeline.

- **Editing an original transition.** If you double-click a transition in the Transitions palette, the changes you make affect every instance of the transition on the Timeline — the change is global. Once it is edited, anytime you then drop this transition onto the Timeline, from that point forward, that use of the transition will also reflect the change.

If you want to revert to the original default settings for your transitions, delete the Preferences file. (We did this in the first chapter. If you need to, refer back to those instructions on how to discard your Preferences file.)

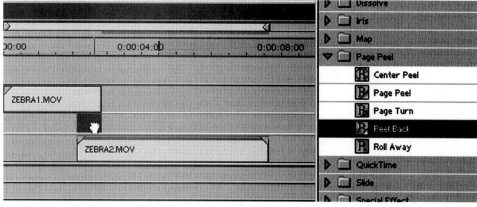

This graphic illustrates editing a single instance of a transition. We first dropped two clips on the Timeline, trimmed them to the desired size and then dragged one of the Page Peel transitions onto the Timeline between the two clips.

Once the transition is in place on the Timeline (in the Transitions track), we're able to double-click it and access that transaction's Settings dialog box. Take a moment to familiarize yourself with the controls.

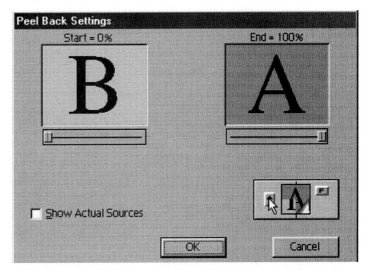

In the lower-right corner of the Settings dialog box is a small rectangular icon. The arrow on the left determines the A/B order of the transition and the front-to-back order of the two clips.

At the top of the Settings dialog box are controls over the start and end percentages of the transition. If you play with these settings some, you'll find that you can't start one transition at a point further then the end of another.

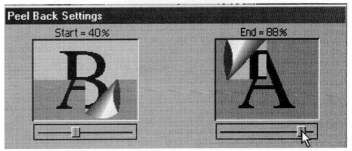

Although we've been showing the use of the generic A/B graphic so far, you can check the Show Actual Sources checkbox to replace the graphic with the actual footage from the Timeline. Checking this is particularly helpful for visualizing the exact effect of changes to the start and end percentages.

You can add borders to transitions and can control the borders' *weight* (thickness) and color.

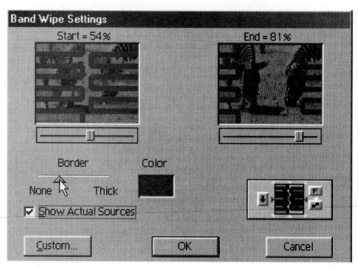

Custom Settings

If you want to experiment with editing settings for specific transitions, it's probably safer to drag an instance onto the Timeline between two short clips and edit it there. That way you'll avoid making changes to the original transitions in the Transitions palette.

Some transitions can be customized, as indicated by the Custom button in the lower left of the Settings dialog box. All transitions can be customized with the general controls, including the start and end percentages of the transition, their stacking order, whether or not Show Actual Sources is activated and borders. In the case of the Band Wipe, for example, you can also control the number of bars used for the transition. Take some time to look at the various transitions available to you by either dropping them on the Timeline or double-clicking them in the Transitions palette. Just make sure that if you use the latter option, you're careful about making changes.

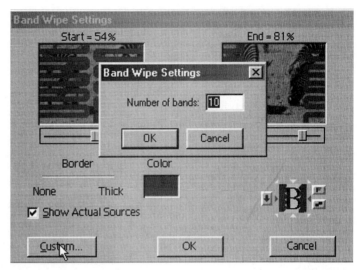

Transitions — particularly custom transitions — can create some pretty dramatic effects. An example of one you may have seen before is the ability to freeze a transition so that you can create picture-in-picture effects. They're frequently used in news broadcasts, for example.

Picture-in-picture

It's the six o'clock news and there's a massive tie-up on the turnpike. The tense newscaster opens with the special news report that all traffic heading west will be delayed until the problem — a protest rally — has ended. As the newscaster speaks, a graphic pops up to enhance the broadcast.

Almost every event that is broadcast is shown with a graphic insert of some kind, typically a still or a video. In television studios this effect is generated using a professional video mixer called a "switcher." Premiere can generate this effect as well. Known as a "split screen" or an "inset," the effect is created by freezing a transition at its midpoint.

Exercise Set-up

In the following set of exercises, you will have the opportunity to create some of the effects you see daily on television broadcasts. You'll create a picture-in-picture or inset effect. With this transition in place, you'll observe two pieces of video playing at once. Finally, you'll add music and adjust it to give your production that professional touch.

Preview the Finished Piece

1. Create a new project using the standard settings we've been using throughout the book. Save it as "broadcastnews.ppj" to your **Work in Progress** folder.

2. Select File>Import>Folder. In the dialog box, select **RF-Premiere>the_news**, and click Choose. The folder, along with its contents, transfers to the Project window.

3. Double-click the_news folder to reveal the three clips with which you will work in this chapter. Double-click NEWSFIN.MOV (or drag it to the Source view). Click the Play button to preview your final project. Close the separate Clip window.

If you have used older versions of Premiere, you may have noticed that a number of special effects are missing in this version. Many of Premiere's older effects have been replaced by After Effects video filters. If you are working on a project created in earlier versions of the program, and your project uses an obsolete effect, you can still use it in Premiere 6.0. All obsolete video effects are in the Obsolete folder in the Video Effects palette.

Place the Clips

1. Drag NEWS1.MOV to the Timeline window, and position it at the beginning of Video 1A.

2. Drag FLAMINGO1.MOV to the Timeline window, and position it on Video 1B at 00:00:10:22. You can do this easily by first dragging the Edit Line to 00:00:10:22. Look at the bottom of the Target view in the Monitor window. As you move the Edit Line, the numbers at the bottom change to 00:00:10:22. Drag FLAMINGO1.MOV from the Project window to the Timeline window. It snaps to the Edit Line.

The term "insert" and "inset" are used interchangeably. They both refer to a split frame technique that allows the display of a still image or video footage within a main clip. A perfect example is a newscast.

Monitor Method

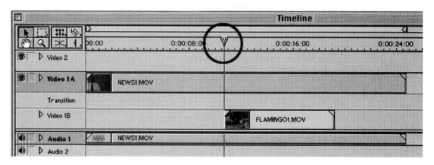

Edit Line Method

3. Use the Scrub tool to view the production. All you see, so far, is the footage on Video 1A. You need to create the split screen that inserts one video clip into another. Save the file.

Add Transitions and Create the Split Screen

1. Drag the Wipe transition from the Wipe folder in the Transitions palette to the Transition track at 00:00:10:22. It should snap into position in the space where the two movies overlap. (If you do not see your transitions, select Window>Show Transitions. You may also need to scroll down to the Wipe transition.)

2. The transition needs to be stretched to the same width as FLAMINGO1.MOV. Position the cursor at the end of the Wipe transition. The cursor turns into a two-sided arrow with a red bracket. Drag the two-sided arrow until the transition is the same length as FLAMINGO1.MOV.

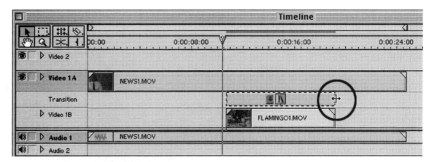

You should notice that there's an audio track at the bottom of the Timeline. Although we won't be working with audio to any major extent until Chapter 7, there are certain situations where we chose to include an audio clip to enhance the exercise.

3. Now let's create the inset for the newscast. On the Timeline, double-click the Wipe transition. A dialog box appears.

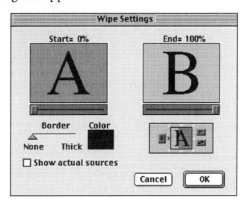

4. Check Show Actual Sources. You will see a preview of your video clips. Set the left slider (Start=) to 50% and the right slider (End=) to 50%, as well. You will see a preview of the final result.

5. We want our newscaster to appear on the left of the screen and the flamingos on the right. Notice that the images are backward. Look to the right side of the screen. You see a small blue "F". Click on it. It changes to an "R," and the pictures reverse on the preview. (Notice also that the small blue Wipe preview stops moving.)

There are other ways to mark the timecode. You can enter the number directly in the Timecode window. On a Macintosh, it turns green when you select it. You can also use the Info palette and the arrow keys to mark the time exactly.

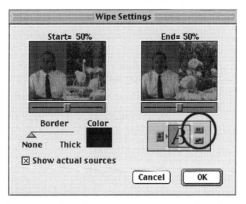

6. At the moment, there is no border to separate the video clips. A border color would help to define the individual sections.

Click on the black rectangle. The Color Picker appears. Set Red: 255, Green: 8, Blue: 31, and click OK.

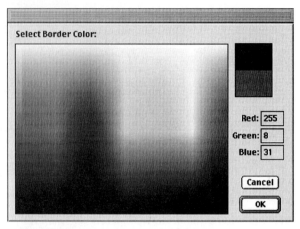

The Start (0%) and the End (100%) that you see in the transition's dialog box represents the beginning and ending of your wipe. By altering these numbers to 20% and 70%, for example, you create a partial wipe that slowly brings a transition onto the screen so that the action can be seen.

7. Move the Border triangle from None to the right, just a little. A thin red border color appears. Click OK.

8. Check to see if the Work Area bar has extended to the end of the production. Extending the bar all the way to the end allows you to view the entire production.

9. Press Return/Enter. It takes several moments for Premiere to render these new changes. This time the entire production plays from start to finish. Now as our newscaster discusses a news event, a split screen appears halfway into the production.

10. Save the file. Leave the file open for the next exercise.

Exporting Video Clips as Single Frames

As you know, in most newscasts the announcer delivers a news story while a single still image is placed in the upper-right corner of the frame. This is usually referred to as a "camera insert."

In your last exercise, you created such an insert with a moving camera-in-camera effect. If you decided that a single-frame insert would be a better choice to tell your story, you could make it quite easily.

Like any video, the flamingo movie is just a series of frames that have been linked together to form a continuous video clip running at 15 frames per second (fps). To make this freeze-frame insert, all we have to do is select a single frame of the movie and transform it.

Create a Freeze-frame Insert

1. Click and delete the following files from the Timeline window: FLAMINGO1.MOV and the Wipe transition. Leave everything else on the Timeline.

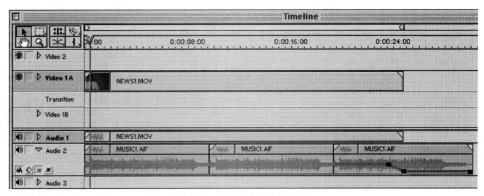

2. Drag FLAMINGO1.MOV from the Project window to the Source view. The movie appears in the window.

3. Move the Scrub tool in the Monitor window until the clock reads 00:00:05:08. (This is the section of the video clip that will turn into a freeze-frame insert.)

4. With the Monitor window active (highlighted), choose File>Export Clip>Frame.

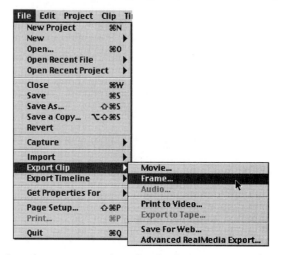

5. You need to select the correct options for the frame you are about to create. Click the Settings box. In this first window, set File Type: TIFF. Click the Next button. Set Frame Size H: 240 and V: 180 for the export size of the frame. Click OK. Check the Open When Finished box.

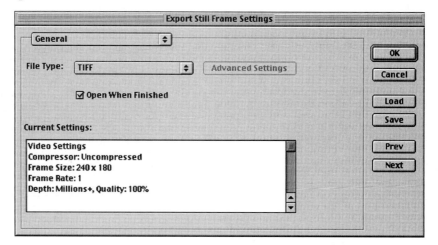

6. Name the file "NEWBIRD.TIF". Save it to your **Work in Progress** folder. A new, single frame of the clip appears as an independent window on your desktop.

7. Click on the Duration box at the bottom left of the Clip window. Change the duration to 00:00:09:00. Drag NEWBIRD.TIF to the Project window. Close the Clip window.

8. Now drag NEWBIRD.TIF to Video 1B at 00:00:10:22. Use the Edit Line to mark the starting spot for the new clip before dragging the file.

9. Select the Inset transition from the Wipe folder in the Transitions palette. Drag it to the Timeline, on the Transition track between NEWS1.MOV and NEWBIRD.TIF. Stretch it the length of NEWBIRD.TIF.

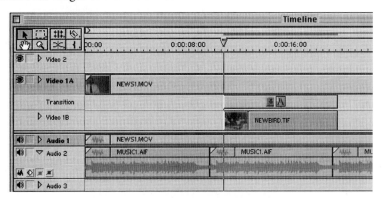

10. Double-click the Inset transition on the Timeline. In the dialog box that appears, click on Show Actual Sources. You see a preview of your video clips. Drag the left slider (Start=) to 56% and the right slider (End=) to 56%, as well. Click on the small white triangle on the right corner at about 2:00. It changes the inset to show the newscaster with the flamingo picture inset.

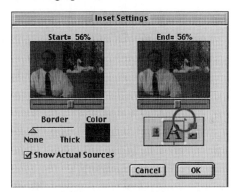

11. At the moment, there is no border to separate the video clips. A border color would help to define the individual sections. Click on the black rectangle. The Color Picker appears. Set Red: 0, Green: 159, Blue: 160, and click OK.

12. Move the Border triangle from None to the right, just a little. When a thin, light-blue border color appears, click OK.

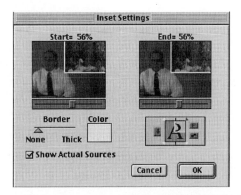

13. Render the production by pressing Return/Enter. You should see our newscaster talking while an inset screen appears halfway into the production. Close the production when you're done. We're going to pick it up again in Chapter 7, when we'll add background music to the piece.

Summary

In Chapter 4 you learned more about transitions — how to control the time when one clip replaces another. You learned to split a picture and create freeze-frame inserts from a video clip. You learned about the options in the transitions dialog boxes and learned to adjust transitions. You also discovered how to create picture-in-picture transitions.

Complete Project A: The Monkey Movie

5 *Superimposing Clips and Stills*

Chapter Objective:

To learn to use the superimposition features to create a variety of effects. In Chapter 5, you will:

- Discover how tracks Video2 through Video97 work like layers in other programs.

- Learn about and use blue screening to put background footage behind actors, after the live footage has been shot.

- Become familiar chroma keys to replace one background with another.

- Learn how to work with transparency and the opacity of clips.

- Study other key types, including non-red, luminance and RGB difference.

- Become familiar with mattes, a method for using one clip to hide or expose clips on tracks 1A and 1B.

- Learn to use alpha channels.

Projects to be Completed:

- The Monkey Movie (A)

- How to Make Spaghetti (B)

- How to Tame a Tiger (C)

- The Gold Rush (D)

Superimposing Clips and Stills

While it must be nice to have a $60 million budget and be able to shoot everything on location, no matter how exotic or logistically difficult that locale might be, there are certain scenes that no one can shoot. Scenes involving great danger to the actors or scenes that don't actually exist are two such impossibilities. Regardless of how much money you have to spend (and most of us don't have access to Spielberg's or Ridley Scott's expense accounts), there are times when you have to create the illusion of reality.

Superimposing allows you to stack multiple clips, stills and graphics. The process works much as layers do in programs like Adobe Photoshop, Adobe Illustrator, Macromedia Freehand and Macromedia Flash. The difference is that instead of using layers, we combine footage and stills on tracks that exist above tracks 1A and 1B (above both numerically and physically).

In older times (before 1970), blue screening wasn't nearly as sophisticated as it is today. Watch a few old movies or television programs, and you'll probably be able to see discrepancies between foreground action and background footage. Check out the "Long, Long Trailer," directed by Vincente Minelli and starring Lucille Ball, Desi Arnez and the Mertz's to see the cast chatting in the car as the California countryside whizzes by at a breathtaking speed of 25 miles per hour.

Among the techniques used to create these illusions of reality is blue screening. Many people have heard about this technique, even people not involved in the film industry. *Blue screening* is a technique that puts an actor, robot, car, plane, boat, house or an action figure in front of a blue (or green) screen. Once that footage is shot, the director can drop out the background and substitute for it background footage. When the two are rendered together, it looks as if the two clips were shot at the same time.

The blue background is used for a good reason — it's a solid color that's easy to select and isolate. This time-honored technique is known as "using a chroma key." You can achieve the effect fairly easily in Premiere by superimposing clips or imposing specific portions of one clip onto another.

The Greek word *chroma* means color, and a *chroma key* is actually another term for color substitution. A *chroma key* is the process that substitutes one color, such as the blue (and in some cases green) of a background, and replaces it with something else — like another clip. It's a great way to put someone in a room that's halfway around the world without sending the entire crew. One person could shoot the footage in India, for example, and then others could use it as a backdrop of a scene they're shooting in Los Angeles, Tampa or Chicago. For all intents and purposes, the final footage shows the stateside actor sitting in the palace of a Pasha in 18th Century India.

Star Wars serves as an excellent example of high-powered chroma-key effects. At an intellectual level we all knew that those scenes weren't really filmed in space, but it sure looked like they were. Using models, actors, interior sets and chroma keys, Lucas took us into the void, and provided us with a nice, cozy seat from which to view the carnage. It wasn't Industrial Light and Magic that invented the process — watch old movies, car chase scenes, war movies or an Alfred Hitchcock classic. Look closely, and you'll see the effect.

Transparency

Transparency is a term that describes one's ability to see through one object to another below it. Exactly how transparent an object (or footage, or still) may be is defined as opacity.

The easiest way to think about transparency is to imagine that you have a photograph and a piece of black cardboard. If you cover a part of the photograph with the cardboard, it would naturally hide that portion of the picture. The cardboard would have an opacity value of 100% (opaque). Nothing behind it could show through. Put clear glass (whose opacity is

0%) on top of the photograph, and it isn't hidden or dimmed at all. Premiere's transparency commands let you define a clip's transparency values. The top clip's opacity determines how much of the underlying video shows through. At 0% opacity, the top image is completely transparent; on the other hand, at 100% opacity the top image is completely opaque; that is, it has no transparency at all.

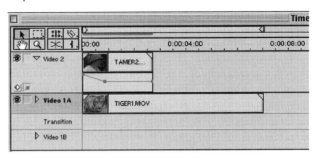

Transparency Keys

You can make clips transparent by using keys. A *key* is a tool that locates pixels of a specific brightness or color and then transforms those pixels; the pixels become transparent or semitransparent, depending on the type of key you select. This process of applying a key to change certain pixels' transparency is called "keying" or "keying out" the color. The most popular type of key is the chroma key. Chroma keys generally use ranges of blue or green to create the transparency effect. (You'll learn more about this under Key Types.) Keys can also use the clip's alpha channel to create the transparency effect.

Clip transparency is activated once the clip is placed in a superimposition track. Each new project, by default, includes one superimposition track — "Video 2." You can, however, add as many as 97 superimposition tracks.

Once a clip has been placed on Video 2, the Transparency Settings dialog box becomes available for use. When Transparency is first selected, the default Key Type is set to None. At this point, no part of the superimposed image is keyed out. A rundown of the different types of keys available in the Key Type menu is shown below.

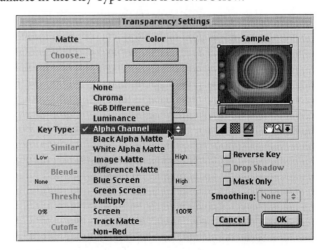

- **Chroma key.** This key is used to replace a color of your choice with an image or video clip. Because chroma keys are difficult to set up properly, Premiere provides a number of settings that can be controlled to create the best possible key effect. These include Similarity, Blend, Threshold, Cutoff and Smoothing. Chroma keys work because they blend similar colors. You will learn more about these in Chapter 8.

- **RGB Difference key.** This key is very similar to the Chroma key — one color is selected and keyed or replaced with an image. You select a range of color, but you do not blend in or adjust transparency in grays. It is best used with day shots, because it requires bright conditions to work.

- **Blue Screen and Green Screen keys.** These keys are used to create transparencies from true chroma blue or green. (True chroma blue is a blue created specially for this purpose.) Television studios frequently use this type of screen for weather segments. The weather forecaster is placed in front of a green wall and weather maps are superimposed on the wall while the information is read.

- **Non-Red key.** This key is similar to the Blue and Green Screen keys, but it fine-tunes images to a greater degree. Images can be softened so that they blend better into the background. This key also allows you to superimpose two video clips on top of the base image.

- **Luminance key.** This key creates transparency for darker values in an image while leaving the brighter areas opaque. This key only works on images that have extremely dark or light colors.

- **Multiply and Screen keys.** These keys create effects by using the underlying image as a map to determine what part(s) of the keyed image to make transparent. The Multiply key creates such an effect based on the lightest areas of the underlying image. The Screen key bases its effect on the darkest areas of the underlying image.

- **Alpha Channel key.** This key is the fourth channel in an RGB image or video clip. The key defines the parts of the image that are transparent or semitransparent. It masks portions of the image partially or completely. When it is removed electronically, another image is revealed, replacing the wholly or partially masked portions.

- **Black Alpha Matte and White Alpha Matte keys.** Similar in process to an Alpha Channel key, these keys use a black or white channel to create the mask effect.

- **Image Matte key.** This key uses a still image or matte to define the area and create the transparency for the portions of the clip that you want to remove. White areas remain intact while black areas become fully transparent, to allow the second image to appear as the superimposition. For example, we could create a picture of a keyhole, then let you look through it to see the action that is taking place inside the room.

- **Difference Matte key.** This key creates an effect by combining two images with similar-looking color pixels. The matching areas are then eliminated. When the Reverse button is selected, a static background can be keyed out to add effect to the foreground picture.

- **Track Matte key.** This matte is used to create a vignette effect on a video clip. A *vignette* is a frame around a picture. It can be soft-edged, like an old-time picture, or hard-edged for a more modern look. The clip plays while surrounded by an opaque frame. This effect is used frequently because it can move or travel with the video shot. Think of the spy movies in the '60s when the black background shot (usually a gun or another spy) travels along with the secret agent.

Additional Transparency Options

These tools, which provide additional options for controlling transparency, are found under the Sample image on the right side of the Transparency Settings dialog box. The first group is represented by icons rather than by a name on a menu. The last four are found as checkboxes or a slider, all in the right column of the same dialog box.

- **Color Key-out tool.** This tool places a black or white background behind the keyed-out image. Click on the button to toggle between black and white.

- **Transparency tool.** This tool displays the checkerboard transparency pattern to help you view transparency in areas that may be difficult to see against a solid background or against the actual underlying image. If necessary, you can click to reverse the checkerboard pattern.

- **Underlying Image tool.** This useful tool displays the actual underlying image in your project. It slows down the render when you set the Transparency slider under the Sample box.

- **Zoom and Hand tools.** These tools are used to zoom in or out on the image in the Sample area. To zoom in, you select the Zoom tool, and then click an area of the image. If you click again, you increase the zoom. To zoom out, you select the Zoom tool, hold down Option/Alt and click the image. To view other areas of the image at the same zoom level, you select the Hand tool and drag the image.

- **Collapse tool.** This tool — available on in the Macintosh version of Premiere — moves the image to the Program view in the Monitor window.

- **Reverse Key checkbox.** This tool allows certain transparent and opaque areas to be reversed. (It is only available for some keys.)

- **Drop Shadow checkbox.** This tool allows you to add a 50% gray/50% opaque shadow to opaque areas. (It, too, is available only for certain keys.) The new shadow is inserted four pixels below and to the right of any adjoining opaque region. Drop Shadow is most effective for titles or simple graphics.

- **Mask Only checkbox.** This tool is used to produce a special effect that displays only the alpha channel matte view of the clip. (It becomes available only when certain keys are selected.)

- **Transparency slider.** When you drag this slider beneath the Sample box, you can sample or preview transparency settings for the clip.

Keying

We've discussed the fact that Premiere provides 14 keys for creating various transparency effects. You can use color-based keys for superimposing, brightness keys for adding texture or special effects, alpha channel keys for clips or images already containing their own alpha channel and matte keys for adding traveling mattes and other creative superimpositions. Your selection depends on the kind of lighting conditions you encounter during a production, or the special effect you are attempting to create.

Chroma keys

Chroma keys are used to replace a color that you choose with an image or video clip. Chroma keys are best used when you have shot a scene against a screen that contains a range of one color, such as a shadowy blue or green screen. A popular use of the chroma key is the nightly weather report. The weather reporter looks as if he or she is standing in front of a large weather map. In reality, the background is a large blue or green backdrop. This color is electronically removed and another image, such as a map, is substituted. The most important aspect of lighting the chroma key set is even background illumination. The background must be carefully lighted to create soft shadows. A key that has not been set properly will cause the weather caster to have a distracting halo effect.

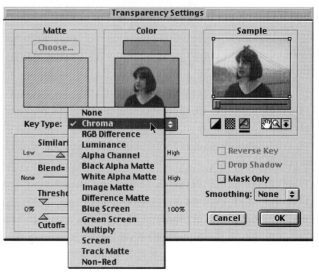

You can quickly access the transparency settings for a clip by clicking Setup next to Transparency in the Effect Controls palette.

As noted above, Chroma keys blend similar colors. Premiere has a number of different settings that can be altered to create the best possible key effect:

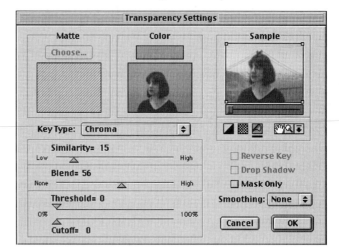

- **Similarity.** The similarity setting looks for similar color values. For instance, similarity looks for a range of blues that can be made transparent.

- **Blend.** The blend setting mixes two clips that are superimposed on top of each other. The higher the value, the more the underlying clip shows.

- **Threshold.** This setting controls the shadows in the clip. A higher values lets some clips slip into the background image more seamlessly.

- **Cutoff.** The cutoff setting controls the shadow areas. Dragging to the right darkens the shadows of your clip. Don't drag beyond the level that is set in Threshold, since doing so turns the pixels gray.

- **Smoothing.** The area between the transparent and opaque regions can be smoothed with this setting. Smoothing finds the similarities in the pixels to produce softer edges. Choose None to produce sharp edges with no anti-aliasing. This is good for type that has sharp lines. Low to High settings produce different effects, depending on the graphic or clip.

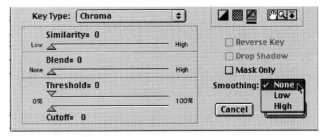

Using the Blue Screen and Green Screen Keys

As you might imagine, Blue Screen and Green Screen keys create transparency using true chroma blue and true chroma green. A video that is created in a studio environment uses these keys to superimpose the actor in front of a different setting. You can adjust the following Blue Screen and Green Screen key settings:

- **Threshold.** This setting controls the overall transparency of the effect. Drag to the left until the background begins to show through.

- **Cutoff.** This setting helps to fill in any stray pixels. Drag this slider in small increments to create subtle effects.

Using Chroma Keys to Combine Footage

The trick in producing chroma-key effects is to think out, in advance, what the two shots will look like when they are assembled. It is important to shoot the actor at the correct angle and at the correct distance. This ensures that when the shots are merged, they will look like they belong together.

Exercise Set-up

The video you are about to create was videotaped in two parts. The first taping involved our actress, Lorna. She was taped in a video-production studio. A blue screen was placed behind her and lighting was carefully applied. The second shot was taken while on a trip to the San Francisco Bay area.

Prepare the Project

1. Begin by setting up a new project. Select File>New Project. The New Project dialog box appears. Select QuickTime/Multimedia for Windows as the Default. Click the Custom button. Click the next button. Set Frame Size H: 240 and V: 180, Compressor: Cinepak, Frame Rate: 15, and click OK. The program finishes loading. A new Project window is created. Save the file as "Using_Keys.ppj" to your **Work in Progress** folder.

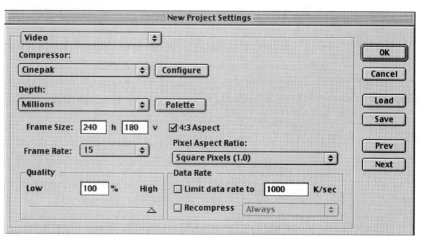

2. Select File>Import>Folder. A dialog box appears. Select **RF–Premiere>Keying**. The folder and its contents transfer to the Project window. You should now have a bin named Keying in the Project window. Double-click it to see the contents.

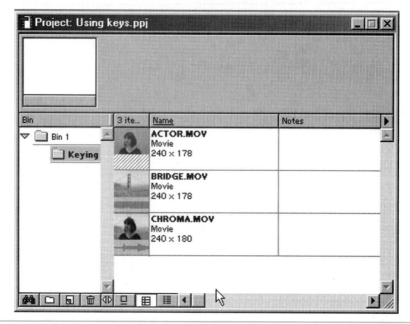

3. Drag CHROMA.MOV to the Source view in the Monitor window. When it has transferred, click the Play button to preview your final project.

4. Close the Clip window and save the file.

5. Drag BRIDGE.MOV to the Timeline window at the beginning of Video 1A.

6. BRIDGE.MOV comes to the Timeline with an audio track that appears on Audio 1. This clip contains a lot of background noise. You will delete the audio track to make room for the new music. Control/right-click on BRIDGE.MOV on Audio 1. When the pop-up menu appears, select Unlink Audio and Video. Make sure the audio track is still selected. Press the Delete key. The audio disappears.

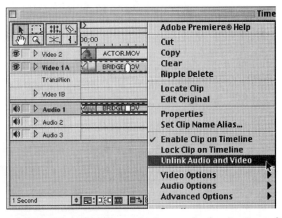

7. Drag ACTOR.MOV to the Timeline window at the beginning of Video 2. Notice that there is no audio for this track.

8. Drag MUSIC8.AIF to the Timeline window on Audio 1, so that it falls at the beginning of the production directly under BRIDGE.MOV.

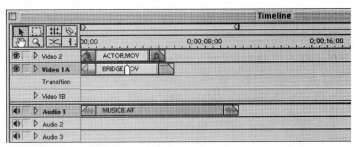

9. At the top of the Timeline window, locate the Work Area bar. If it has not automatically extended to the end of the project, extend the bar all the way to the end of the video, or about 10 seconds. This allows you to view the entire production as you create it.

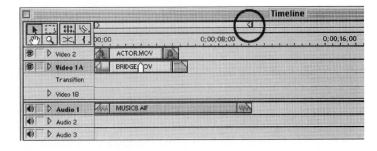

We'll cover audio in much greater detail in Chapter 7. This exercise does require that you perform a simple audio edit — changing one piece of background audio for another, more appropriate selection.

Special effects such as chroma keys should always be created in the Video 2 or 3 tracks.

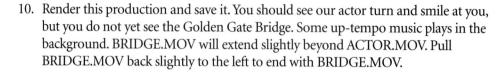

10. Render this production and save it. You should see our actor turn and smile at you, but you do not yet see the Golden Gate Bridge. Some up-tempo music plays in the background. BRIDGE.MOV will extend slightly beyond ACTOR.MOV. Pull BRIDGE.MOV back slightly to the left to end with BRIDGE.MOV.

Superimpose with the Chroma Key

This main shot of our actor was created in a video studio. It's a rather ordinary shot. The actor simply smiles at you, but we'll change all that! Now we'll take a great shot of the Golden Gate Bridge and superimpose it behind our actor.

1. Highlight ACTOR.MOV in the Video 2 track. Select Clip>Video Options>Transparency to display the Transparency Settings dialog box.

2. At the moment, the Key type is set to None. Click on None. A new list of choices will appear. Select Chroma as the key type.

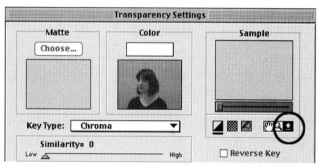

3. In the center of the Transparency Settings window, directly above our actor, you will see the Color box. At the moment, it is set to white. This is the color that is keyed out so that a new color can be substituted.

4. Roll the cursor over the blue background that surrounds the actor. It changes to an eyedropper. Click on the blue background. That blue now appears in the previously white Color box. Now click on the Color box. The Select Transparent Color dialog box appears.

There are actually two ways to create a Chroma key: (1) with the Eyedropper tool clicked on the background color or (2) by typing numbers directly into the Select Transparent Color dialog box.

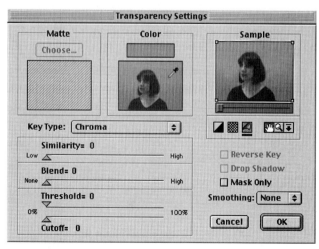

5. Notice the numbers in the RGB mode boxes. Set Red: 92, Green: 185, Blue: 210, and click OK. That new color now appears in the Color box.

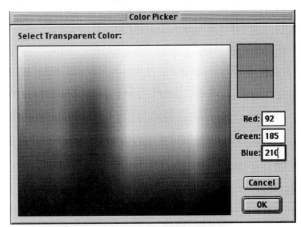

6. Now let's complete the blending process. Set Similarity= 12, Blend= 41, Threshold= 5, Cutoff = 0, and click OK.

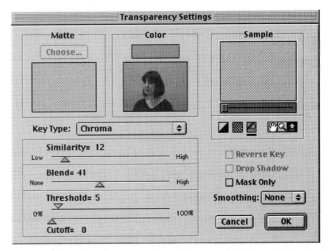

7. Save and render this production so that you can see this effect in action. After several moments, you should see our actor and the Golden Gate Bridge. It looks like she is really at the California location.

8. Close the file.

Alpha Channels

Every commercial and program you see starts with a 10-second countdown. The producer (or the engineer running the video computer) uses it to cue productions before they air. Since it takes roughly three to five seconds for a videocassette device to come up to speed, this gives them just enough time to get the next footage ready to go. Done correctly, it results in the commercial beginning just nanoseconds after the show fades to black.

All images composed for television or the Web are created using the RGB color model. RGB images consist of three separate images, called "channels," that contain the red, green and blue components of the image. An *alpha channel* is a fourth channel that is used to determine what portions of the underlying (RGB) channels can be seen, and at what opacity.

Many third-party applications, such as Adobe Photoshop, use alpha channels to mask or make transparent specific portions of the image. Premiere can read alpha channels created in programs like Photoshop and import them directly onto the alpha channel of the Timeline.

This illustration, created in Photoshop, shows a background image on the left, and one of ten foreground images in the center. An alpha channel in the oblong shape of the old television screen lets the videographer superimpose the changing numbers onto the set's screen.

Exercise Set-up

In the following exercise we're going to create a 10-second countdown clip. Feel free to customize the finished product with filters or transitions, but be sure to follow the specified steps first so that you get a good grasp of the concepts involved.

Preview and Begin the Project

1. Begin by setting up a new project. Select QuickTime/Multimedia Video for Windows as the default, and click the Custom button. Set Frame Size H: 240 and V: 180, Frame Rate: 15 frames per second, and click OK. The program finishes loading and a set of new Project windows appears. Save the file as "countdown.ppj" to your **Work in Progress** folder.

2. Select File>Import>Folder. A dialog box appears. Select **RF-Premiere>television**, and click Choose. The folder and its contents are brought into the Project window. Double-click the imported folder to see the clips we're going to use for this exercise.

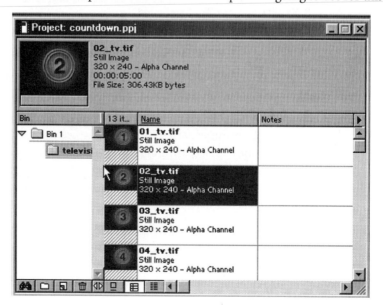

3. Select Countdown.mov, and double-click it or drag it to the Source view. When it has transferred to a unique window, click the Play button to preview your final project. After you've seen the movie, close the Clip window.

If your Project window looks different than ours, it's probably just because we change our view settings from time to time to create screen shots.

4. Leave the project open for the next exercise.

Using Still Images

By default, all still images imported into Premiere are automatically assigned a duration of five seconds. Once the clip's on the Timeline, this duration can be adjusted to any length of time required.

Set the Duration Options for Still Images

1. In the Project window of the open file, double-click on TV.TIF. The still image TV.TIF displays in the Clip: TV.TIF window.

2. Click on the Duration rectangle at the bottom left of the image. In the dialog box, change the number from 0:00:05:00 to 0:00:13:00, and click OK.

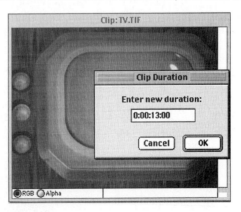

3. Position your cursor inside the TV screen. Drag the picture to the Video 2 track on the Timeline. It should stretch out to the 13-second mark. Close the Clip: TV.TIF window.

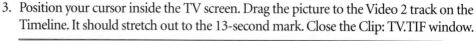
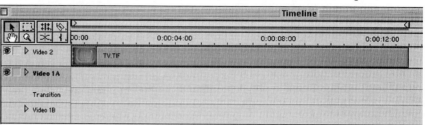

4. Double-check that the Work Area bar extends all the way to the end of the production, allowing you to view the entire production as you create it.

5. In the Project window, double-click on TV-BLANK.TIF. The still image Clip: TV-BLANK.TIF displays.

6. Click on the Duration rectangle at the bottom left of the image. In the dialog box, change the number to 00:00:02:00, and click OK. This shortens the clip to two seconds.

7. Position your cursor inside TV-BLANK.TIF, and drag the picture to the beginning of the Video 1A track on the Timeline. It should stretch to fill two seconds. Close the Clip: TV-BLANK.TIF window.

8. Return to the Project window, double-click on 10_tv.tif, and look at the still.

9. Click on the Duration rectangle at the bottom left of the image. In the dialog box, change the number to 0:00:02:00, and click OK.

10. Drag 10_tv.tif to the Timeline window on Video 1B at 00:00:01:00. (You can do this easily by first setting the Edit Line to 00:00:01:00.) Close the clip's window.

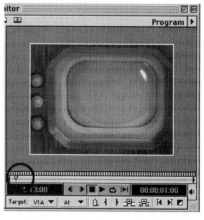

Option/Alt-click on the Work Area bar to extend it quickly to the end of the production.

11. Back in the Project window, double-click on 09_tv.tif. The still image appears.

12. Click on the Duration rectangle at the bottom left of the image. In the dialog box, change the number to 0:00:02:00, and click OK.

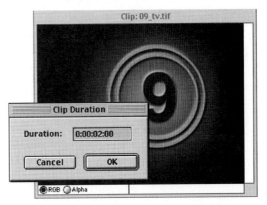

13. Drag 09_tv.tif to the Timeline window on Video 1A at 00:00:02:00. It snaps next to TV-BLANK.TIF. (Remember, you can also accomplish this by setting the Edit Line to 00:00:02:00 and dragging the clip to the Edit Line.) Close the Clip window.

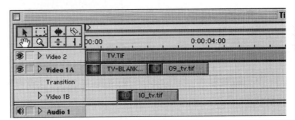

14. In the Project window, double-click on 08_tv.tif. The image Clip: TV-EIGHT.TIF will display.

15. Click on the Duration rectangle at the bottom left of the image. In the dialog box, change the number to 0:00:02:00, and click OK.

16. Drag 08_tv.tif to the Timeline window on Video 1B at 00:00:03:00. It snaps next to 10_tv.tif. Close the Clip window.

17. Repeat steps 14 through 16 for each of the remaining countdown numbers. Continue to place them on the Timeline alternately on the Video 1A and Video 1B tracks. Place TV-BLANK.TIF as the last picture at the end of the Timeline.

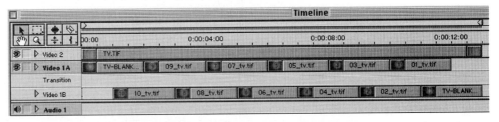

18. Leave the file open for the next exercise.

Use Alpha Channels to Generate Special Effects

1. In the open file in the Project window, double-click on TV.TIF. Click on the Alpha button. Take a look at the black mask. This black area is where new image data can be substituted. Anytime an image that has an embedded alpha channel comes to Premiere, that image's black or white channel can be altered. Click the RGB button to return to the TV picture. Close TV.TIF.

2. On the Timeline, click to select TV.TIF. You should see the "walking ants." Select Clip>Video Options>Transparency.

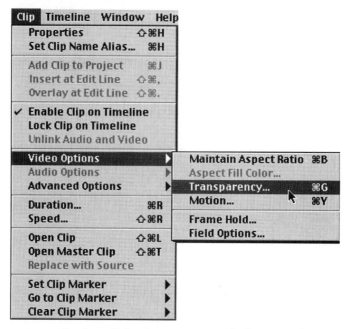

3. The Transparency Settings dialog box appears with the TV in the Sample box.

4. Notice that the Key Type is set to None. Set Key Type to Alpha Channel. Click on the Underlying Image icon (a small button that looks like a page curl and is found under the Sample box). Your first picture, TV-BLANK.TIF, suddenly appears inside the television screen. Click OK to close the Transparency Settings dialog box.

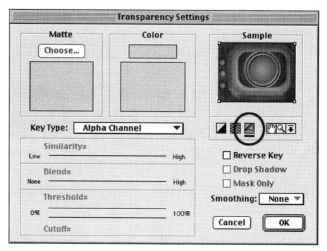

5. Want to see what you have accomplished so far? First, as always, save your work.

6. Now render this production by pressing Return/Enter. After your project renders, you should see your countdown playing inside a television without transitions. The only problem is that the even numbers aren't showing — we need to add transitions to bring in the remaining characters.

7. Open the Slide folder in the Transitions palette, and drag the Band Slide transition to the Transition track of the Timeline. Place it at the one-second mark on the Timeline. You should see it snap into position in the space where the first two clips overlap.

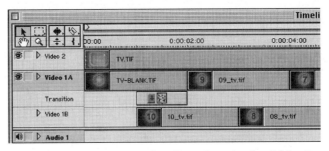

8. The second transition is Cross Dissolve, from the Dissolve folder. Drag this transition to the Transition track, at the two-second mark on the Timeline. You should see it snap into position in the space where your second and third clips overlap. Click the Up Arrow on the transition to ensure that the arrow is pointing up.

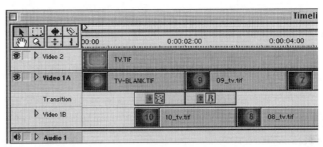

9. As you may have noticed, a familiar pattern is emerging. Each transition starts at the beginning of one clip and overlaps to the next. Continue to select and drag transitions onto the Timeline. This production requires 11 transitions. You may choose any transitions from the Transitions palette for your production.

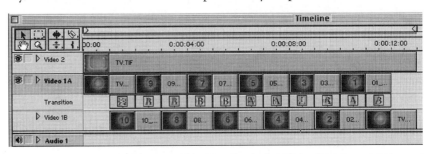

The transition must stretch to cover only the overlap of the two video clips. If the transition is too long, ugly sections of black will show through.

Want to find those transitions quickly? Use the Find Transition icon located at the bottom of the Transitions palette.

If you are having difficulty seeing the transitions properly, you might want to zoom in on the Timeline. Use the Zoom tool (Z) or hold the cursor on the Time Zoom Level, at the lower-left side of the Timeline window.

10. Save your project by pressing Return/Enter to render these new changes. After building the preview, you should see your countdown playing inside a television with all of the new transitions.

11. Take a moment to change any of the transitions with which you are not happy. When you are satisfied with the results, save the final production and close the file.

Summary

In Chapter 5 you learned how to superimpose clips using a number of techniques. You became familiar with transparency, and how to control transparency of a clip or still over time. You learned about chroma keys, and how they're used to combine footage in blue screening. You learned to use alpha channels and to combine them with still images and assorted transitions for special effects. You also learned how to control the duration of still images on the Timeline.

Free-Form Project #1

Assignment

A local multimedia company is creating an educational product that showcases their ability to construct complex, CD-ROM based projects. The project will feature 24 different lessons, each on a different subject.

To make it more compelling and interesting to potential clients, and to garner some community support, the creative team is gathering work from different content experts in the area. You're one of them.

Your assignment is to create a one-minute video that teaches the viewer to do something. The subject can be anything that you know well enough to teach: gardening, fishing, riding a bike, repairing a screen door, building a boat or climbing a ladder. As long as you can fit the content in the allotted time, the choice is yours.

Applying Your Skills

You will create the training video by:

- Creating a storyboard
- Developing a shot list
- Picking or preparing a location
- Shooting the video
- Capturing the video
- Assembling the video clips
- Using the Title window to superimpose instructions over the scenes
- Adding a split-screen sequence with content relative to the lesson
- Creating a QuickTime movie

Specifications

Complete your project as follows:

- Finished length: 1 minute
- At least 10 to 12 video shots
- Easy-to-read instructions appearing where necessary
- Transitions placed on all clips
- Color added to transitions, as needed
- One split-screen sequence
- At least two filters applied to footage

Included Files

No files have been included with this assignment. It's up to you to collect and capture the video. For information about capture, see Chapter 10.

Publisher's Comments

Educational video is widely used — videographers experienced in this specialty area are in demand across the country. In this assignment, you'll get a feel for what's important and what's not — there's no room for extraneous video, effects or transitions. Everything has to be compact. Furthermore, since you haven't yet worked with audio, you'll have to use the Title window to create succinct, easy-to-read instructions for each scene.

Review #1

Chapters 1 through 5

In Chapters 1 through 5, you've learned the basic operations necessary to create a simple Premiere production. You've become familiar with many of the principal tools, menus, dialog boxes, windows and palettes, as well as how to navigate among them. You understand how to assemble the initial clips, and apply filters and transitions, transparency and opacity to create specific effects. After reading the discussions, performing the hands-on exercises and working through the projects, you should:

- Be familiar with the Premiere working environment, and be able to reset the program's defaults by deleting the Preferences file and creating a new one. You should understand custom settings and how to maximize the interface to suit the way you work. You should also understand the A/B editing workspace and how to preview your productions.

- Be comfortable creating a simple production, and importing video clips into the Project window, both individually and several at once. You should be familiar with the concept of aspect ratio and the importance of proper file and folder organization.

- Know how to work with and apply native and After Effects filters. You should be familiar with and able to use the Video Effects palette, the Effect Controls palette and keyframes.

- Understand transitions, have practiced working with several of the more than 70 transitions available in the Transitions palette, and be able to customize the palette to your needs. You should be familiar with a number of different categories of transitions, including dissolves, fades, wipes and blends. You should also be able to customize transitions on the Timeline or in the Transitions palette.

- Know how to use the Video 2 through 97 tracks to superimpose video footage or still images on the Timeline. You should know about and be able to use blue screening and chroma keys. You should be familiar with and have worked with transparency and opacity of clips, and understand how to replace one background with another. You should also be comfortable using alpha channels and understand that they can be brought in from other applications.

6 Titles and Graphics

Chapter Objective:

To explore the Title window — a powerful feature that provides control over type objects, font selection, rolling titles, and more. To become familiar with the functionality of the Title window. In Chapter 6, you will:

- Learn the components of the Title window.

- Discover how to add type elements, or titles, directly into the Project window.

- Become familiar with the difference between static and rolling or crawling titles, and how to create each.

- Learn about the basic shapes available to you from the Title window, including hollow and solid shapes.

- Learn to color objects and select shades from the Color palette.

- Become familiar with creating gradients — fills that change from one color to another, or from one tint of a color to another.

- Discover how to control the transparency of objects you create with the Title window.

- Become familiar with and experiment with attributes such as line thickness, fills, font size, type effects, alignment, positioning and more.

- Learn to adjust character and paragraph spacing.

Projects to be Completed:

- The Monkey Movie (A)

- How to Make Spaghetti (B)

- How to Tame a Tiger (C)

- The Gold Rush (D)

Titles and Graphics

Almost all of today's movies start with titles — the names of the actors, the producer and the director. When the movie ends, we see the credits. Besides repeating the names of the actors and directors, they often give us insight into the people and logistics behind the scenes — special effects artists, costume designers, set locations, music and wardrobe. You learn about who acted, cast the show, got the coffee and more. Titles are a critical component of your productions.

In addition to titles, simple graphics — rectangles, ovals, lines and polygons — are often used to isolate titles and draw the viewer's attention to specific elements. A good example might be placing a newscaster's name in a rectangle that fades back into the scene. Using the superimposition techniques we learned in the last chapter with the graphic and text tools available from the Title window makes achieving highly-professional results straightforward.

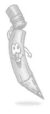

Text and graphic objects created with the Title window are vector graphics — the same as Macromedia Flash, Adobe Illustrator, Macromedia Freehand and other illustration programs. You can also create graphics and text elements in those applications and import them directly into your Premiere productions.

Creating Titles and Graphics

In Premiere, titles (and graphics) are created via the Title window. To create a new title or graphic, you just select File>New>Title. Alternately, you can click the Create Item icon at the bottom of the Project window and select Title from the pop-up menu.

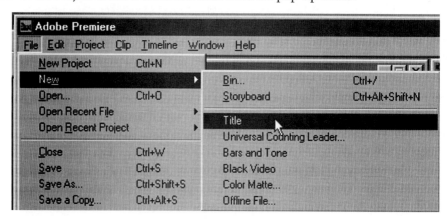

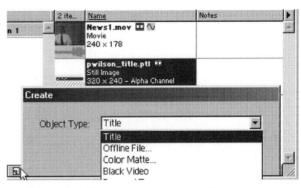

Graphics and titles are both created in the Title window. Because titles are components like any other clip or still, you have to save them, preferably into the same folder as the rest of the project's assets. In the following example, we named the title pwilson_title.ptl.

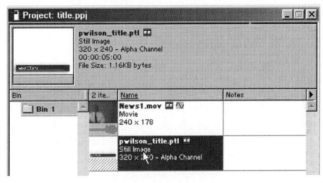

Once you create a title, you use it in your project just like any source clip, by editing it into your video program, using cuts and transitions, or by superimposing it over clips. You can also use the Title window options to specify the size of the title area and the background color.

The Title Window

Let's take a brief tour of the Title window.

If you're working on a Windows system, with file extensions enabled (visible), the .ptl suffix appears automatically. Windows uses these suffixes to connect data files with their creator applications. If you're working on a Macintosh, you don't need to use them, but we recommend that you do. Most editing environments are cross-platform, and the extensions ensure compatibility between the Macintosh and Windows computer workstations.

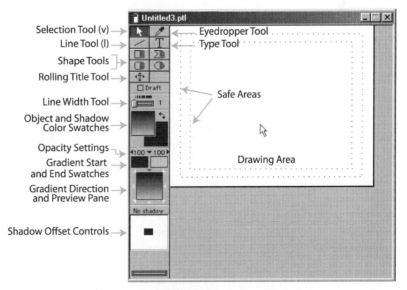

The Title window provides a workspace for creating titles, credits and graphics.

- **Selection tool.** The default tool is the Selection tool that is used to select and move text and graphic objects.

- **Eyedropper tool.** Use this tool to select a color from anywhere on the screen. Once selected, this new color can be applied to other objects or type.

- **Line tool.** This tool draws straight lines. Drag to draw the line, or hold down the Shift key as you drag to draw a constrained line at 45° increments.

Type and Rolling Title Tools

Two of the tools on the Title window are used to create text elements:

- **Type tool.** This tool is used to create static (non-rolling) text elements. Once text is on the drawing area, you have full control over its attributes, including color, font, size and a host of others.

- **Rolling Title tool.** Dragging this tool creates a region within which your titles will roll or crawl; the object is empty and requires formatting the text.

Shape Tools

The next several tools are used to draw primitive shapes:

- **Shape tools.** The basic shape tools let you draw ovals and rectangles by clicking and dragging the tool. Each of the tool icons has two parts: select the right side of the icon and the tool creates solid or filled shapes. Select the left part of the tool icon and the shapes you draw will be hollow, displaying a line but no fill. If you want to draw a perfect circle or a perfect square, hold the Shift key while dragging the shape.

- **Polygon tool.** You can use this tool to create fairly complex shapes. Realize, however, that Premiere isn't meant to be a drawing program. If you need a background or a really complex graphic, consider using a program like Adobe Illustrator or Macromedia Freehand to create the object and import it into your project.

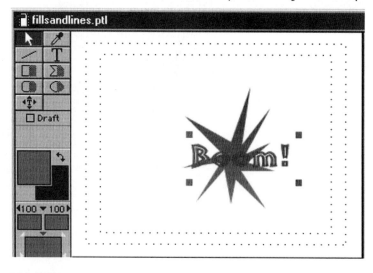

The Line tool reverts to the Selection tool after one use unless you double-click it.

- **Line Width tool**. You can use this slider to change the width — often called the "weight" — of a line. You can select an existing line and change its width, or set a width for new lines.

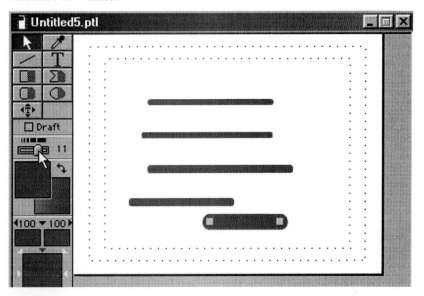

Coloring Objects and Gradients

- **Object and Shadow color swatches**. The chip on the upper left controls the color of solid objects and lines, and the chip on the lower right controls the color of shadows. You can swap the two using the curly arrow icon.

- **Opacity Start and End swatches**. The next two icons are settings for creating transparent gradients. The one on the left provides a slider for setting the start opacity, and the one on the right controls the opacity of the end color.

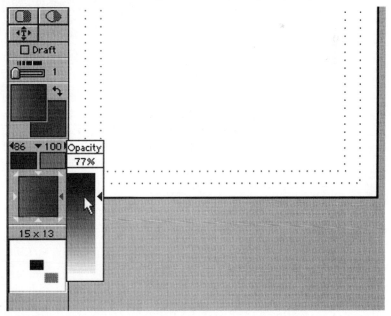

- **Gradient Start and End swatches**. Underneath the gradient opacity sliders are the two gradient color swatches. The left swatch is the starting color of the gradient and the right swatch is the ending color.

- **Gradient Direction and Preview Pane.** The large color chip in the center shows you how the gradient will appear. Around the Preview pane are a number of directional arrows — clicking them will move the starting point of the gradient to that orientation.

Shadows

Using the Shadow offset tools, you can position an object's shadow anywhere in the drawing area by clicking and dragging it within the small preview window. Changes occur immediately in the Title window.

Safe Areas

Safe areas are zones defined by dotted rectangles displayed in the drawing area. The outside rectangle is the Action safe zone, where objects will still be visible to the viewer. The inside, or Title safe zone, defines the maximum region where type will be properly displayed in the final production. To access the Title Window Options dialog box, select Window>Window Options>Title Window Options.

You should remember that all TVs have slightly different safe-action areas. It's wise to stay well within the safe area display lines.

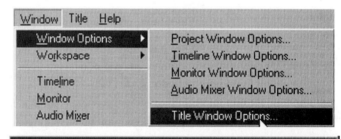

Title Attributes

Premiere enables you to control many attributes of your titles. You can change typefaces, control the size and color of text, add gradients and drop shadows and use the object like any other clip.

Font Selection and Type Size

You can use any font on your system for your titles. To set the font, simply select the copy you want to change, and select Font from the Title menu.

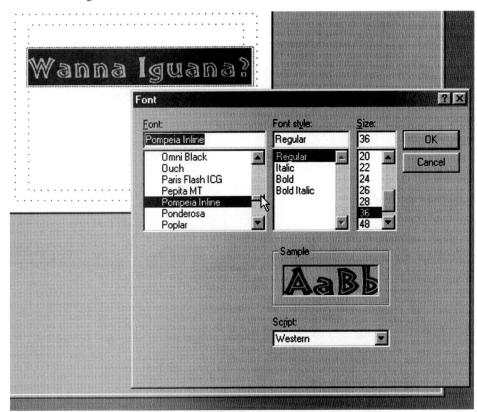

Type size is controlled from the same dialog box, or by selecting Title>Size. Try to avoid using very small type, since it's hard to read.

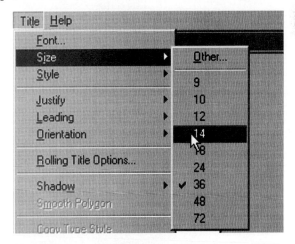

Letter Spacing — Tracking and Kerning

The amount of space between characters is a subtle but important detail to consider when you're developing your productions. It makes sense to pay attention to every title that you create, and be sure to fix the spacing — they almost always benefit from the extra attention.

Letter spacing is controlled with the Increase/Decrease Tracking tools, which appear in place of the Line Width tool whenever you select text with the Type tool.

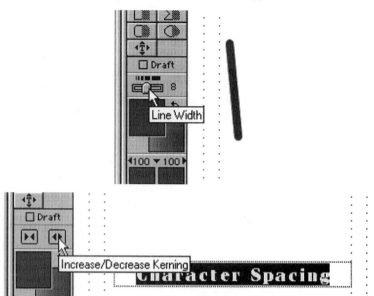

There are two aspects to letter spacing: tracking and kerning. Tracking controls the overall space between the letters of a title. To track a title, click the Type tool inside the word or phrase, and press Command/Control-A to select all. Once it's selected, simply click the appropriate icon to increase or decrease the letter spacing. Two examples of identical titles using different tracking values are shown below.

The second category of letter spacing or kerning controls the spacing between pairs of letters. Many fonts come with kerning values already built in; for example, there's a bit of space removed between the capital "W" and the letter "a" or "o." At times, however, you'll want to adjust that space yourself. To do so, click the Type tool between the letters you want to kern, and then click the appropriate tool to increase or decrease the spacing between the letters.

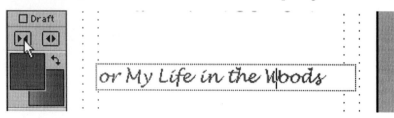

Alignment and Orientation

Text can be aligned vertically or horizontally using the drop-down menu found by selecting Title>Orientation.

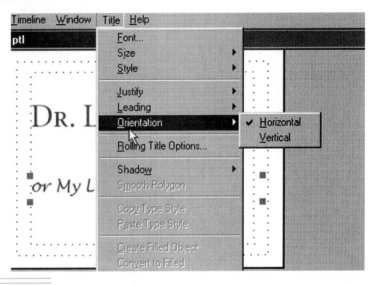

Begin the Project

1. Begin by setting up a new project. Click Custom. Select File>New Project. In the New Project dialog box, select QuickTime/Multimedia Video for PC as the Default, and click the Custom button. Set Frame Size H: 240 and V: 180, Frame Rate: 15 frames per second, and click OK. The program finishes loading. A set of new project windows is created. Save it as "using_title.ppj" to your **Work in Progress** folder.

2. Select File>Import>Folder. When the dialog box appears, select **RF-Premiere>the_lizard_speaks**, and click Choose/OK. The folder, with everything inside it, transfers to the Project window in a bin of the same name. Double-click the bin to see the three clips it contains.

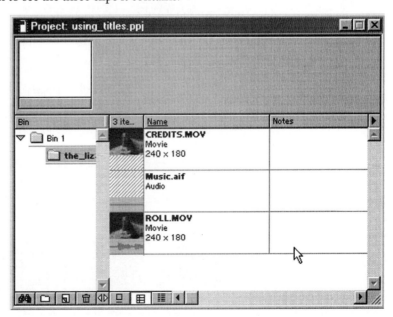

3. Double-click ROLL.MOV or drag it to the Source view. Click the Play button to preview the end result of this exercise.

You can also preview a video clip in the Bin window. Click the Play button to see the movie.

4. Drag CREDITS.MOV to the Timeline window at the beginning of Video 1A.

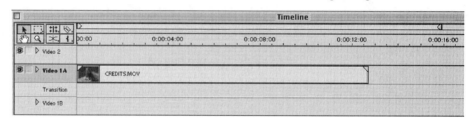

5. Make sure the Work Area bar is extended to the end of the production so you can view the entire production as you create it.

6. Press Return/Enter to render the production and see how it looks. Save it when you're done.

7. Select File>New>Title, and the Title window appears.

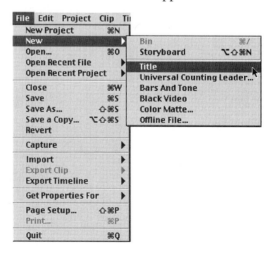

8. We need to make sure that the Title window is the same size as the rest of the production. If not, the type will look small and peculiar when it joins the rest of the movie on the Timeline.

    Click on the Untitled Title window to make it active. Choose Window>Window Options>Title Window Options.

9. In the Title Window Options dialog box, set Drawing Size H: 240 and V: 180, NTSC-safe Colors: checked, Aspect Ratio: Square Pixels, Show Safe Titles: checked. The Background should be set to white. Click OK.

Clicking on the background color box allows you to choose a specific color for the entire background.

10. Now that we know that the title will be the same size as the actual production, we can create the first title. Click on the Type tool. As you move your cursor to the right onto the drawing area, it will change to an I-beam (much like a cursor in a word processor). Make sure you are safely within the Title safe zone.

11. Click on the upper one-third, at about at the center of the drawing area. You will see a blinking insertion line. Make sure you are safely within the Title safe zone.

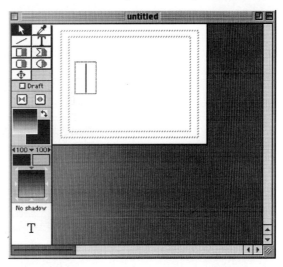

12. We want the type to be centered on the page, so select Title>Justify>Center, and type the following text. Press Return/Enter at the end of each line.

A
Lizard Goes
Home

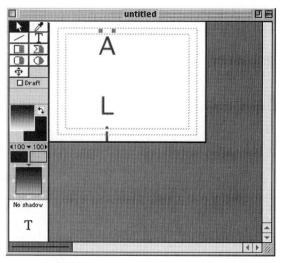

You can gain access to most formatting options by Control/right-clicking in the drawing area and choosing a command from the contextual menu.

13. How does your type look now? Is it running off the page? To fix this, click on the Selection tool, and then click on your new type. You will see a set of black squares or handles. Grab the handle at the upper-right corner of the type, and pull it toward the right side of the screen. The type should stretch to fill the screen correctly.

14. Once the words are properly spaced, they need to be centered on the screen. Premiere does this for you automatically. Make certain the words still have handles on them. (If not, reselect the Selection tool, and click on the type.) Select Title>Center Vertically, and then Title>Center Horizontally.

15. Let's color the title with a solid bright green. Double-check that the words still have handles. Click on the center of the Object Color palette (the main color palette at the left). The Color Picker box appears.

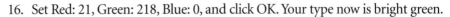

16. Set Red: 21, Green: 218, Blue: 0, and click OK. Your type now is bright green.

17. How about adding a drop shadow? Again, ensure that the handles are still showing on the words. At the lower-left side of the Tool menu, you will see a "T" with the words "No shadow" just above. Position your cursor on the "T," and drag down slowly. A drop shadow appears under both the "T" and your words.

18. To make the drop shadow more pronounced, select Title>Shadow>Solid. Now your words have a sharp gray shadow.

19. The words may still be quite large. Let's make them smaller. Make certain the handles still show on the words. Select Title>Size>Other. Type "30" pt., and click OK.

20. Save the file and leave it open for the next exercise.

Want to stretch your type a bit? Use the Selection tool with Option/Control as you drag any of the object handles. The Selection tool changes to a Stretch tool and resizes your type.

Importing Titles from External Applications

Many videographers use external applications to create titles, feeling that programs like Adobe Illustrator, Macromedia's Freehand and Flash applications are better suited to producing high-end text and graphic effects.

Some programs can generate a series of numbered sequence of still images, such as Adobe After Effects and Adobe Dimensions. These files start out as individually saved files. Once they are imported to Premiere, they are converted into a numbered sequence. You can import individual still images or convert a numbered sequence of still images into a single animation as you import. If you create 30 still images, you will have 1 second of video, because video runs at 30 frames per second. It's a lot of work, but well worth it if you are seeking a special effect for your project.

When you import an individual still image, it uses the duration specified in the dialog box that appears when you choose Edit>Preferences>General & Still Image. You can change the duration of a still image after you import it. In the Still Image section, specify the number of frames you want as a default duration for a still image. The projects in this book have been set up at 15 frames per second. So, the default of 15 frames per second at 150 frames equals 5 seconds.

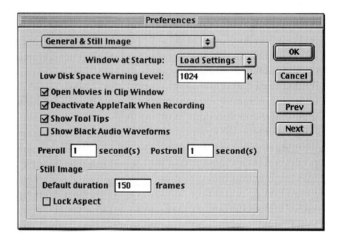

You can also change the speed or duration of an animated sequence once it is on the Timeline. To change the duration of a still image you have already imported and placed, select the clip and choose Clip>Duration. Type the new duration and click OK. You will see the time of the clip extend on the Timeline.

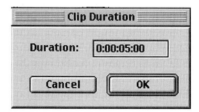

By default, Premiere will attempt to change the size and proportions of your still image to match the current project. This can cause some unexpected and ugly results. If you know that the final project will be 240 × 180, create the numbered stills at the same size. This is particularly important if there is type involved. Images that are resized within Premiere can end up looking very pixilated. You should specify that still images retain their original aspect. Try not to resize an image to a size other than the size of the frame.

If you're planning to use many still images that use different aspect ratios from your project frame size, you can lock the aspect ratio of each still image before you import it into your production.

To lock the size or aspect ratios of still images before you import them, choose Edit>Preferences>General and Still Image. Select Lock Aspect to preserve the proportions of a still image in Premiere. When you import a still image that has a different size than the project, Premiere resizes the image to fit, whether you want it to or not. Just remember: be careful! Don't resize images if you don't have to.

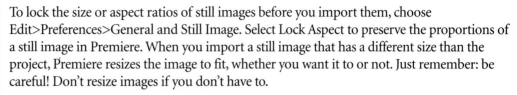
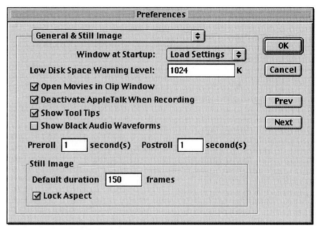

Importing Images to Create a Sequence

Let's take a moment to discuss animations. An animation is different from live-action video because it is generated synthetically. What does that mean? Well suppose you wanted to create a battle sequence with the good guys and the bad guys fighting it out with light sabers. You can't exactly go to the local mall and buy a "real" light saber, but you can create the look of one. You start by slowly creating and saving a series of stills. These stills are then imported into Premiere where they are reassembled into one complete sequence or animation.

As mentioned earlier, some programs, such as Adobe After Effects and Adobe Dimensions, can generate a series of numbered sequences of still images. A still-image sequence cannot include layers, so you must flatten images (in Photoshop, for example) that will become part of the new animation.

When creating stills, always use broadcast-safe color filtering standards.

When importing numbered stills, there are different rules for Macintosh and PC users. In Windows, begin the process by creating a unique directory to hold each of your numbered sequences. As you create your numbered files, make sure that each still-image file name has the correct file extension, and make sure that all file names in the sequence shows the same number of characters at the end of the file name — for example, file000.bmp, file001.bmp and so on. To create the animation, choose File>Import>File. Locate and select the first numbered file in the sequence, select Numbered Stills and click Open. Premiere will create the sequence with the information you have provided.

The rules are similar for Macintosh users. Create a unique folder for each of your numbered sequences. Make sure that all file names in the sequence also have a name, plus a period. Then add the same number of digits — for example, File000.gif, File001.gif. Choose File>Import>File. Locate and select the first numbered file in the sequence, select Numbered Stills and click Open. Premiere will assemble the animation based on your numbered stills.

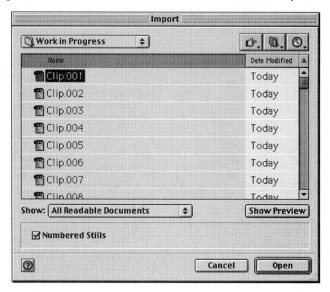

If you want your project to be cross-platform, be sure to add the .ptl suffix (or extension) after the name. Without it, Premiere for Windows won't see the file in the open dialog box and won't launch Premiere if you double-click the file's icon to open it.

Adding Titles to the Project Window

Once you have type, you need to save and add it to the Timeline. When you have it on the Timeline, you can create and apply the actual effect.

Add Titles to the Project Window

1. In the open file, save your title as "TITLE1.PTL" to your **Work in Progress** folder. You will need to move it into the lizard bin. Your new title should automatically transfer to the Project menu. If it does not appear, select Clip>Add Clip to Project. Close the Title window.

2. You should now have TITLE1.PTL in the Project window along with your other clips. Save your file.

Superimposing Titles

As you've learned, the Video 2 track is used for superimposing additional footage or graphics onto the normal A/B Timeline. You can create up to 97 additional video tracks, and they're numbered sequentially.

You can add titles directly to the Project window (as you just did) or by selecting File>Import>File as you did in earlier chapters. It makes no difference.

One of the most important uses for superimposing footage onto your production is for titles and graphics.

Alpha Channels and Titles

1. Drag TITLE1.PTL to the Timeline window, and position it at the beginning of Video 2. Click to highlight it. Select Clip>Video Options>Transparency.

2. The Transparency Settings dialog box now appears with TITLE1.PTL in the Sample box. Set Key Type: White Alpha Matte. Click on the Underlying Image tool (turned-down page icon) so that you can see your transparency applied to the credit. Click OK to close the Transparency Settings dialog box.

If the project's folder is not selected (showing its contents), the title appears outside the folder. If the contents are showing, the title joins them in the folder.

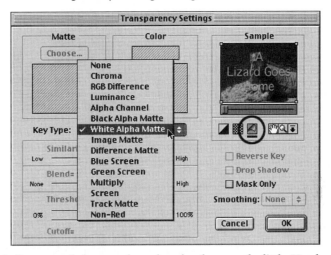

The title is five seconds long and needs to be shortened a little. You last accomplished this by clicking on the Duration box. As you may have noticed, however, there is no Duration box in the Title window. You will change the time in another way.

3. Click to select TITLE1.PTL on the Timeline. Select Clip>Duration, set the Duration to 00:00:03:00. Click OK, and your credit will now fill three seconds.

Title files, created in Premiere, automatically come with an alpha channel to set controls.

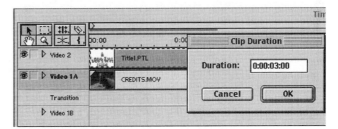

4. Save your project and render this production. You should see your title superimposed on top of Sam the Lizard.

Title Opacity and Fade Controls

Being able to control the opacity of titles is an important technique and a very common one in contemporary video production. Some excellent examples of transparent titles and graphics can be seen in professional sports footage — names, statistics, colored boxes, rules and other graphics are often defined to be slightly transparent. This transparency enables the viewer to see them without the information totally obscuring the action and images in the background.

Set the Opacity for the Titles

As you see, the title graphic of the video starts and ends rather abruptly. What we actually want to achieve is a smoother, more professional start. We will accomplish this by having the graphic ease in. In video lingo, this is referred to as a "fade-in" and "fade-out" effect. Premiere has built-in controls for managing the opacity of the graphic.

The keyboard shortcut for Duration is Command/ Control-R.

1. Expand Video 2 (by clicking the triangle at the left of the track name). It expands to show the opacity levels for TITLE1.PTL.

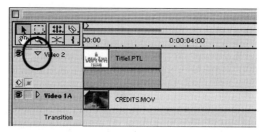

2. You should see a thin red line at the top of this window. This shows the title at 100% opacity. At the far left of the red line, notice a red handle.

3. Move the cursor slightly to the right of this handle, and click on the red line. A second handle appears.

4. Position the cursor over the far-left handle, and drag the handle to the bottom of the window. This will be the fade-in for the title.

5. Move the cursor slightly to the left, and click again on the red line. A fourth handle appears.

6. Position the cursor over the far-right handle, and drag this handle to the bottom of the window, as well. This is the fade-out for the title.

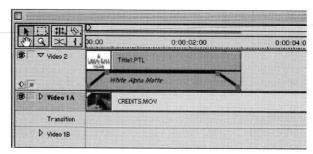

7. Save your project and render this production. You should see your title fade in and fade out on top of Sam the Lizard.

Create Rolling Credits

For the next part of this exercise, you will create a set of credits that scrolls up as the rest of the video plays.

1. Select File>New>Title. The Title box appears.

2. Click on the Rolling Title tool (at the bottom left of the Tool palette).

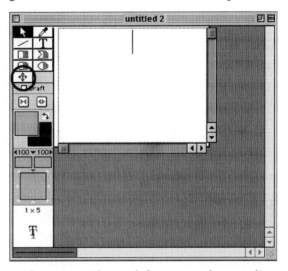

By holding the Shift key as you select the red line, you can fade the entire clip at once. This is especially helpful for superimpositions and special effects.

Draw a dotted square that starts at the top-left corner and moves diagonally to the lower-right corner of the drawing area. This defines the rolling area for the titles you will be adding.

3. The gray corner handles disappear, indicating that you are ready to type some text. A set of scroll bars also appears.

4. The green that you created earlier should still be available on the Object Color palette if you're on a Macintosh. If you're on a PC, click on the center of the Object Color palette. In the Color Picker box, set Red: 21, Green: 218, Blue: 0, and click OK. Your title now has a bright green color. As long as your title has handles on it, any new color will be applied automatically.

5. The words are going to be too large for this section of the project unless we reduce them. Select Title>Size>24 points.

6. It is time to type the actual credits — the words you see below. Be sure to add your name as the director to the credit list. Press Return/Enter once after the Starring line and Produced by line, but twice after the Directed by line and Stunt Double line. This will give the viewer time to read each of the credits as they appear. (The credits run slightly off the screen. You can scroll up or down if you wish to look at them.)

Starring: Sam the Lizard
Directed by: Your Name

Produced by: Your Name
Stunt Double: Lizzie the other Lizard

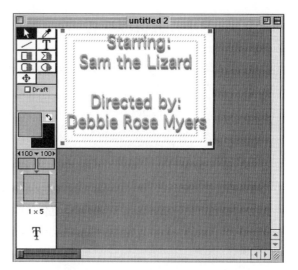

7. The credits need a setting so that they will roll. Select Title>Rolling Title Options. Click the Move Up button, and then click OK.

8. Select your title as "TITLE2.PTL" to your **Work in Progress** folder. Your title should automatically transfer to the Project menu. (If it does not appear, select Clip>Add Clip to Project.) Close the Title window and move the title into the Lizard bin.

9. You should now have TITLE2.PTL in in the Project window along with your other title and video clips. Save your file.

10. Drag TITLE2.PTL to the Timeline window after the end of TITLE1.PTL on Video 2. Click to highlight it, then select Clip>Video Options>Transparency.

11. The Transparency Settings dialog box appears with TITLE2.PTL showing in the Sample box. Set Key Type: White Alpha Matte, and click OK to close the Transparency Settings dialog box.

12. The title will last only five seconds, unless you again change its duration. Click to select TITLE2.PTL on the Timeline, then position your cursor at the end of the TITLE2.PTL. The cursor changes to a two-sided black arrow with a thin red line. Drag this clip to the end of the CREDITS.MOV on Video 1A. Your credits expand to fill the remaining time.

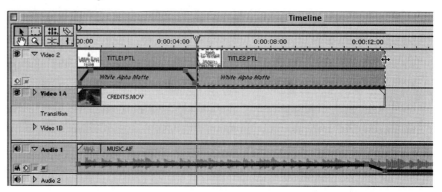

13. Save and render this production. You should see your title superimposed on top of Sam the Lizard.

Smooth the Effects with Fade-in and Fade-out

As before, this second title graphic starts and ends too abruptly. We want this graphic to fade in and fade out as the first one did.

1. You should see a thin red line in the transparency area of the Video 2 track. This shows the title is at 100% opacity. At the far left of the red line, you should see a red handle.

2. Move the cursor slightly to the right, and click on the red line. A second control handle appears.

3. Position the cursor over the far-left handle, and drag the handle to the bottom of the window. This is the fade-in for the title.

4. Move the cursor slightly to the left, and again click on the red line. A fourth control handle appears.

5. Position the cursor over the far-right handle, and drag the handle to the bottom of the window. This is the fade-out for the title.

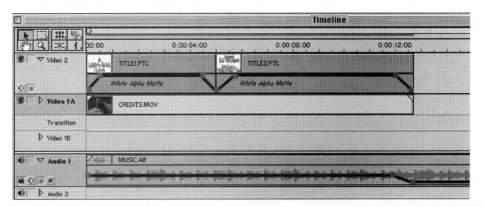

7. Render the production, then save and export it as a QuickTime movie. You should see both of your titles fade in and fade out on top of Sam the Lizard. Close the file.

Summary

In Chapter 6, you learned how to create and save movie titles. You became familiar with how to set the opacity for the titles, and add and merge them with video clips. You discovered how to create rolling credits. You also explored adding and fading audio clips.

Notes:

7 Audio

Chapter Objective:

To expand your knowledge of audio and audio editing. To become familiar with the audio workspace and tools. To learn how to edit and adjust audio clips. In Chapter 7, you will:

- Explore the predefined audio workspace.

- Discover how to import audio clips into the Project window.

- Learn to listen to audio tracks in the Monitor window.

- Discover how to view waveforms, and observe their importance in the audio-editing process.

- Become familiar with audio tracks and their role on the production Timeline.

- Explore the general audio settings.

- Become familiar with and practice using the Audio Mixer to combine, edit and sweeten audio tracks.

Projects to be Completed:

- The Monkey Movie (A)

- How to Make Spaghetti (B)

- How to Tame a Tiger (C)

- The Gold Rush (D)

Audio

Sound creates atmosphere; it establishes reality, sets mood and supports all visual footage. Without sound and music, there would be no scary scenes in horror movies, no tears as the hero embraces the woman of his dreams. Even in the days of silent movies, sound effects and background music (often created and played right in the theatre) was used to embellish the video production.

Although many beginning videographers wait until the end of the production to add music, it's arguably among the most critical components of any professional production and should be considered from the start. Many of the most memorable movies derive their power as much from the subtle impact of the soundtrack as from the visuals.

This version of Premiere adds considerable horsepower to its built-in audio-editing functions. It offers a real-time Audio Mixer window, and a broad selection of After Effects filters and special effects. Pan and fade controls are easy to select, and you can turn on a waveform display when you need to apply fine edits or synchronize your soundtracks more accurately to the footage in the Timeline.

Remember the girl going for a swim at the beginning of *Jaws*? The scene contained a very simple soundtrack — the splashing of the swimmer, the gentle lapping of the waves on a warm summer night, the distant laughter, subdued conversations and guitar music from the people partying up the beach. In the meantime, below the surface, a silent and effective killer approaches. No sounds are emitted by the beast, but the soundtrack for that scene contained strong, deep horns — duundunn, dundun. Dundun dunndun. It successfully instilled such a sense of impending horror that it remained imprinted on the consciousness of millions for some time after the release of the movie. If you heard that sound, it was time to get out of the water — and fast.

The star of Jaws was a beast of few words, but add deep horns and underwater footage and his message of fear and doom was easily established.

Another great example of a powerful sountrack was Spielberg's *Close Encounters of the Third Kind* — the method of communication chosen by our extraterrestrial visitors were musical notes — no words, just sounds.

The Audio Workspace

Premiere offers a predefined audio workspace. When you're working with the background music, sound effects or dialog boxes, selecting this option positions the Audio Mixer in the center of the working area. To select this option, select Window>Workspace>Audio.

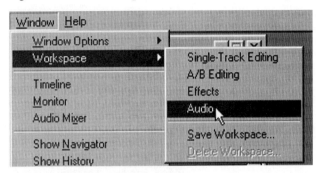

By default, new Premiere projects contain three audio tracks. You can, however, add 96 more, for a total of 99 possible audio tracks. Add to that the ability to render multiple tracks, transitions, fades and other effects into a single track, and there's really no limit to what you can accomplish with the program's audio-editing features.

Viewing Clips and Waveforms

A waveform is a visual representation of an audio track. Using vertical bars, the waveform displays volume and tonal ranges on a horizontal graph. As you work through this chapter, you'll have an opportunity to use waveforms and see how they translate what you're hearing into a visual-editing aid.

Audio clips are imported into Premiere just like video footage, and appear in the Project window. When you select one, a small version of its waveform appears in the upper-left corner of the Project window, complete with a Play button. Clicking it plays the audio in the window.

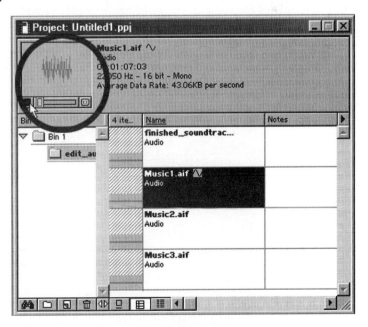

Audio Clip Windows

Double-clicking the clip in the Project window opens an audio Clip window, similar in appearance and function to a regular video Clip window. The difference here is that instead of seeing the footage play, you see the clip's waveform.

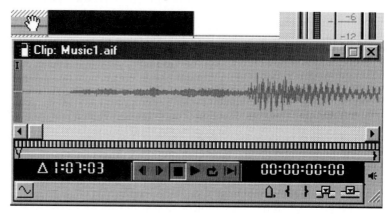

You can use the Zoom icon in the lower-left corner of the audio Clip window to move in on and out from a waveform. This helps you position in/out marks more accurately. As you work more with audio, you'll come to understand the relationship between the waveform and the sound, and be able to focus instantly on the specific piece of audio you need.

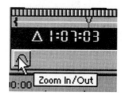

Audio Channels

To place audio tracks into your movies, simply drag them from the Project window to one of the audio tracks. Although Premiere provides 3 audio tracks by default, you can add up to 96 more — plenty to meet the demands of any project.

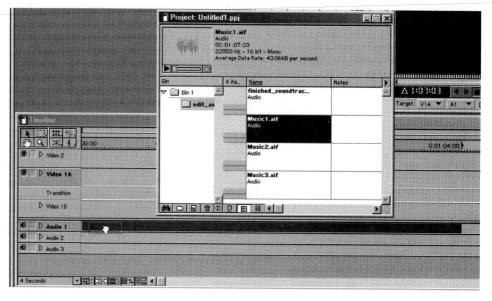

Editing Audio

Editing audio is essentially the same as editing video footage. You can create in/out markers, adjust volume, control *panning* (the movement of sound from the left to right channel and back again) and fade one track into another.

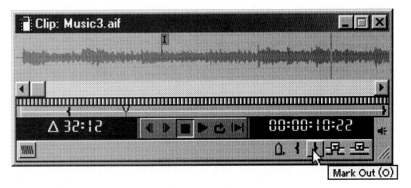

Timeline View Options

Just like video tracks, audio tracks can be expanded to display more information for the clip. Clicking the small triangle to the left of the track's name expands that track. You can keep any or all tracks expanded or collapsed, without having any effect on the clip itself.

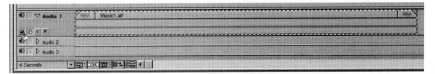

If you expand an audio track and look in the lower-left corner, underneath the Mute and Lock checkboxes, you'll see four small buttons.

You'll find yourself using these buttons frequently. Starting on the left:

- **Show/Hide Waveform.** The Waveform button toggles the display on and off in the Timeline. We find that it's usually easier to work with the waveform in an audio Clip window, instead of on the Timeline itself, but it's a matter of personal preference.

- **Display Keyframes.** Since you can apply effects to sounds clips in much the same way as you do to video footage, keyframes are equally important in your audio tracks. This button toggles their display on and off.

- **Display Volume Rubberbands.** This rubberband controls the overall volume of a clip on the Timeline. Note that if you're using the Audio Mixer to adjust a track's *gain* (volume), the rubberband settings take effect first, then the Audio Mixer's adjustments.

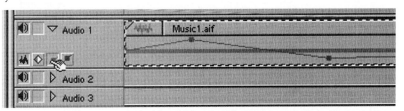

- **Display Pan Rubberbands**. Panning refers to sound moving from the right speaker to the left, or vice versa. Click the rubberband to display a change point, and drag the marker up to shift the sound to the left speaker or down to shift it to the right speaker. Set in the middle, the sound balances between the two speakers, based on the original recording. Panning is also critical to keeping sound environmentally accurate. For example, as a car moves by from right to left, the sound can't move from left to right, nor should it stay in the middle.

Exercise Set-up

It's time to apply some of these concepts to a real-world assignment. A while ago, we put together a news broadcast using footage of a newscaster, a number of very angry flamingos and several split-screen effects.

The footage of the newscaster came complete with its own audio track. Now we're going to take that production and fine-tune the audio — specifically, we're going to add background music. To do so, we'll have to use several of Premiere's audio functions.

Add Background Music

1. Open the project named **broadcast_news.ppj** from your **Work in Progress** folder.

2. Drag MUSIC1.AIF to the Audio 2 track. The music expands to its finale. Click on the triangle at the left side of the Audio 2 track to expand the track. When the triangle points down, you should be able to see the music.

3. Render the production by pressing Return/Enter. Now our newscaster discusses a news event while music plays.

Option/Alt-click on the Work Area bar to extend it quickly to the end of the production.

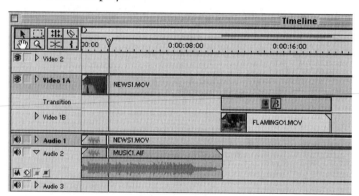

4. You may have noticed that the music does not play long enough to cover the entire newscast. There is a dead spot at the end of the broadcast. We'll solve this problem by duplicating the music. This extra music clip will be placed at the end to complete the production.

5. Drag another copy of MUSIC1.AIF to the Audio 2 track. Place it where the last piece of music concludes. Drag a third copy of MUSIC1.AIF to the Timeline. The music expands beyond the end of the video.

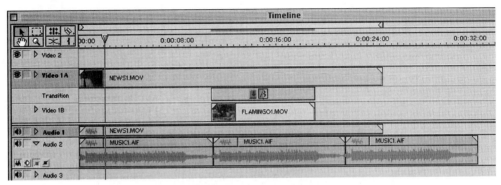

6. Render the production. You should see our newscaster discussing an item while the news music plays. Save your project.

7. On the Timeline, move the Edit Line into the first piece of music on Audio 2. The Target clock (on the right in the Monitor window) should read 00:00:09:20.

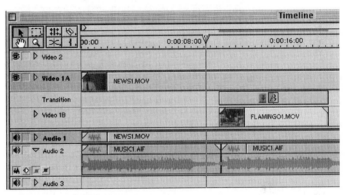

8. Position the cursor just at the end of MUSIC1.AIF. The pointer changes to a two-sided arrow with a red bracket. Drag the music to the left until it snaps to the Edit Line.

9. Now that the music has been shortened, a hole has opened up. Let's fix that.

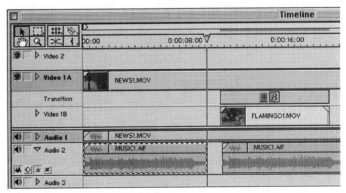

Select the second MUSIC1.AIF. Move it to the left so that it bumps up against the first music clip.

10. Let's trim this copy of MUSIC1.AIF as well. Position the Edit Line at 00:00:19:10. Drag the right corner until it snaps into position. Drag the third (farthest right) copy of MUSIC1.AIF to the left to cover the newly created gap.

11. Render the production. Our newscaster discusses a news item while the news music plays continuously. Save your file.

12. The music ends abruptly at the finish of the newscast. It needs to fade out instead.

    Move the Edit Line to 00:00:24:29 and click. A second small red square appears. Click again at 00:24:30, and drag that handle (red square) to the bottom of the audio area. This creates a fade-out between the two marks.

13. One more frame must be altered. Position the Edit Line at the end of the production and click. Drag that last handle as well to the bottom of the audio area. This keeps the music from fading back in.

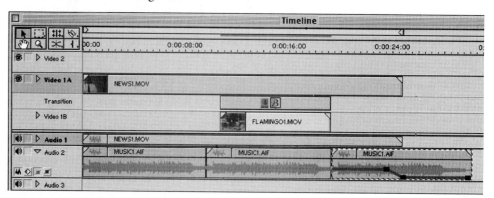

14. Render the production. As your newscast plays, the background music plays and then fades out.

15. Save the project and close it.

General Audio Settings

The higher the rate you specify, the better the sound quality you get, but at a cost. Stereo requires much more disk space than mono. It is important to decide what the final use of the project will be before selecting a sample rate for your sound. Projects that will be placed on the Web do not need the same sound quality as a production played on television or on a CD. Sound can always be resampled or changed to a different rate. Resampling is usually done at the end of a production.

When you begin a project, you have a number of different options to process audio. These options include Compressor, Interleave, Enhanced Rate Conversion and Use Logarithmic Audio Fades. Each option provides a way for Premiere to give you the best possible sound for your production. Let's look at these settings.

The first option is the Compressor setting. Notice that its default is set to Uncompressed. In general, most productions are created in this basic format. When a project is ready to be exported, you can select a compression option or choose not to use one. The setting selected depends on how the sound will be used by the particular output equipment.

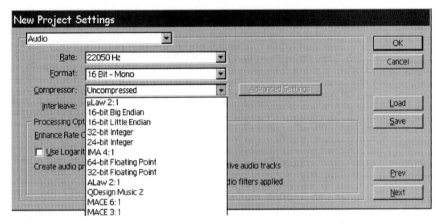

The Interleave option specifies how often audio information is inserted among the video frames in a preview file. The default for this option is 1 Second. This number indicates that when Premiere plays back a frame, the audio for that frame is loaded into RAM. It then stays in RAM and plays until the next frame appears. The smaller the number, the more smoothly your production plays, but also the more RAM you will need — very possibly a lot more RAM then your computer has.

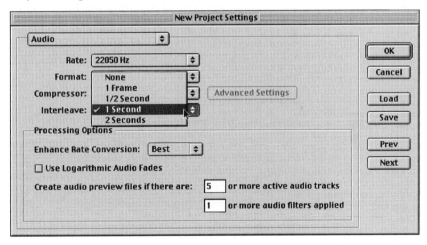

The Enhanced Rate Conversion option allows you to select the level of quality for your sound as it is imported. The options are Off, Good and Best. Each option resamples the audio. Off is the fastest, but generates only average sound. The Good options tries to balance both quality and overall processing speed. The Best option resamples audio at the highest level but requires huge amounts of RAM. Most videographers select Off while editing.

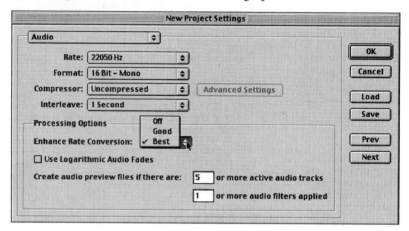

The Use Logarithmic Audio Fades checkbox controls how audio gain increases or decreases are perceived during playback in Premiere. Selecting this option creates a more natural overall sound, but the downside is that it also increases the time it takes to render a file.

You can tell Premiere how to display your audio tracks on the Timeline using the Create Audio Preview Files If There Are setting. This function specifies when Premiere will create an audio preview instead of real-time playback, based on how many audio tracks are active. This function number directly affects the time you will wait for a preview to generate. You will know when you have overloaded your RAM. You will hear pops and clicks while playing back audio in Premiere.

Mixing Audio Clips

Commercials are frequently created with a musical effect called a "bridge." A *bridge* is a section of music that is repeated several times until the end of the commercial, when the final main chorus is played. Bridges are usually created to give an announcer time to speak about the product. A bridge is easily created using a longer piece of music that is trimmed precisely so that the overlap gives no evidence that two ends have been connected.

Edit Music

1. Open **RF-Premiere>Audio>mixing_audio.ppj**. Once it opens, select Window> Workspace>Audio.

2. There are four audio clips inside the project's bin: MUSIC1.AIF, MUSIC2.AIF, MUSIC3.AIF and finished_soundtrack.aif. Double-click the finished_soundtrack.aif clip. Click the Play button, and listen to the finished track. When you're done, close the Clip window.

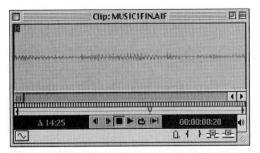

3. Drag MUSIC1.AIF to Audio 1. The music extends to 1:07:02 on the Timeline. This is much too long for our music bridge. Let's tighten things up a bit. Double-click MUSIC1.AIF, so that it opens as a separate Clip window, and slowly drag the left Set Location button to the right until it reads 00:00:15:01. Click the Mark In bracket.

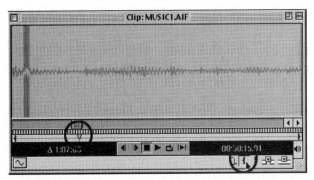

4. Next drag the Set Location button to the right again until it reads 00:00:29:25. Click the Mark Out bracket. You will see a blue rectangle marking the file's new boundaries.

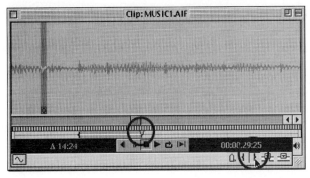

5. Click the Apply button. This will shorten MUSIC1.AIF from the Timeline. Drag MUSIC1.AIF left to the beginning of the Timeline.

6. From the open MUSIC1.AIF Clip window, drag another copy of MUSIC1.AIF to Audio 1. Notice how much shorter it is on the Timeline. The two copies should be lined up, side by side.

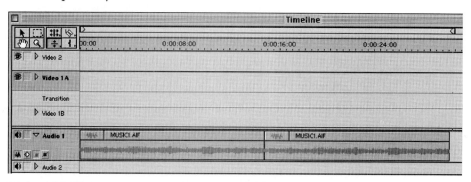

7. Save this file to your **Work in Progress** folder as "BRIDGE.PPJ". Render the file and listen to the results. If you listen carefully, the two files blend together seamlessly. Leave the project open for the next exercise, but delete all the audio clips from the Timeline.

Using the Audio Mixer Window

Premiere provides an Audio Mixer window that gives a high level of control over the audio tracks in your productions. Changes made in the Audio Mixer are also visible in the Timeline.

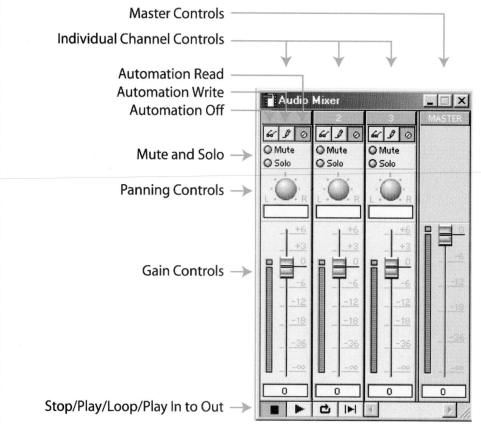

The sliders control the gain or volume of each clip.

By default, the Audio Mixer displays a set of individual controls for each track you create in the Timeline. In addition, it provides a Master control that affects all of the channels at one time.

Each track of the Audio Mixer comes with a pan/balance control. You may have a monophonic sound, but you can simulate stereo by applying panning controls. Change the setting of this control either by dragging clockwise or counterclockwise, or by typing a value from -100 to +100 in the box below the control, and pressing the Return/Enter key.

Automation States

One of the easiest and most interactive ways to control sound levels in Premiere is with the Automation state buttons. For each audio track, three buttons determine the sound state during the mixing process. These buttons are Automation Read, Automation Write and Automation Off.

Automation Read translates the audio information for an audio track and records any adjustments you make in the Audio Mixer window. In other words, Automation Read starts with the initial changes you have made to the audio on the Timeline, then shows the adjustments visually as the music plays.

Automation Off is the default mode for Premiere, allowing use of the Audio Mixer without the limitation of the rubberbands on the Timeline.

These adjustments are stored as a set of handles under the audio on the Timeline track. Simply click the triangle to the left of the track name to expand the audio track with which you want to work, and your changes will be available for you to edit.

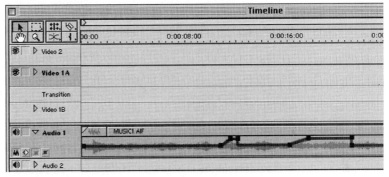

Automation Write works in the opposite way. In Automation Write mode, you start the music and make the changes in the Audio Mixer as the music is playing. The changes are available immediately on the Timeline.

Mute and Solo are two of the channel-specific settings available on the Audio Mixer window. Mute does just what it sounds like — turns off the sound for that channel. This is particularly useful if you're working on a project that has a lot of audio tracks. Solo is exactly the opposite — it mutes all other tracks in the production, leaving only that specific channel playing.

Ganging Tracks

Besides using the Master gain control, you can *gang* (or connect) two or more channels, so that you can adjust their gains simultaneously.

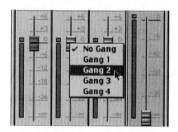

Adjusting Audio Levels on the Timeline

If the change you wish to make is a simple one, you might want to work directly on the Timeline. You may have noticed that all audio clips include two handles that you can't remove — one at the beginning of the clip and another at the end. You can also *cross-fade* two audio clips automatically so that one fades out as another fades in. The rubberband in the Timeline corresponds to the volume fader in the Audio Mixer window.

Here are a few extra methods to help you adjust your sound. To adjust volume in 1% increments, position the pointer over the volume handle, hold the Shift key, and drag the volume handle up or down. A numeric display appears over the audio track to indicate the current volume level as you drag. To adjust two handles simultaneously, just select the Fade Adjustment tool and position it between the two handles you want to adjust. Drag that segment up or down. The sound adjusts for the entire clip.

Naming Audio Tracks

Premiere gives you the ability to incorporate up to 99 video and 99 audio tracks on the Timeline. Working with so many tracks can make a production confusing. With that in mind, Premiere enables you to name both your audio and video clips. By default, all of your tracks are named Audio 1, Audio 2, etc. To rename an audio track, you choose Track Options (in the Timeline) or access the Track Options Dialog box. To rename a track, just select it, click Name, type a new name and click OK.

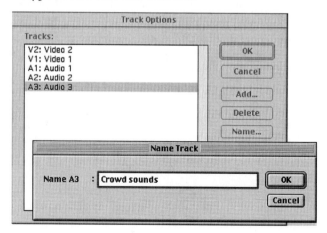

New audio tracks appear on the Timeline underneath existing tracks. Deleting a track removes all clip instances on the track but does not affect the source clips stored in the Project window.

Cross-fades

You will discover that there are times when your music does not play long enough for the production. One of the easiest solutions is to extend the music by cross-fading two pieces. *Cross-fading* is causing the sound of one audio to fade away as another is fading in. If cross-fading is done cleverly, the viewer will never notice that two pieces have been spliced together.

Cross-fade Audio Clips

1. Play the music clipping MUSIC2.AIF to get a feel for the music. Drag MUSIC2.AIF to Audio 1. The music extends out to 00:00:10:22 on the Timeline. This is very short and ends too abruptly for production. If necessary, click the triangle to the left of each track name to expand the audio tracks you want to cross-fade. Drag a second copy of MUSIC2.AIF to Audio 2. Position the music to start at 00:00:08:13 on the Timeline.

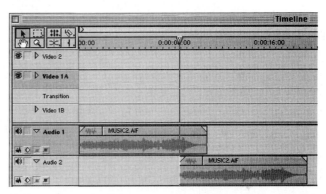

You can add or remove tracks at any time, except for the Video 1, Video 2, Transition, Audio 1, Audio 2 and Audio 3 tracks, which cannot be deleted.

2. Select the Cross-Fade tool. Click on MUSIC2.AIF in Audio 1. This is the fade out. Click on MUSIC2.AIF in Audio 2. This is the fade in. Premiere automatically creates and adjusts volume handles on both clips.

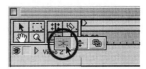

3. Save this file in your **Work in Progress** folder as "BRIDGE2.PPJ". Render the file and listen to the results. The two files cross-fade and blend together nicely. Leave the project open for the next exercise, but delete all of the audio from the Timeline.

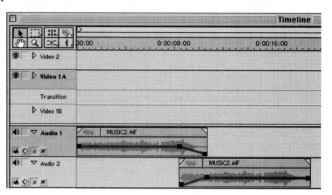

Audio Special Effects

As you know, music really adds to your production, but sometimes the music you select isn't at the sound quality you need. Adobe Premiere includes a variety of audio effects (located in the Audio Effects palette) designed to alter or enhance the properties of audio clips. Here are some of the most useful audio enhancement effects.

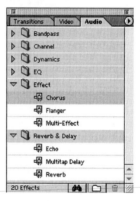

Two clips cannot overlap on the same track, so you must place each audio clip on a different audio track.

When creating a cross-fade, the order in which you select the clips is not important.

- **Auto Pan**. This effect (located in the Channel folder) makes audio sound much richer by automatically panning or moving an audio track cyclically between the left and right audio channels. Several options are available to you in this area. Depth specifies how much of the audio clip is moved back and forth. Rate specifies how quickly the pan will occur.

- **Bass & Treble**. If your sound is a little too tinny, you can make basic adjustments to audio tone with this option. Bass (located in the EQ folder) specifies the amount of sound that is applied to the low frequencies of the audio clip, while Treble specifies the amount of sound that is applied to the high frequencies of the audio clip. Flat restores the clip to its original state without any adjustment.

- **Boost**. This option (located in the Dynamics folder) compensates for weaker sounds. It accomplishes this while leaving the loud sounds untouched.

- **Chorus**. Does your audio sound a little flat? Chorus (located in the Effect folder) will add depth to your audio clip. This effect applies a copy of the sound and plays it at a sound level slightly higher than the original. Mix specifies the overall balance. A value of 50 is the default. Depth specifies the amount of delay. If you want a deeper chorus sound, try increasing this number. Regeneration applies an echo effect.

- **Compressor/Expander**. This option attempts to compensate for the differences between sounds. It is sometimes referred to as "dynamic range" and is located in the Dynamics folder. Use this effect to raise the level of a soft sound without affecting a louder sound in the same clip.

This option is sometimes used to reduce noise. Ratio affects how quickly the change occurs. Threshold specifies where the compression begins or expansion ends. Adjusting Gain affects the overall output level.

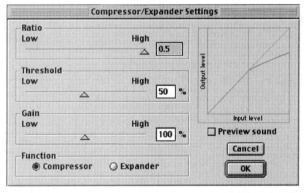

- **Echo**. This option (located in the Reverb & Delay folder) plays the same sound repeatedly during a defined period of time. This effect might create the effect of a ball bouncing up and down in a room with a lot of echo. Moving the Delay slider from Short to Long lengthens the delay between the original sound and its new echo effect.

- **Equalize**. This effect polishes the overall tonal quality of your audio. It is located in the EQ folder. It attempts to attune the highs and lows of the audio clip using presets that measure the frequency settings.

- **Fill Left and Fill Right**. These effects play the entire audio clip in the left or right stereo channel. They are located in the Channel folder.

- **Flanger**. This option can add interest to your audio by reversing audio signal. It accomplishes this effect in a similar manner to the Chorus effect. It sometimes adds an underwater effect to the audio. Additional options in this effect include Mix, Depth Change and Rate. It is located in the Effect folder.

- **High Pass and Low Pass**. The High Pass effect (located in the Bandpass folder) removes low frequencies from an audio clip, and the Low Pass effect removes high frequencies. These effects are used to correct shooting situations for which you might not otherwise be able to compensate. One such situation might be nearby high wires that generate a sound that affects the quality of the audio.

- **Multi-Effect**. This option can generate novel echo and chorus effects by allowing you to change audio rhythm and emphasis. The controls include Delay, Feedback, Mix, Modulation, Rate and Waveform. It is located in the Effect folder.

- **Multitap Delay**. This one effect (located in the Reverb & Delay folder) actually contains a number of different controls for managing delay effects in the soundtrack. It can be useful for effects such as adding an extra touch to scary-sounding music. These controls are called "taps."

Taps turn on a delay on an audio effect. Each tap can include a unique combination of delay, feedback and stereo-channel balancing. By combining multiple taps, you can originate new and elaborate sound effects.

- **Noise Gate**. This option (located in the Dynamics folder) removes faint background noise during the quiet moments of an audio clip. Threshold is the control point at which the unwanted effect is triggered and removed. It is especially useful if important audio is cut off at the end of the track.

- **Notch/Hum Filter**. *Hum* is the sound created when you are shooting too close to audio cables or equipment that is improperly shielded or grounded. Use the Notch/Hum Filter effect to remove any annoying sound from an audio clip. It can be found in the Bandpass folder.

- **Pan**. This effect allows you to control how much of the music plays from either the left or right speaker. Use the slider to control how far to the left or right the sound plays. It is located in the Channel folder.

- **Parametric Equalization**. If you have a good ear for music, this is the effect for you. The Parametric Equalization effect (located in the EQ folder) allows precise isolation of frequency ranges. It enhances up to three different bands of the audio clip. Other controls in this effect area include Enable, Frequency, Bandwidth and Boost/Cut.

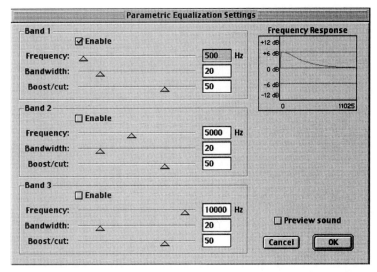

- **Reverb**. Want to simulate the sound of a big auditorium? The Reverb effect can accomplish this for you. It can effectively simulate sound that is being produced in a large room. You input the room size, and then adjust the other settings accordingly. Reverb can be found in the Reverb & Delay folder.

- **Swap Left & Right**. This effect (located in the Channel folder) swaps the left and right channels of a clip imported as stereo. This effect can be useful during special-effect sequences such as a train moving through a tunnel.

Applying Effects

Unless you have access to an orchestra, chances are you will have to compromise with your musical selections. Music that you can use for free or for a small amount of money is referred to as "royalty-free" music. Royalty-free music is available from many different sources. There are many excellent companies offering literally thousands of music clips. You can find these companies in the yellow pages or on the Internet.

Let's take a moment to mention copyright law and music. No matter what type of project you work on, you must pay for the music you use. It is the law and is designed to protect the musician. An artist writes music as a source of income, so using that music without the express permission of the artist is the equivalent of stealing. Most of the royalty-free music companies offer very attractive rates for smaller projects. Frequently special promotions are available. Don't be afraid to ask about them. The bottom line is that no matter what type of project you work on, audio is an important part of your overall success.

Sweetening Music

There is a fine art to working with voice, sound effects and music. In fact, entire books have been devoted to the subject. The process of enhancing or *sweetening* music involves the method of modifying bad music to make it better and improving good music to make it the best. There is only one thing to keep in mind: if you can hear the improvement clearly, you've improved it too much! This is a subtle process.

Using Two Methods to Adjust Audio Gain

1. Play MUSIC3.AIF to get a feel for the music. Drag MUSIC3.AIF to the Audio 1 track.

2. In the Audio Effects palette, expand the Dynamics folder. Drag the Compresssor/Expander filter onto MUSIC3.AIF. If it is not already open, the Effect Controls palette pops up.

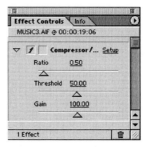

3. Click Setup in the Effect Controls palette. A dialog box appears. Set Ratio: .39, Threshold: 87%, Gain: 138%, and click the Preview Sound checkbox to be able to hear your changes. When you are satisfied with the results, click OK.

4. Render the file and listen to the results.

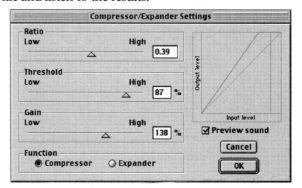

5. Take a moment to listen to the music as it sounded both before and after the effect was applied. Select Edit>Undo Filter setting. Render the file once again, and listen to the results.

6. Let's adjust the gain a second way, using the Audio Mixer. With the Timeline and clip active, click the Trashcan in the Effect Controls palette to clear the effects placed on MUSIC3.AIF. Click Yes.

7. Select Window>Audio Mixer. Click on Automation Write in the first section, and then click the Play button.

8. Music begins to play. Raise the Audio Fader bar up and down to raise and lower the volume of the music.

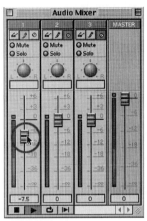

9. When you are finished, click the Stop button. Expand the Timeline and take a look at the audio. Zoom in to 2 seconds to really see the results. Fine-tune the newest changes with the handles on Audio 1.

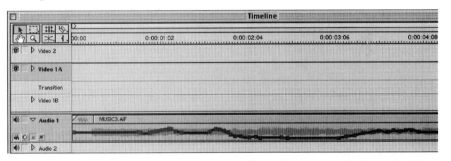

10. Leave the project open for the next exercise, but delete the audio from the Timeline.

Custom Audio Effects

Sometimes, no matter how hard you try, you just can't find the right music. A solution to your problem is at hand. Premiere has controls to let you completely alter existing music to create a new set of sounds.

Create New Audio Effects

1. Play the audio clipping MUSIC1.AIF once again to get a feel for the music. Drag MUSIC1.AIF to Audio 1.

2. In the Audio Effects palette, expand the Effect folder, and drag Multi-Effect onto MUSIC1.AIF. If it is not already open, the Effect Controls palette pops up.

3. Click Setup in the Effect Controls palette. A dialog box appears. Set Delay Time: 44, Feedback: 60, Mix: 70, Modulation Rate: 2.07, Modulation Intensity: 100.

4. Click the Preview Sound checkbox to hear your changes. Click OK. Render the file and listen to all of the modifications.

5. With the Timeline active, click the Trashcan in the Effect Controls palette to clear the effects placed on MUSIC1.AIF. Click Yes.

6. In the Audio Effects palette, expand the Reverb & Delay folder. Drag Multitap Delay onto MUSIC1.AIF.

7. Click Setup in the Effect Controls palette for Multitap Delay. A dialog box appears. Place a checkmark in Tap 1, 2, 3 and 4. Place a checkmark in the Cross box for Tap 1, 2, 3 and 4 as well. Set Mix: 100% Effect, Time Signature: 4/2, and click the Preview checkbox. Click OK. Render the file and listen to all of the modifications.

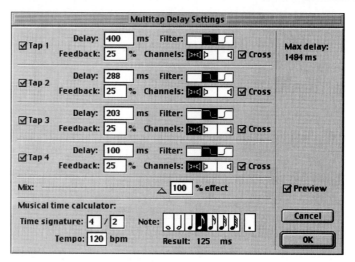

8. Save and close this file.

Summary

In Chapter 7, you have explored Premiere's audio controls. You learned about the importance of music and its ability to enhance a production. You produced an audio bridge and created a cross-fade.

You practiced ways to create new and unique sounds. You discovered the many audio options in Premiere and used these options to sweeten music. You then used the Audio Effects palette to create a set of new sounds.

Complete Project B: How to Make Spaghetti

⑧ Creating Footage

Chapter Objective:

To discover how Premiere can be used to create scenes and objects that appear to be something that they're not. To learn how to use familiar and new techniques to create new scenes, movement within stills and custom effects. In Chapter 8, you will:

- Become familiar with the Pan and Zoom controls, and how they can be used to create a sense of movement in still images.

- Learn about and practice using the Title window to create stills.

- Explore how to use filters to simulate effects such as moving water and lens flares.

- Discover how to use alpha channels for superimposing stills and graphics created with the Title window.

- Become familiar with and practice adding mood and feeling to productions using advanced effects and motion.

Projects to be Completed:

- The Monkey Movie (A)

- How to Make Spaghetti (B)

- How to Tame a Tiger (C)

- The Gold Rush (D)

Creating Footage

It's one thing to learn to edit clips, fade audio and use filters — becoming technically adept at using a program like Premiere is possible for almost anyone. Using the tools to create art, however, is quite another matter. Throughout this chapter, you're going to move into the realm of true creation — using Premiere to make elements that didn't exist before you started the project.

Why would you need to be able to create material? There might be any number of reasons. You might find that your project is due, but some of your shots didn't live up to your expectations so you're short usable video. You might realize that a still image you had planned to import and incorporate in your production was not strong enough by itself, so you would like to animate it. You might want to give a custom look or tone to your production with original backgrounds, titles and other graphics. You might even plan to underscore the playful or somber mood of an underlying concept for your production.

Imagine, for example, that you want to create a production that would convey the sense of a poem or quotation. How could you do this? You might shoot footage of a discussion between several people about the poem or saying. But the poetic language, itself, has the ability to convey powerful visual images and meanings. You could, instead, choose to represent the words graphically, and use your creative insight to cause the backgrounds, images, fonts and colors to highlight the tone and meaning of the words. In all of these cases, it is important to be able to use the functions of Premiere effectively to convey your creative vision. But your creative vision must begin with a clear understanding and thoughtful, sensitive approach to the poem or saying itself.

In this chapter, you will explore a number of the advanced features of Premiere while creating new elements and altering existing elements. You will learn how to create movement and scenes that don't really exist. They'll be crafted by combining stills with graphics created within Premiere. You'll manufacture backgrounds, make your own combinations of images and titles, add motion to words and images, and even have the opportunity to illustrate a Native American proverb. You'll also learn how Premiere can work effectively with other software to enable you to add functions like rotoscoping, color correction, editing and more.

Simulating Motion with Static Images

It is a beautiful day. The sun is shining, and you are on the road to a client site to complete a video shoot. You just need a couple of background shots to finish things up. Everything is great — until you realize that you've run out of battery on your video camera. The final project is due in the client's hands the next day and you are short video footage.

Premiere comes to your rescue. With its special-effect filters and other tools, in fact, even the most mundane picture can be given new life in Premiere. You can add backgrounds, animate still images and generate effects after the fact. Even the simplest still images can be manipulated to get a custom look — it's just a question of knowing how to use Premiere. As you remember, the best part is that, no matter how much you experiment, all of your footage remains intact, so you can try out new effects without destroying your clips.

One of the most versatile features is the ability to add a variety of animation or motion effects to still images.

Creating Custom Stills within Premiere

The first step to giving static images motion is to import or create the image. Armed with nothing more than a still image and an ability to visualize what you want, you, the intrepid videographer, can nonetheless produce impressive video. The secret lies in using the Title window, Character window and motion controls to build your effects. Still images can be imported or created from scratch with the Title window or the drawing tools in the Character window, and then given movement with motion controls.

One of the most common challenges facing any videographer is creating custom backgrounds. Used in a wide variety of productions and for many different purposes, backgrounds can be created from imported stills, by drawing within Premiere itself or by a combination of the two.

Exercise Set-up

In the following exercises, as you work with four different sets of pictures, you'll have the opportunity to generate an entirely different effect with each image. The first effect we'll explore is creating a graphic using the Title window and give it life using a few of Premiere's motion controls. We'll start by creating a rising sun, complete with lens flares from a non-existent light source.

Preview and Begin the Project

1. Open **RF-Premiere>reality>creating_reality.ppj** from within Premiere. The program prompts you to find the file **Adobe1.tif**, which is in the same folder. Once you select it, the program finds all of the other clips it needs and imports the folder as a bin in the Project window. Double-click the sequence_edits bin to reveal the components we're going to use for this exercise.

2. Drag FINAL12.MOV to the Source view in the Monitor window, and click Play to view the final project before you start. Leave this file open for the next exercise.

Create a Custom Imaginary Background with the Title Window

1. In the open file, select File>New>Title to display the Title window dialog box.

2. Let's draw the sky first. Select the right or filled side of the Rectangle tool. Draw a small rectangle in the drawing area.

Each drawing-tool shape is divided in half. Click the left half for an outline shape or the right half of a tool for a filled shape. Once a color is selected, you move to the drawing area and draw the shape you need.

3. With handles still showing on the rectangle, select a beginning and ending gradient for the sky. Click on Gradient Start Color. In the Color Picker, set Red: 10, Green: 0, Blue: 56, and click OK.

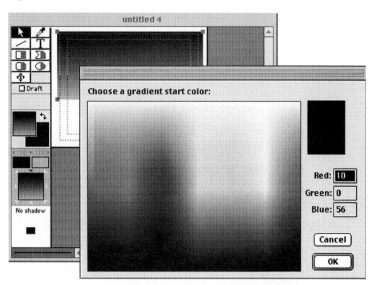

For the darker color, click on Gradient End Color. Set Red: 0, Green: 0, Blue: 0. This creates a night sky that changes from a deep blue-purple to black. On the left side, pull the shadow representation over to cover the black rectangle so that it reads No Shadow.

4. The rectangle needs to cover the entire drawing, including the entire safe area. (See Chapter 6 for details on the safe areas.) Grab the top-left or bottom-right handle, and drag it until the rectangle covers the entire drawing area — outside the safe areas.

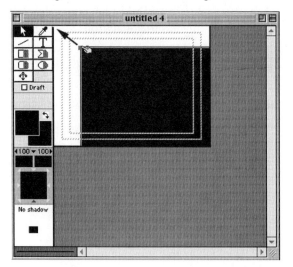

Pull the bottom-left handle until it also extends off the safe area. It should extend down to cover the entire page. If necessary, reverse the direction of the gradient so that the color is light at the bottom and dark at the top.

Holding the Shift key constrains the circle or rectangle.

5. Let's draw the moon. Select the filled side of the Oval tool. Draw a small round moon over the background. (Hold the Shift key to constrain the shape.) Fill it with a gradient composed of start and end gradient colors of your choice. (Our example was created with the following gradients — Red: 7, Green: 194, Blue: 185. For the lighter color, we set Red: 255, Green: 255, Blue: 255.)

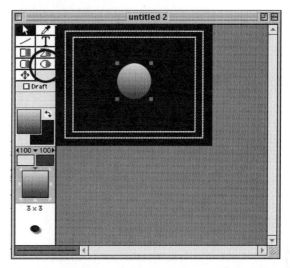

6. The moon needs to be moved so that it sits at the top left of the screen. Click the moon so that the handles appear, and then move the moon until it is in the upper-left corner of the screen. (Do not accidentally grab the handles themselves to move the moon or you will resize the oval instead of moving it.)

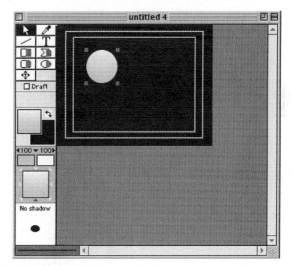

7. We need some stars and a couple of small planets to give the picture depth. Select the filled side of the Oval tool. Draw a small round planet over the background. Fill it with a gradient composed of start and end gradient colors of your choice. (Our example was created with Red: 255, Green: 126, Blue: 154. For the lighter color, we set Red: 255, Green: 255, Blue: 255.)

8. Click the planet so that handles appear on it. Move the planet (not using the handles) until you are satisfied with its new location.

9. Let's create another planet. With the original planet still selected, choose Edit>Copy, then Edit>Paste. This will give you another planet to place where you prefer. If it is on top of the original, drag it to a new position.

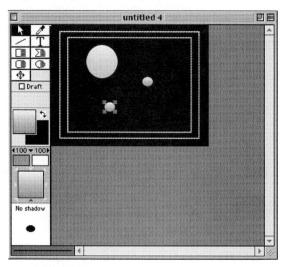

Having trouble moving that tiny star? Here is an easy way. You can move a selected item around in the Title window with the arrow keys. By pressing the Up, Down, Left or Right Arrows, you can easily move a shape into position.

If you hold down the Shift key while pressing the arrow keys, the item is moved in larger increments.

When trying to move selected objects, wait until the cursor touching the object becomes an arrow shape instead of a hand shape.

10. Let's create some stars. With the filled side of the Oval tool, draw a small round star over the background. Fill it with a gradient composed of start and end gradient colors of your choice. (Our example was created with Red: 255, Green: 243, Blue: 255. For the lighter color, we set Red: 255, Green: 255, Blue: 255.)

11. Let's create more stars. With the first star selected, choose Edit>Copy, and then Edit>Paste 12 times. Move these twelve stars around until you are satisfied with their locations, creating an image of a universe.

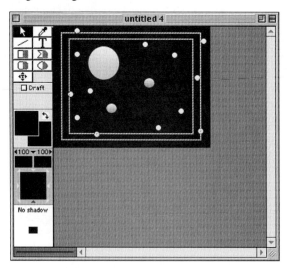

12. The new background must be saved and added to the Project window. Save your title as "SPACE.PTL" to your **Work in Progress** folder.

13. Once named and saved, your title automatically transfers to the Project window. Close the Title window. You now see SPACE.PTL displayed in the Project window.

14. Leave this file open for the next exercise.

Assemble and Trim the Components

Now that you have created an interesting space background, it's time to place the pieces on the Timeline and trim them appropriately.

1. You should now have ADOBE1.TIF, ADOBE2.TIF, CIRCLE.PTL, FINAL12.MOV, SKY.PTL, SPACE.PTL and WATER.TIF in the Project window. In the open file, drag SKY.PTL to the Timeline window at the beginning of Video 1A.

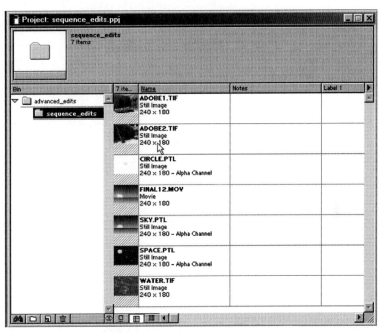

2. The still image has a five-second duration, which you will shorten to three seconds. Click on SKY.PTL so that it is highlighted. Select Clip>Duration, and set it to 00:00:03:00. Click OK, and the clip shortens on the Timeline.

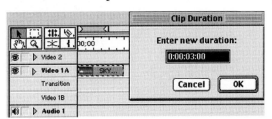

3. Drag SPACE.PTL to the Timeline window on Video 1B, under and to the right of SKY.PTL at 00:00:03:00.

4. This new still image also has a five-second duration. Shorten it to three seconds by setting it to 00:00:03:00.

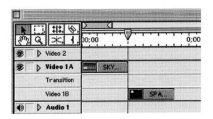

You can select the duration for a clip before it is moved to the Timeline. You just select the clip in the Project window, then select Clip>Speed. You can then specify the duration. It saves time and is very accurate.

5. Drag CIRCLE.PTL to the Timeline window on Video 2 at 00:00:03:00, directly above SPACE.PTL. Shorten this clip to one second. Copy and paste copies of CIRCLE.PTL so that you have three pictures of one-second duration each on the Video 2 track on the Timeline.

6. Drag WATER.TIF to the Timeline window, to the right of SPACE.PTL on Video 1A at 00:00:06:00. Shorten its five-second duration to three seconds.

7. Drag ADOBE1.TIF to the Timeline window on Video1A at 00:00:09:00. Shorten the duration to three seconds.

8. Drag ADOBE2.TIF to the Timeline window on Video 1B, so that it overlaps ADOBE1.TIF. Shorten its duration to three seconds.

9. Add an Additive Dissolve transition (from the Dissolve folder) to the overlap between ADOBE1.TIF and ADOBE2.TIF.

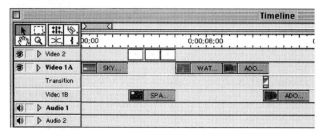

10. At the top of the Timeline window, check the Work Area bar, which should be extended to the right. Make certain that the bar extends to the end of the background title or about 15 seconds.

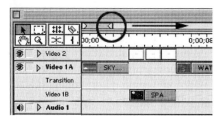

11. Save your project as "EFFECTS.PPJ" to your **Work in Progress** folder.

12. Render this production. Leave the file open for the next exercise.

Use the Lens Flare

1. In the open file, click on SKY.PTL on the Timeline. From the Render folder in the Video Effects palette, drag the Lens Flare filter onto SKY.PTL.

2. A new dialog box appears. Move the small bright "+" over to the sun, and click OK.

3. In the open Effect Controls palette, click the Enable Keyframing box to add a clock. On the Timeline, click the triangle to expand Video 1A. Create a keyframe at the end of SKY.PTL on the Timeline. Click on Setup in the Effect Controls palette.

4. In the main Lens Flare dialog box, move the bright "+" over to the right of the sun as the ending point of the filter. Set the Brightness slider bar to 170%. Click OK again to close the Lens Flare dialog box.

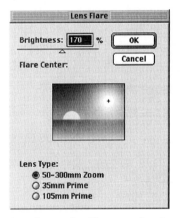

5. Save and render this project. Leave the file open for the next exercise.

Use Alpha Channels to Generate Special Effects

We've worked previously with alpha channels. As you recall, the Video 2 track serves as a special-effects track that enables you to combine or superimpose videos atop one another. By creating additional video tracks, we are able to generate some impressive video effects.

1. In the open file, click on the first CIRCLE.PTL, and select Clip>Video Options>Transparency.

2. The Transparency Settings dialog box appears with the CIRCLE.PTL file in the Sample box. Set Key Type: White Alpha Matte, and click OK to close the dialog box.

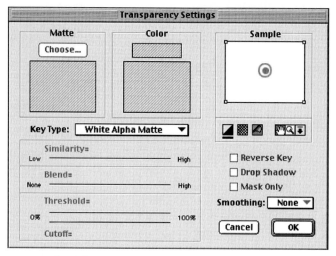

3. Select, in turn, each of the three copies of CIRCLE.PTL from the Timeline window, and choose Clip>Video Options>Transparency to be sure that each clip is set to White Alpha Matte.

4. Save and render this production. You should see your planets superimposed on your background. Leave the file open for the next exercise.

Work with Motion Settings

Now let's add movement — we'll make the planets zoom through space.

1. In the open file, click on the first CIRCLE.PTL on the Timeline. Select Clip>Video Options>Motion to display the Motion Settings dialog box.

2. Watch the planet fly across the screen from left to right. Notice that the Use Clip's alpha channel is selectcd. Let's change the motion effect.

Title files created in Premiere automatically come with an alpha channel.

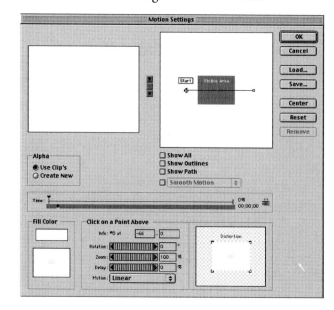

Click on the Start keyframe, and move it to the center of the screen. Click on the End/Finish button, and move it to the left, above the Start keyframe.

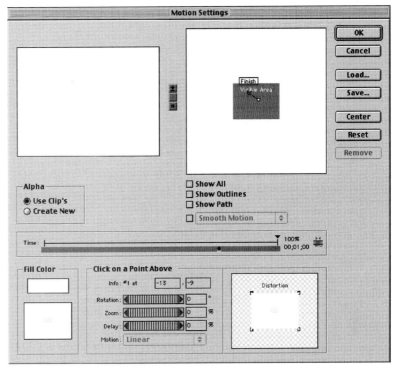

The keyboard shortcut to access the Motion Settings dialog box is Command/Control-Y.

A red line appears under a video clip when a motion effect has been added. This is Premiere's way of letting you know that you have applied a special effect.

3. Click on the Zoom control, and enter 0%. The planet should seem to travel from right to left, and recede into the distance. Click OK.

4. Click on the second CIRCLE.PTL on the Timeline. Select Clip>Video>Motion to display the Motion Settings dialog box.

5. This time drag the Start keyframe to the lower-left center of the visible drawing area. Now drag the Finish/End keyframe to the top center area.

6. Click on the Zoom control, and enter 0%. The planet now moves from left to right, from bottom to top. Click OK.

7. Click on the third and final CIRCLE.PTL, and again access the Motion Settings dialog box.

8. Drag the Start keyframe to the top-right center of the visible drawing area. Now drag the Finish/End keyframe to the lower-left center area.

9. Set the Zoom control to 0%. The planet now moves from right to left, from top to bottom. Click OK.

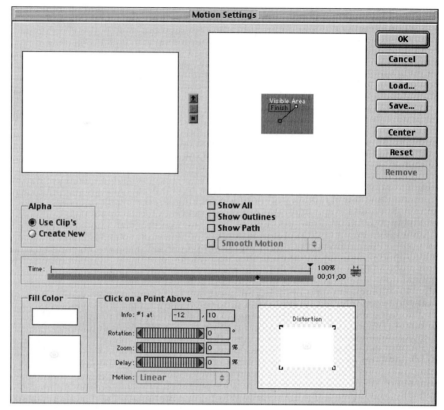

10. Save and render this production. You should see your three planets moving through space. Leave the file open for the next exercise.

Using Filters to Add Motion

One of the most powerful assets of Premiere is its set of special-effect filters. These filters can be used individually and in combination, on still images or whole clips, giving the imaginative individual an almost unlimited set of video effects. Through the creative use of filters, for instance, it's fairly simple to simulate motion using only still images. If you start with quality photographic images (such as JPEG, GIF, TIF or PNG files), the resulting footage can seem quite realistic.

Of course, working with filters and gaining experience in using them to enhance transitions and create special effects is important, but it's only half the story. Like many aspects of Premiere, simply understanding what buttons to press doesn't generate compelling content. It's when you apply those tools in an imaginative way that you begin to evolve from a camera operator or an editor to a videographer.

Exercise Set-up

In the following series of exercises, we're going to create rippling water where there isn't any, and make the viewer believe that we were shooting a live scene while panning with the camera dolly.

*A **camera dolly** is a wheeled platform to which the camera is mounted. The wheels enable the camera operator to move the camera around a set, quickly and smoothly, and position it as needed for individual shots. Since such cameras are often heavy equipment, these dollies also make it possible to sustain shots that might otherwise wear on the shoulders of the camera operator.*

Use the Find Video Effect button at the bottom of the Video Effects palette to locate the filter you need quickly.

Create Motion with the Wave Filter

1. In the open file, click on WATER.TIF on the Timeline. From the Distort folder in the Video Effects palette, drag the Wave filter onto WATER.TIF on the Timeline.

2. The Wave dialog box appears. Set Number of Generators: 3, Wavelength Min.: 10, Wavelength Max.: 140, Amplitude: 5 and 35, Repeat Edge Pixels: selected. Click OK.

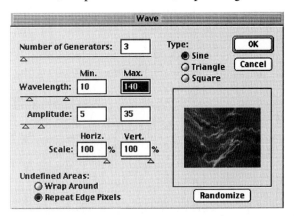

3. In the Effect Controls palette, click the Enable Keyframing box to display a clock in it. Click on the keyframe at the end of WATER.TIF on the Timeline. Click on Setup in the Effect Controls palette. You are now back in the main Wave dialog box. This is the Out Point of the Wave effect. Set Number of Generators: 7, Wavelength Min.: 22, Wavelength Max.: 321, Amplitude: 5 and 35, Repeat Edge Pixels: selected. Click OK.

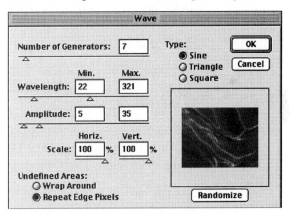

4. Save and render this production. You should see your still picture of water rippling as if it really has movement. Leave the file open for the next exercise.

Making Stills Move with Created Pans and Zooms

If you're on-site, and you have a good dolly setup or another method of moving the camera smoothly across or towards an object or scene, you can get fairly creative with pans and zooms. Pans and zooms involve the audience by letting them feel that they're moving across the location, viewing the scene from different angles.

You can use Premiere's filters to create the illusion of a panning camera, using only still images. The following still images from New Mexico are a good example. They are pretty to look at but lack movement. With filters, you can create the illusion that you had a video camera on the scene.

Exercise Set-up

In the set of images we brought into this project, we also have two still images from New Mexico. They are impressive images but could be improved by adding movement. You will use the Camera View filter to create the illusion of a zoom-out and a pan from right to left.

Create Movement with Filters

1. In the open file, highlight ADOBE1.TIF on the Video 1A track. Open the Transform folder in the Video Effects palette, and drag Camera View onto ADOBE1.TIF.

2. Click Setup in the Effect Controls palette. The Camera View Settings dialog box appears. Set Zoom: 0.40, leave the other settings as they are, and click OK.

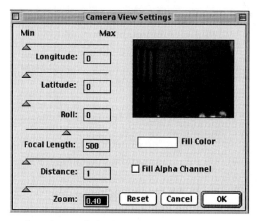

3. In the Effect Controls palette, click the Enable Keyframing box to display a clock in it. Expand Video 1A, if necessary. Click on the keyframe at the end of ADOBE1.TIF on the Timeline. Click on Setup.

4. You are now back in the main Camera View Settings dialog box. This time, set Zoom for 1.00, and click OK. This zooms the picture out to its actual size at the completion of the three-second duration.

5. Let's use the Image Pan filter, which enables you create left to right movement on a still image. Highlight ADOBE2.TIF on the Video 1B track. From the Transform folder in the Video Effects palette, drag the Image Pan filter onto ADOBE2.TIF.

6. In the Effect Controls palette, click the Enable Keyframing box to display a clock. Click on the keyframe at the beginning of ADOBE2.TIF on the Timeline. Click on Setup. You are now in the main Image Pan Settings dialog box. Set Left: 0, Width: 182, Top: 0, Height: 180, and click OK.

7. If necessary, expand Video 1B. Click the keyframe at the end of ADOBE2.TIF on the Timeline. Click on Setup. In the Image Pan Settings dialog box, set Left: 56, Width: 182, Top: 0, Height: 180, and click OK.

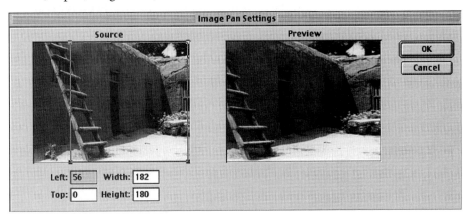

8. Save and render. You should see all of your filters plus a zoom effect and a pan effect on the adobe house. It should now look as if a camera had been placed there to record the movement. If you like, export the production as a QuickTime movie, and save it for posterity. Close the file.

Creating Moving Objects

Not only can Premiere add motion to still photographic and graphic images, but it can also generate a variety of type effects. Two of the best such effects include two- and three-dimensional movement. Type can be made to maneuver around the screen from any direction or seem to fly off the screen toward you.

Exercise Set-up
Creating a production around the following proverb will give you the opportunity to explore some of the most advanced features of Premiere. When you are finished with the assignment, your newly created type will zoom in from all over the page.

You will create a complete set of titles that will contain all of the words in the proverb. Each title will contain one word only. That way you will have the most flexibility to move the type around the screen. Again, here is the Native American proverb:

"To touch the earth is to have harmony with nature."

Create Movie Titles

1. From within Premiere, open **RF-Premiere>poetry>poetryinmotion.ppj**. Premiere prompts you to find the file Audio7.aif, which is in the same folder as the project. Double-click **Audio7.aif**, and the program will find the rest of the assets. Open the poetry_assets bin, and look at the contents.

2. Select File>New>Title. The Title window appears.

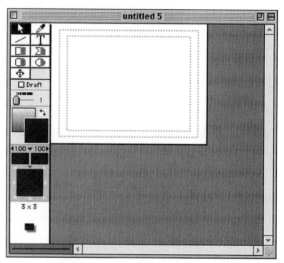

3. We need to make certain that the Title window is the same size as the rest of the production. If not, the type will look rough when the production is built. If it is not already highlighted, click on the untitled title.

4. Select Window>Window Options>Title Window Options. A dialog box appears with some new options for this area of the program.

5. Double-check that the dialog box is set as follows, making any changes necessary — Size H: 240 and V: 180, Background: white, Show Safe Titles: selected, NTSC-safe Colors: selected. When you are finished, click OK.

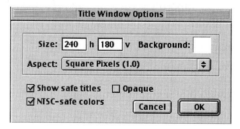

6. Let's create the first title. Click on the Type tool. As you move your cursor to the right onto the title area, it changes to an I-beam.

Be certain that any fonts used in your production are installed not only on your system, but also on any other system where you plan to open and/or continue working on the file. This especially applies to cross-platform work. Once the file has been compressed into a QuickTime movie, however, there is no need to be concerned with this issue.

7. Click on the upper third, at about at the center of the title area. You will see a blinking insertion line.

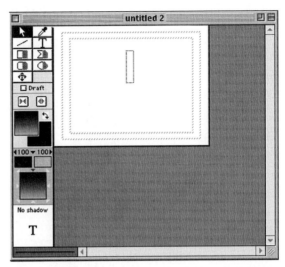

8. Select Title>Justify>Center. Type the word "To". You may still have a small point size left over from a previous project. Select a larger size (such as 72 points) for your type. Double-check that you've selected the text object — handles appear when you have.

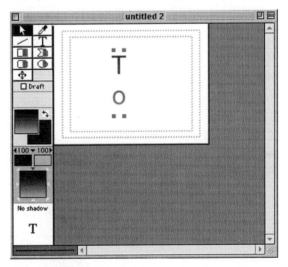

9. Does the layout look OK? If your type is running down the page (like the above example), read on. If not, skip ahead to step 10. Let's review how to fix that problem.

You can edit the existing text by double-clicking it with the Selection tool. Your Selection tool will change to the Type tool so that you may highlight and alter the text.

You can't color individual characters using the Type tool — Premiere colors the entire block at one time. If you want titles that have different colored letters, create them as individual titles, and then put them together on the stage.

You can change the direction of the gradient using the Gradient/ Transparency options on the lower portion of the Toolbox.

Click on the Selection tool and then on your new type. When a set of black squares or handles appear, drag the handle at the upper-right corner of the type further toward the right corner of the screen. When you let go, the type should resize itself to fill the screen correctly.

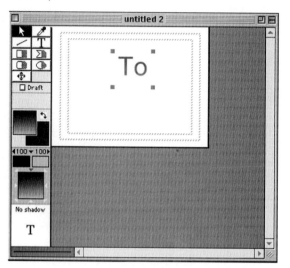

10. Once the word is spaced properly, it needs to be centered on the screen. Premiere does this for you automatically. Be certain the word still has handles on it. (If not, reselect the Selection tool and click on the type.) Center the title using Title>Center Vertically and Title>Center Horizontally.

11. At the moment your type is probably in black and white (or a color left over from a previous assignment). Let's create a blended earth-green for the type. Again, check that the words still have handles on them. Click on the Gradient Start color on the Color palette at the left. A Color Picker box appears.

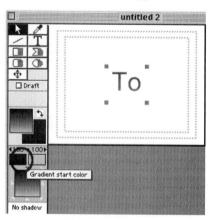

12. Set Red: 0, Green: 133, Blue: 52, and click OK. Your type is now a medium green.

13. Let's make that color a gradient moving from light green to medium green. Click on the Gradient End Color, just to the right of the Gradient Start Color box. Set Red: 189, Green: 255, Blue: 224, and click OK. Your type now has a gradient that shades from light green to medium green.

14. Let's add a drop shadow. Double-check that the word still has handles. At the lower-left side of the Toolbox, you will see a "T" with the words "No shadow" just above. This is the Shadow Position tool. Position your cursor on the "T," and slowly drag down and to the right. When you release the mouse button, a drop shadow appears under both the "T" and your words.

15. To make the drop shadow a little softer, select Title>Shadow>Soft. Now your type has a soft shadow. Let's make it dark green.

16. Click on the Shadow Color box to the right of the Object Color box. Set Red: 0, Green: 87, Blue: 0, and click OK. Your type now has a gradient that progresses from light green to dark green with a dark green shadow.

Save Movie Titles, and Add Them to the Project Window

1. Save your title as "TO.PTL" to your **Work in Progress** folder. As it is saves, it should automatically be added to your project bin. (If not, you can transfer it by selecting Clip>Add This Clip.)

2. Close the Title window. You should now have TO.PTL in the Project window. It is the first of your title clips. Leave this file open for the next exercise.

Creating Graphic Objects

The Title window Toolbox offers a number of tools to help you create drawings and back-grounds. You see tools that create shapes such as straight lines, rectangles, ellipses and polygons. These shapes are vector-based objects, similar to those created in Adobe Illustrator, Macromedia Freehand, Macromedia Flash and others. If you are familiar with this manner of drawing, you will have no difficulty working with the Title window. If you are unfamiliar with vector-based drawing, you will enjoy the ease with which you can create graphics. The main benefit of vector-based graphics is that they use little space.

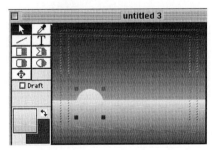

It's important to develop an awareness of the nature of your subject matter. This proverb reflects the Native Americans' respect for nature. As you choose the colors for the type, try to think about colors that would reflect the feeling expressed by the words. Sensitivity to subject matter is very important to video production.

When saving a poem, it's a good idea to use a word from the poem as the saved name. That way, when you look at the Project window, it is easy to recognize.

As you create your designs, you will notice that you have a variety of different options. Your shapes can have sharp, defined corners or corners smoothed into curves. These shapes can also have gradient and shadow attributes.

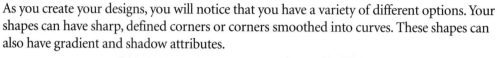

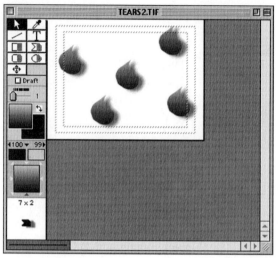

Once you draw a shape, you can apply color. You may change the color of the fill as well as the outline. When you change the color and outline of a graphic, the change affects the next shape you draw. In other words, each time you wish to change a color, you must select new fill and outline colors for the new shape or text block. A graphic object can be either *framed* (outlined with no fill) or *filled* (solid with no outline).

Each rectangle, rounded-corner rectangle or ellipse shape tool is divided in half. Click the left half of the tool for an outline shape or the right half for a filled shape. Once a color and style is selected, you move to the drawing area, and draw the shape you need.

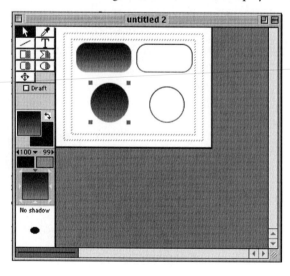

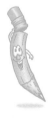

The same rules apply to drawing a polygon. Click the left half of the Polygon tool for an outlined polygon, or click the right half for a filled polygon. When you are ready to begin drawing, move to the drawing area and click a starting point. This creates a point and a line segment leading out of it. Position the Polygon tool where you want to place the next line segment, and click. Repeat these steps until you have only one segment left to draw. To finish the drawing, position the cursor over the first point you created (a small circle appears next to the cursor when it is over the first point) and click.

To smooth the newly created polygon, choose Title>Smooth Polygon. To edit the polygon, select the graphic object. Drag any handle on the object to make a change to the shape. The more points you create as you draw, the more natural the object will look when you have completed the drawing.

To create a straight line, select the Line tool in the Toolbox. Drag to draw the line, or hold down Shift as you drag to draw a line constrained to 45° increments. One of the quirks of the Line tool is that it always reverts to the Selection tool after a use. To keep this from occurring, double-click on the Line tool when you first select it.

Arranging Text and Graphic Objects

As you create your design, Premiere stacks the objects in the order that they were drawn, from bottom layer to top layer. This might cause problems, but the Title window provides methods for changing the order of the text and graphic objects.

To change the order of text and graphic objects, you just select the object, then from the Title menu, choose either Bring to Front or Send to Back. Select each of the shapes you wish to reorder until type and objects are stacked in the way you want.

It would be difficult to center type perfectly on the page without the help of some other extremely useful tools. You can also center your type automatically once you have created it. To center type or objects in the drawing area, select the object. Now you can choose any of the following options from the Title window: Center Horizontally, Center Vertically or Position in Lower Third.

Exercise Set-up

We will continue to create more words for the proverb in a moment. Let's build a custom background that can be used for the production. Although Premiere's Title window may seem limited in capability, it can actually produce many different creative drawings. You will build a background that includes a night sky and a rising moon.

Create a Custom Background with the Title Window

1. Select File>New>Title to display the Title window dialog box.

2. Let's draw the sky first. Select the filled side of the Rectangle tool from the Toolbox. Draw a small rectangle in the drawing area

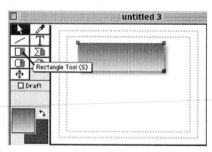

3. With handles still showing on the rectangle, select a beginning and ending gradient color for the sky. For the lighter color, set Red: 106, Green: 195, Blue: 255. For the darker color, set Red: 0, Green: 8, Blue: 166. (You do not need a drop shadow for this background.) On the left side, pull the shadow position over to cover the black rectangle so that it reads No Shadow.

4. The rectangle needs to cover the entire drawing, including the safe area. Drag the top-right handle up and to the right, until the rectangle extends off the page. Drag the bottom-left handle correspondingly until it, too, extends off the page. It should extend down about two-thirds of the page.

If necessary, reverse the direction of the gradient so that the color is light at the bottom and dark at the top, using the triangles on the Gradient/Transparency Direction icon.

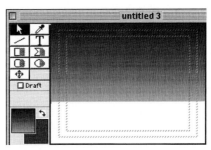

You can also set the direction of the gradient by clicking on the small white triangles arranged around the Gradient/Transparency Direction icon.

5. Let's paint in the ground. Select the filled side of the Rectangle tool from the Toolbox. Draw a small rectangle in the drawing area under the sky. With handles still showing on the square, select a beginning and ending gradient color for the ground. For the darker color, set Red: 0, Green: 92, Blue: 112. For the lighter color, set Red: 234, Green: 255, Blue: 172.

6. This new rectangle needs to cover the rest of the drawing. Drag the top-right handle to the right until the rectangle extends off the page. Drag the bottom-left handle until it, too, extends off the page. The rectangle should cover the rest of the page.

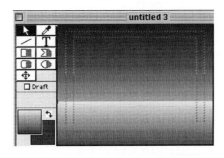 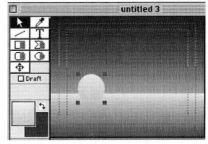

7. To add the moon, select the filled side of the Oval tool. Draw a small round moon over the background. Fill it with Start and End Gradient Colors of your choice. The example was created with the darker color of Red: 227, Green: 255, Blue: 0, and the lighter color of Red: 243, Green: 255 Blue: 174.

8. The moon is sitting atop everything but needs to be stacked beneath the ground. Click to select the handles for the ground. (You may not be able to see them because they are outside of the drawing area. Don't worry, the handles are there.) Select Title>Bring to Front. The picture should now look correct. If necessary, move the moon down until it is just at the horizon.

Hold the Shift key as you draw your shape with the Oval tool to form a perfectly proportioned circle.

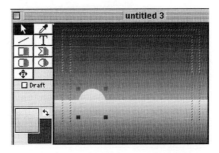

9. Save your title as "BACK.PTL" to your **Work in Progress** folder. Your title should transfer to the Project menu. (If not, you can also transfer it by selecting Clip>Add Clip to Project.) Your title should transfer to the Project menu. Close this Title window.

10. BACK.PTL should now display in the Project window as the second of your title clips. Leave the project open for the next exercise.

Create the Remaining Titles

Let's continue to prepare the rest of the titles that will make up the proverb. As before, each title will contain only one word.

1. In the open file, select File>New>Title to display the Title window.

2. Double-check that the Size is still set to H: 240 and V: 180. Click on the Type tool. As you move the cursor to the right, onto the title area, it changes to an I-beam.

3. Click on the upper third of the title area, at about the center. You will see a blinking insertion line.

4. Center the type on the page. Select Title>Justify>Center, and type the word "touch".

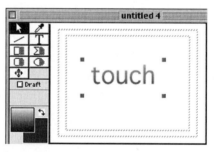

5. In the Title menu, select a larger point size for your type so that it fills the screen. If the type is running downhill, drag the handle at the upper-right corner of the type toward the top-right corner of the screen. When you let go, the type should resize to fill the screen correctly.

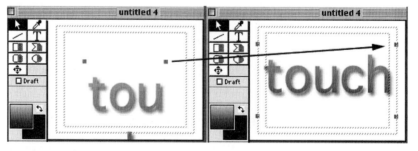

6. Once the word is spaced properly, it needs to be centered on the screen. Make certain the words still show handles. (If not, reselect the Selection tool, and click on the type.) Select Title >Center Vertically, then Title>Center Horizontally.

7. At the moment your type is probably yellow, a color left over from drawing the moon. Let's create a blended purple for this new type. Again, ensure the words still show handles. Click on the Gradient Start Color. A Color Picker box appears.

It's always a good idea to close each Title window after you have saved it. The file will be waiting for you in the bin of the Project window, and it takes lots of extra RAM to hold all of this information in memory.

8. Set Red: 118, Green: 0, Blue: 111, and click OK. Your type now has a gradient shading from purple to yellow.

9. Let's change the yellow to a more interesting color. Click on the Gradient End Color. Set Red: 252, Green: 216, Blue: 255, then click OK. Your type now has a gradient that progresses from light pink to dark violet.

10. Let's add a drop shadow. Make sure the word still shows handles. At the lower-left side of the Toolbox, you will notice a "T" with the words "No shadow" just above it. Position your cursor on this "T," and slowly drag downward. A drop shadow appears under both the "T" and your words.

11. To make the drop shadow a little softer, select Title>Shadow>Soft. Now your type has a soft shadow. Let's make it dark purple.

12. Click on the Shadow Color box to the right of the Object Color box. Set Red: 76, Green: 0, Blue: 118, and click OK. Your type now has a gradient that moves from light purple to dark purple with a deep purple shadow.

13. The words are still not quite the ideal size. Make sure the words still show the handles. Select Title>Size>48, then click OK. Drag the upper-right handle toward the top-right corner to see all of the type.

14. Save title as "TOUCH.PTL" to your **Work in Progress** folder. Your title should transfer to the Project menu. Close the Title window.

15. It is time for you to generate the rest of the word titles that will become your final project. Repeat steps 1 through 15. (You may find 48-pt. type too small for certain words. Adjust type points sizes as necessary.) Again, here is the proverb:

    "To touch the earth is to have harmony with nature."

16. Save each title naming it for the word it contains. For example, when you create the title for the word "harmony", save it as "HARMONY.PTL". Also note that the word "to" appears twice in this proverb. Save it as "TO.PTL" and as "TO-B.PTL". That way, you can have two words with different colors and effects. Try to select colors that reflect the feel of the proverb.

Don't forget: if you wish to change the direction of the gradient, click on any of the triangles to the left of the drawing area. Each time you select a different location for the triangle, the direction of the gradient changes and a small red square appears to show you the new direction.

Alpha Channels and Compositing

In the last chapter, we looked at alpha channels and the ability of the Video 2 track (and higher) to enable superimposing videos. By creating additional video tracks, we are able to generate some most impressive video effects, but first we need to create alpha channels for the titles.

When you need to create space for superimposing, Premiere makes this easy. The program allows you to establish up to 99 additional video tracks and up to 99 additional audio tracks. These extra tracks enable you to generate special effects using multiple transparent clips.

Exercise Set-up

You have just constructed all of the titles that will become the proverb. There are 11 titles in all — the 10 words that comprise the proverb and the one background. We need to create a space on the Timeline for all of the titles, so that they can be superimposed on top of each other.

Add Video Tracks

1. Click on the Timeline to make it active. Under the Timeline window Options menu, select Track Options. A dialog box appears.

2. Click the Add button. In the Add Video Tracks dialog box, type in the number "2". You have just created two new video tracks for your production. Click OK to close the Add Tracks box, and then click OK to close the Track Options dialog box.

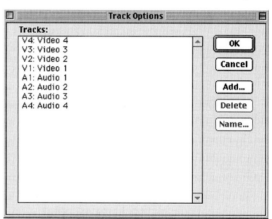

3. On the left side of Timeline, you should now see Video 3 and Video 4. Leave the file open for the next exercise.

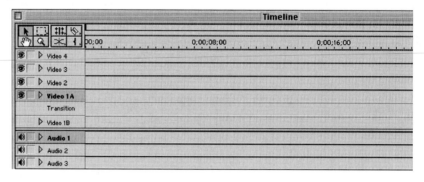

Add Titles to the Timeline Window

It is time to construct the final production. Begin by positioning the background picture on Video 1A, and then place all of the individual title clips on Video 2, Video 3 and Video 4.

1. In the open file, drag BACK.PTL to the Video 1A track on the Timeline. It stretches out to five seconds.

2. Click BACK.PTL to select it on the Timeline. Select Clip>Duration, set its duration to 00:00:25:00, and click OK. Your credit expands to 25 seconds.

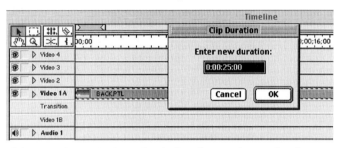

3. At the top of the Timeline window, check that the Work Area bar has automatically extended to the end of the production. If not, drag the bar to the end of the background title — about 25 seconds. This enables you to view the entire production as you create it.

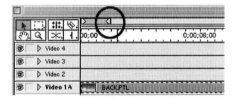

4. Save your project as "poetry.ppj" to your **Work in Progress** folder.

5. Let's add the words to the background. From the Project window, drag TO.PTL to Video 2 on the Timeline. Shorten this five-second clip to about three seconds. (Remember: your cursor will change to a red line with two black arrows.)

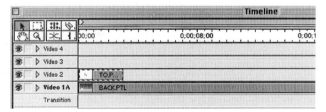

6. Now you'll continue adding the words of the proverb to the background. From the Project window, drag TOUCH.PTL to Video 3 on the Timeline. Make sure it overlaps TO.PTL on Video 2. Change its five-second duration to about three seconds.

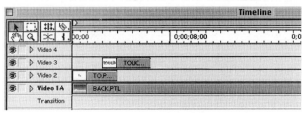

7. Drag the next title, THE.PTL, to Video 4, so that it overlaps TOUCH.PTL and extends about three seconds.

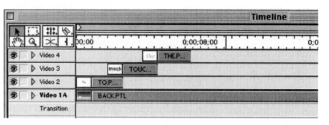

8. Drag EARTH.PTL to the Timeline on Video 2. (As long as EARTH.PTL overlaps THE.PTL, it actually makes no difference on which track it is placed.)

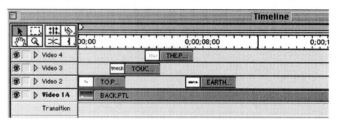

9. Continue to place each of your titles onto the Timeline. If you need to make the background a little longer, simply drag the right side until you reach the desired length. Don't forget to extend the Work Area bar as well.

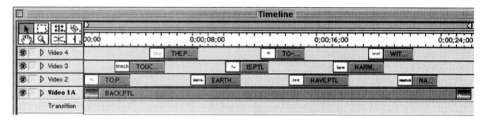

10. Save your project. Leave it open for the next exercise.

Use Alpha Channels to Generate Special Effects

1. In the open file, highlight TO.PTL, and select Clip>Video Options>Transparency.

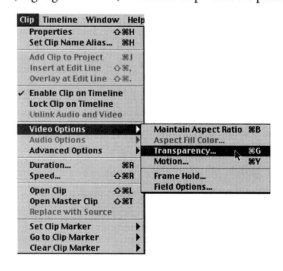

Notice that your titles are placed on every video track except Video 1 A or 1B. These tracks will not display the special Alpha key and Chroma key effects.

Title files created in Premiere automatically come with an alpha channel.

2. The Transparency Settings dialog box appears, and TO.PTL displays in the Sample box. Double-check that Key Type is set to White Alpha Matte; if it isn't, correct it. Click on the turned-down page icon so that you can see your transparency applied to the background. Click OK to close the Transparency Settings dialog box.

3. Continue selecting each of your words from the Timeline menu. For each, select Clip>Video Options>Transparency. Each individual clip should have a White Alpha Matte. (If it doesn't, correct it.)

4. Save and render this production. You should see your titles superimposed on your background. Leave the file open for the next exercise.

Combine Filters

1. In the open file, click on EARTH.PTL on the Timeline. From the Video Effects palette, select the Pinch filter from the Distort folder. Drag this filter onto EARTH.PTL, and click OK. The Effect Controls palette appears.

2. Next to the Pinch filter in the Effect Controls palette, click the Enable Keyframing box to display the clock.

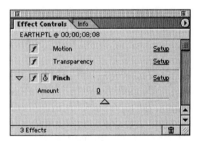

On the Timeline, click the Display Keyframes triangle.

You can always tell if you have placed an alpha matte on a video clip correctly. Click on the gray triangle next to Video 2, 3 or 4. The track expands. If you see a red line just under the video, you know that some type of effect has been generated.

3. Click the first keyframe, and set the slider to 0%. Click the second keyframe, and set the slider to -70%. You are setting the Out point or ending point of the effect.

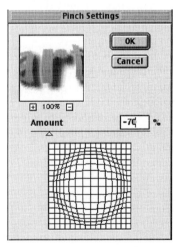

4. Press Return/Enter to render the production. After you preview the file, leave it open for the next exercise.

Set the Opacity for the Titles

1. In the open file, expand the Video 2 track on the Timeline to show the opacity levels for TO.PTL.

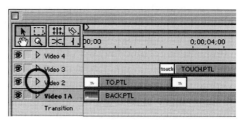

2. You should see a thin red line at the top of this window. This shows the title at 100% opacity. At the far left, notice a red handle.

3. Move the cursor slightly to the right, and click on the red line. A second handle appears.

4. Drag the first handle down to the bottom of the window. (This will be the fade-in for the title.)

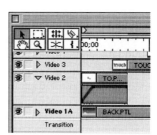

5. Let's repeat the last couple of steps for the last title, NATURE.PTL. This time let's have the title fade out.

   Double-check that Video 2 on the Timeline is still expanded and shows the opacity levels for the title.

6. You should see a thin red line at the top of this window. This shows the title at 100% opacity. At the far left, notice the red handle.

7. Move the cursor slightly to the left, and click again on the red line. A second handle appears. Drag the far-right handle down.

8. Save and render this production. You should see your title fade in on top of your background. Leave the file open for the next exercise.

Add Audio Clips

1. In the open file, drag AUDIO7.AIF to the Timeline window, and position it on Audio 1 at the beginning of the production, directly under TO.PTL.

2. The music extends much longer than the project. Drag the right edge of the audio so that it extends slightly longer than the project. Fade the music in (at the beginning of the production) and out (at the end) to add a professional touch to your production. Once again, save and render. You should see your titles fade in while some music plays to set the mood. Leave this file open for the next exercise.

Animating a Clip

Now that you know how to create objects and type, let's turn our attention to the animation effects you can apply to a clip. You can create these effects through the Motion Settings dialog box. With motion settings, you can specify the path for any object. You can make the object move entirely within the viewable area of the screen, or even extend the movement outside this viewable area so that the clip seems to enter and exit at the borders. In addition, you can specify rotation, zooming, delays and distortion to give your shape even more complex motions.

Motion Controls

Press the Tab key to toggle through each keyframe from the Start to Finish/End positions along the motion path. Hold the Shift key and press Tab to move from keyframe to keyframe in the opposite direction.

To create motion for a clip, you first select the clip in the Timeline window. You then either click the box to the left of the word Motion in the Effect Controls palette, or choose Clip>Video Options>Motion. When a new dialog box appears, notice, in the top-left corner, a sample of the selected clip as it moves along the default motion path. You also see Start and End keyframes just outside the viewable area of the video area. The clip moves into the viewable area from the left, scoots straight across and exits on the right.

You can change this movement. In fact, you can design the path your object travels by dragging the Start and Finish/End keyframes to any location within or outside the visible area. You can have the object travel top to bottom, bottom to top, even diagonally. You can also increase the movement of the object by adding more points. Position the cursor anywhere on the motion path. The cursor turns into a pointing finger. Click to add a new keyframe to the path, and drag it to adjust its position, creating a new segment along which the object will travel. You can add as many keyframes as you wish.

The arrow key can be used to adjust an individual keyframe's position, 1 pixel at a time in the direction of the arrow. If you hold down the Shift key and press an arrow key, you will move the keyframe in 5-pixel increments. If you want to make your measurements precise, type the coordinates for the keyframe's position in the Info boxes below the Timeline. To delete a keyframe on the motion path, select the keyframe and press Delete.

Rotating, Zooming, Delaying and Distorting

You can set the numbers that determine an object's rotation, zoom and delay as it makes its way across the screen. You can also change its shape as it travels. As you change these values, you can rotate, zoom, delay and distort the clip all at once or at different times.

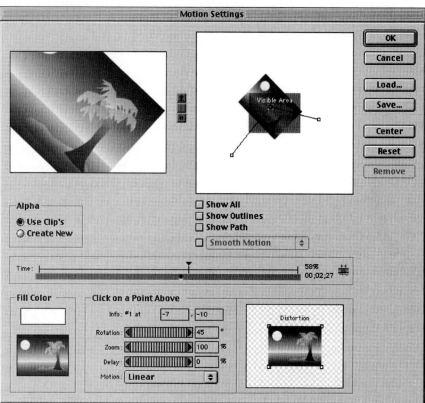

You can use the normal keyboard shortcuts for copying and pasting if you want to apply one keyframe's motion settings to another.

To rotate, zoom or delay the clip, select one of the control points for the object. Drag any of the sliders or type a value to create the effect you need. You can rotate an object 360° on any given point. This means that your shape can tumble over and over. You can specify up to eight full rotations, clockwise or counterclockwise. The Zoom controls allow you to have your object start out tiny and grow larger as it comes toward you or visa versa. Type a number between 0 and 500. At 0, the clip is not visible; at 100, the clip is at its original size, at 500 it is huge!

Suppose you want to show someone run, stop momentarily, then start running again. You can cause type to mimic that motion as well. This start-and-stop motion is created by applying a pause control to your object. The delay is based on the running time of the clip and varies from clip to clip. You'll want to experiment to find the best way to achieve the effect you have in mind. A blue bar appears on the Timeline when you add a delay . You can also achieve smooth motion when zooming by speeding up or slowing down the movement of your object. Accelerate works well when going from small to large. Decelerate works when zooming from large to small.

If you wanted to show leaves falling gently on a crisp fall day, you might want to use the Distort area to help the leaves to appear to waft across the screen.

To distort a clip, you first select the keyframe at which you want to add the distortion. You then drag one or more of the four corner points to other positions. Your object morphs to this new shape. You can also spin this twisted little image around a center point, by holding the Option/Alt key. You would position the cursor on a corner point, and then drag the image to spin it around a center point.

Command/Control-Y displays the Motion Settings dialog box.

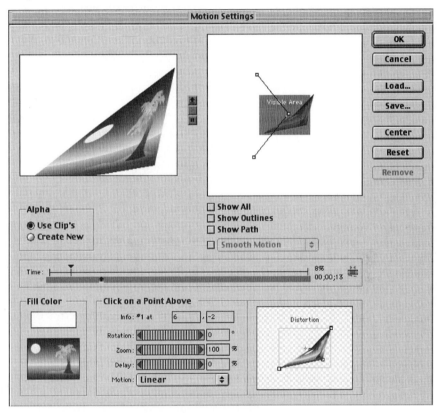

Saving, Loading and Deleting Motion Settings

Premiere comes with a number of preset paths for your convenience. Use the Load button in the Motion Settings dialog box to open the custom motion settings you need for a clip. To remove all motion settings from a clip, click Remove in the Motion Settings dialog box. New motion effects can be saved for later use.

Exercise Set-up

You have all of the components you need on the Timeline to build a great production. Now what you need is some movement. Let's make the words zoom around the screen from all directions by applying the motion settings.

Apply Motion Settings

1. Select TO.PTL on the Timeline. Select Clip>Video Options>Motion to display the Motion Settings dialog box.

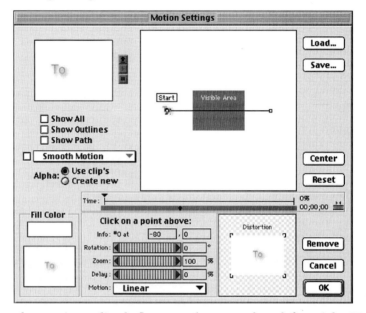

2. You see the type immediately fly across the screen from left to right. Notice that the Use Clip's Alpha channel is selected. Let's use this motion effect just as we see it. Click OK.

3. Click on TOUCH.PTL on the Timeline. Select Clip>Video Options>Motion. The Motion Settings dialog box appears.

4. Let's try something a little different. Drag the Start keyframe over just above the top center of the visible area. Drag the Finish/End keyframe to the bottom-center area, just under the visible area. The type now travels from top to bottom. Click OK.

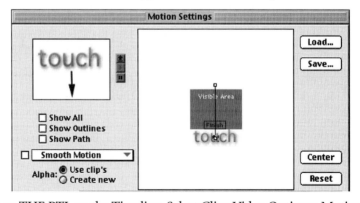

5. Click on THE.PTL on the Timeline. Select Clip>Video Options>Motion to display the Motion Settings dialog box. This time, click on the center of the line that the type follows. When a new handle appears, drag it to the top.

Your type starts to follow this new path. Pull each of the side handles down to the corner. This will form a triangle for the type to travel along.

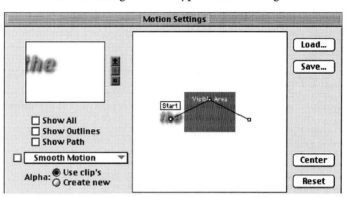

6. Save and render this production. You should see your first three titles moving on top of your background.

7. Now let's click on EARTH.PTL on the Timeline, and display the Motion Settings dialog box again.

8. This time we will load one of the preset motions. Click the Load button, and then navigate to the **Premiere** application folder on your hard drive. Once you have found this folder, open the **Motion Settings** folder (on Windows workstations, it's called the **Motion** folder). Scroll down and select **Whoosh1**.

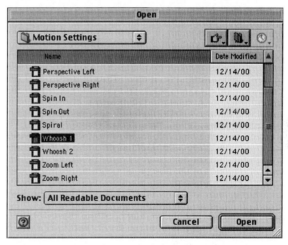

9. Click Open. You should now see your type following this new path. Make certain the Use Clip's Alpha is checked. Click OK.

10. There are more interesting effects that you can create with the Motion Settings. Let's try another. Click on IS.PTL on the Timeline. Select Clip>Video Options>Motion.

11. Drag the Start and Finish/End keyframes to the ends of the visible drawing area. The type should move just off the page.

12. Set 360 in the Rotation dialog box. Now, click on the Finish/End control point. The point turns red. This causes the word to rotate one full turn as it moves from left to right. Click OK to accept this new effect.

A red line appears under a video clip when a motion effect has been added. This is Premiere's way of letting you know that you have applied a special effect.

13. Now let's try some three-dimensional tricks. Click on TO-B.PTL on the Timeline. Again access the Motion Settings dialog box. Pull both the Start and Finish/End keyframes to the middle of the drawing area. Place the End keyframe slightly under the Start keyframe. Type 10 in the Zoom box at the bottom. Click the Start keyframe. The type will begin very small and get bigger as it travels toward you.

14. The Finish control point is in the center, just under the Start button. Type 200 in the Zoom box at the bottom. Click the Finish control point. ThewYpe will start very small and get much bigger as it travels toward you. Click OK.

15. Save and render this production. You should see your first six titles moving on top of your background.

16. It is time for you to experiment. Repeat steps 12 through 14, but tinker with the different motion controls. Remember to select Use Clip's Alpha after selecting Premiere's motion settings. Work on all of the words. When you are satisfied with the results, save and close the file.

17. Now that you have worked with the Title window, motion controls, filters and music, it's time for you to apply your skills to another proverb. The proverb is:

    "The soul would have no rainbow if the eyes had no tears."

    This time create another production. Continue to explore the imact of your choices of color, motion controls, filters, etc. as you apply them. Remember to think about the spirit of the proverb as you make your choices.

    We have also provided two sample preview files that use these concepts. Review both **SOUL.MOV** and **POEM2.MOV** for ideas. Feel free to use **AUDIO7B.AIF** as audio for this assignment.

Rotoscoping

Rotoscoping is another way to extend the capabilities of Premiere. The term *rotoscoping* actually comes from a machine called a "rotoscope," and both the machine and the term have been around far longer than Premiere. Essentially a modified projector, a rotoscope is able to display one frame at a time onto an artboard.

The concept is elegant and simple. Live-action footage can be used as a template, resulting in drawings that are spatially and physically accurate. Imagine footage of a horse running, a person throwing a javelin or any of the thousands of instances of real-life action footage. Once individual frames of the footage are projected onto the board, the artist either draws lines and shapes to replace the video, or paints objects onto acetate, which is then superimposed over the original. Naturally, using Premiere makes the compositing and superimposing process fairly straightforward. The results can be highly realistic and compelling.

Masterpieces such as *Who Framed Roger Rabbit*, *Jurassic Park* and many others were created using the technique. Hitchcock's acclaimed 1963 masterwork *The Birds* is another example of rotoscoping; the birds were rotoscoped over the New England backdrops to create this hair-raising production.

Like other film techniques, the idea of a rotoscope easily translates to the digital world. The shift to computer-based rotoscoping began in the early 1990s. The same earlier hand-drawn techniques can now be performed with digital imaging.

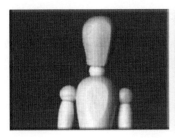

Premiere allows you to export with ease a video clip or a section of the Timeline as a filmstrip — ready for editing, color correction, painting or creating line-art animations. A *filmstrip* is a single file that contains the frames of the Timeline or clip. To export a clip or the timeline as a filmstrip, you use File>Export (Timeline or Clip). Just select Filmstrip as the File Type, and tell the program how many frames you want to export.

Once you've created a filmstrip file, it can be opened directly in Photoshop.

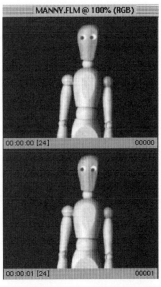

Photoshop displays filmstrip files in a long, tall, thin strip. If the clip is long enough, you'll see more than one column. Zoom in closely to ensure that you can see enough detail.

Photoshop can be a little picky when it comes to saving files back out as filmstrips. To avoid problems, keep a blank filmstrip file on hand, and copy and paste your edited, rotoscoped footage into the file. It should save properly from that point.

While this isn't a book about Adobe Photoshop, this program is an essential component in any production where rotoscoping is required to achieve a particular look or effect. Adobe After Effects can also perform magic on your files. Premiere integrates well with other applications, so rotoscoping, color correction, editing and other functions can be performed in other applications and then imported into a Premiere production. Materials may be exported from Premiere, acted on by another application, then imported back into Premiere, or it may initially be created in another application and then brought into Premiere. Typical applications that compliment Premiere include Adobe Photoshop, Adobe After Effects, Adobe Illustrator, Macromedia Freehand and many others.

Summary

In this chapter, you learned how to use Premiere's motion controls. You learned how credits can be overlapped. You also learned how to create and enhance movie titles with motion controls and special effects including alpha channels.

You practiced creating custom backgrounds with the Title window. You learned how to add video tracks, create motion settings and animate type. You also discovered that effects can be combined.

You explored the use of filters and motion controls. You learned how to adjust motion controls to create movement. You also practiced creating custom backgrounds with the Title Window.

Finally you learned about rotoscoping and extending the abilities of Adobe Premiere by using complimentary functions from other programs.

Complete Project C: How to Tame a Tiger

(9) *Advanced Editing*

Chapter Objective:

To enhance your knowledge of editing techniques for individual clips or many clips at once. To learn to control the impact of trims on duration. To become familiar with efficient options for moving, reworking and replacing clips. To learn the value of planning the placement of shots through logging individual shots in available footage. In Chapter 9, you will:

- Become familiar with nonlinear editing and its role in post-production.

- Learn the difference between rolling and rippling edits, and to distinguish which is appropriate for a particular situation.

- Explore editing more than one clip at a time.

- Learn how to and practice removing, replacing and reworking clips on the timeline.

- Discover and practice using options for synchronizing audio to edited video footage.

- Become familiar with common types of shots and camera movements and the purposes of each.

- Learn the value of logging shots both for identifying what is available on footage and planning the final production.

Projects to be Completed:

- The Monkey Movie (A)

- How to Make Spaghetti (B)

- How to Tame a Tiger (C)

- The Gold Rush (D)

Advanced Editing

There is nothing quite like a good story. Boy meets girl… boy loses girl… boy finds girl… boy wins girl… they live happily ever after. What you have just read is the essence of many a movie or television program. It begins with a plot or storyline. Somehow along the way, a tale is told and a truism is expressed.

There is a beginning, middle and an end. Every narrative — fable, novel or epic movie — must tell its story in a logical sequence. As you watch the plot unfold, you must be able to understand why the characters act as they do. At the end of the story, you must be able to understand why events unfolded as they did. After all, a story does not customarily *begin* with "they lived happily ever after."

Telling the story logically, cogently and compellingly is where editing comes into play. You shoot a series of video clips composed of different types and lengths of shots, assemble audio, create titles and then edit them together to structure a story. If you do your job well, you create a great video production.

So far, you have completed lessons in the basics of editing, such as the trim feature of Premiere. In this chapter, you will learn some advanced editing techniques, like working with both rolling and ripple edits. These techniques will enhance your video vocabulary and enable you to become a better storyteller. Not only will you be able to tell a good story, but you'll also be able to tell it in such a way that it will win over the viewer.

Editing and Run Times

Although it would be great if you could shoot all of your clips in the order in which they will be used in the final production, that is not generally possible. Most video is shot out of order. Why? Not every actor is available on any given day, nor is it always economically efficient to have an actor sitting around for one scene on one day and one scene four days later. Lighting conditions change during a shoot. Sometimes a new shot has to be added after the fact, to enhance or strengthen the story. It is common practice to overshoot a production, sometimes as much as 5 to 1. It is also common practice to shoot video clips with extra footage at the beginning and end, to allow for more precise editing later.

Nonlinear editing allows video to be shot in any order. It is then the skill of a great editor that takes the story and brings it to life — truly a fine art.

Let's take some time to look at two forms of editing commonly used in video production.

We will begin with a scenario in which you have placed three pieces of video on the Timeline. They are PELICAN1.MOV, PELICAN2.MOV, and PELICAN3.MOV. You decide to add another clip — PELICAN4.MOV. You now have a choice.

You can insert PELICAN4.MOV so that it simply pushes the other clips over to make room and lengthens the overall production. This process is a *ripple edit*. Alternately, you can insert PELICAN4.MOV in such a fashion that the entire production remains the exact duration. This is a *rolling edit*.

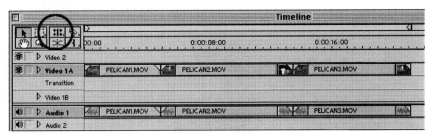

The Rolling Edit Tool

Ripple Edits

A ripple edit trims the selected clip without changing the duration of the other clips on the Timeline. In other words, a ripple edit lengthens or shortens the overall running time of your production.

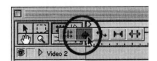

The Ripple Edit Tool

It accomplishes this preservation of the running times of all other clips by changing the program duration. You drag the Edit Line, and the overall program duration is lengthened or shortened by the number of frames you add to or subtract from the clip you are editing.

To execute a ripple edit, you select the Ripple Edit tool and position it on the In or Out point of the clip you want to change. You then drag it left or right. The program duration is extended or shortened to compensate for your edit, but the duration of adjacent clips remains unchanged.

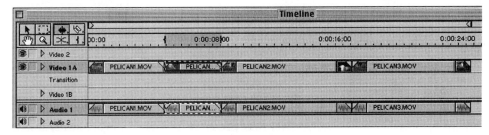

Rolling Edits

The Rolling Edit tool trims both sides of an edit equally. It does not affect the overall running time of a production. A rolling edit keeps the program duration constant and also preserves the combined duration of the two clips you are editing.

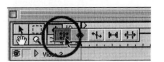

The Rolling Edit Tool

You adjust the Edit Line, and the frames you add to or subtract from one clip are subtracted from or added to the clip on the other side of the Edit Line.

To complete a rolling edit, you select the Rolling Edit tool and position it on the edge of the clip you want to change. You then drag left or right. The same number of frames are added to the clip and subtracted from the adjacent clip.

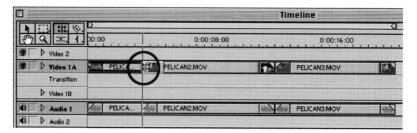

Preview the Project and Assemble the Components

1. From within Premiere, open the **RF-Premiere>advancededits>rippleandroll.ppj** file. Look at the Project window.

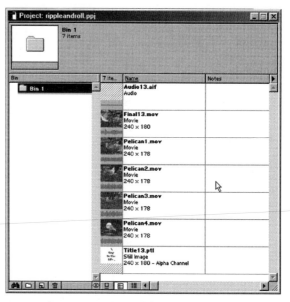

2. Drag final13.mov to the Source view of the Monitor window, and click the Play button to preview the final movie.

3. Drag PELICAN1.MOV to the Timeline window at the beginning of Video 1A. Drag PELICAN2.MOV to the Timeline window, next to PELICAN1.MOV, on Video 1A. It should fall at 00:00:04:27.

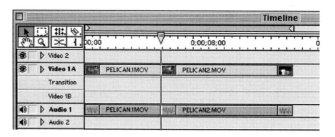

4. Drag PELICAN3.MOV to the Timeline window on Video 1A at 00:00:13:13.

5. Drag PELICAN4.MOV to the Timeline window next to PELICAN3.MOV on Video 1A. It should fall at 00:00:21:05.

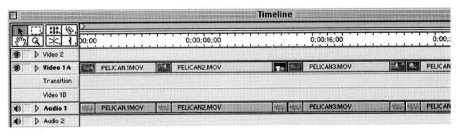

6. Save your project as "BIRDS.PPJ" to your **Work in Progress** folder.

7. Press the Return/Enter key to render this production. You should see a selection of pelicans enjoying life.

Ensuring You Have Enough Footage

If you shoot more footage than you need, Premiere makes it simple to trim the excess to fit your exact creative vision. If you shoot too little video, it's more difficult to fit the footage to the production.

Exercise Set-up

You can work around the problem of having too little footage. Creative use of stills, using filters to simulate motion, and tasteful use of dissolves and other transition methods can often work to fill in gaps. Just be careful not to overuse these techniques, though. If you do, they'll distract the audience.

You have already worked with trimming footage (shortening its run length). Now we'll look at using trim techniques in combination with other advanced-editing tools in the next series of exercises.

Trim a Clip

1. Double-click PELICAN1.MOV on the Timeline. Click the Play button. Notice the brackets at the bottom of the window.

Set Location Brackets

2. Play the clip. Slowly move the right bracket to the left. The Set Location bracket scrubs through the PELICAN1.MOV clip so that you can look at it frame by frame. When you reach 00:00:02:16 on the timecode, you are at the point where you will make the edit.

3. Click the Out point bracket. When the Apply box appears at the bottom of the Clip window, click Apply. Your clip shortens in the Timeline window to accommodate this new trim.

4. Save and render the file. Notice the results of the edit. Close the Clip window. Leave this file open for the next exercise.

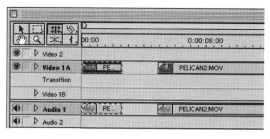

Trimming a clip does not shorten the original footage. It remains in your computer, whole and intact.

Editing Ranges on the Timeline

There are many times when you'll find yourself needing to edit more than one clip at a time — moving them on the Timeline, for example, or changing their run times. There are several techniques available that let you change or move multiple clips at the same time. Among them is the Range Select tool.

Use the Range Select Tool

1. In the open file, on the left side of the Timeline, select the Range Select tool.

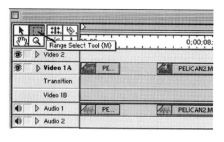

2. Position your cursor at the lower-right side of the video and audio clips, and hold down the mouse button. Slowly drag diagonally, up and to the left, until all of your clips, except PELICAN1.MOV, are selected.

3. The cursor turns into a pointer with a plus sign. This is the Range Select tool in action. Drag all of these selected clips to the left, until your video is at the end of PELICAN1.MOV.

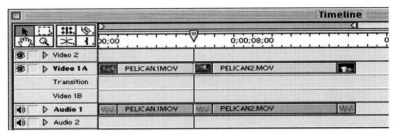

To activate the Range Select tool, press the "M" key. To return back to the Selection tool, press the "V" key.

4. Deactivate the Range Select tool by reselecting the Selection tool. Save and render the file. Notice the results of the edit. Leave this file open for the next exercise.

Edits and Production Length

We've discussed rolling and rippling edits, and how they impact the length of a movie. Again, if you insert a clip and use a rippling edit, the other clips aren't affected in any way. The movie becomes longer or shorter, depending on whether you trim an existing clip or insert a new one. If you use a rolling edit, the length of the production stays the same — to accomplish this requires that you make changes to one or more of the remaining clips.

Complete a Ripple Edit

1. You've changed your mind: you want to put the entire piece of video back at the beginning of the production and you want to move the rest of the video out of the way. In the open file, delete PELICAN1.MOV from the Timeline. Be sure to delete both the audio and the video.

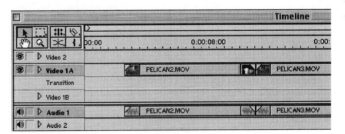

To activate the In point, press the "I" key. To activate the Out point, press the "O" key.

2. Delete PELICAN1.MOV from the Project window as well.

3. Import PELICAN1.MOV.

4. Drag PELICAN1.MOV to the Timeline window, and position it at the beginning of Video 1A. All of the other video and audio clips will ripple to the right to make room for PELICAN1.MOV.

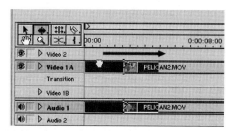

5. Save and render the file. Notice the latest changes. Leave this file open.

Complete a Rolling Edit

1. Position the Selection tool on the Timeline at 00:00:10:15 over PELICAN2.MOV and click. Using the Selection tool, shorten PELICAN2.MOV to 00:00:10:15.

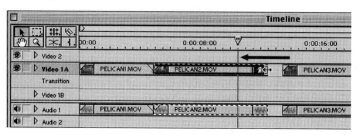

2. With the Range Select tool selected, reposition PELICAN3.MOV and PELICAN4.MOV so that they are adjacent to PELICAN2.MOV.

3. Click on the Rolling Edit tool. Position the Rolling Edit tool so that it lines up with the end of PELICAN2.MOV and PELICAN3.MOV. Drag it either left or right. Notice that PELICAN3.MOV continues to expand or shrink to make room, but the total production time never changes.

The Arrow keys can be used to move or "nudge" video clips to the left or right.

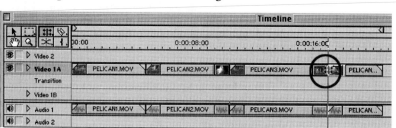

4. Let's try one more rolling edit. Position the Selection tool on the Timeline at 00:00:17:00 over PELICAN3.MOV and click. Using the Selection tool, shorten PELICAN3.MOV to 00:00:17:00.

5. With the Selection tool active, reposition PELICAN4.MOV so that it is adjacent to PELICAN3.MOV.

The shortcut for the Rolling Edit tool is the "P" key.

6. Activate the Rolling Edit tool and position it so that it lines up in between PELICAN3.MOV and PELICAN4.MOV. Drag it either left or right. Notice that PELICAN4.MOV once again continues to expand or shrink to make room.

7. Save and render the file. Observe the results of the edit. Close this file.

Telling a Story

Telling a story requires a great deal more than shooting some footage and assembling it. Placing the footage and judging what should be used in what order, trimming individual clips to just the correct length, moving and reworking the order and the length to make a finished production — all of this and more are essential to the ultimate goal: telling a story and telling it effectively.

When all of the footage in this chapter is placed in combination, a story begins to unfold. It is the story of a pelican and dinnertime. The only problem is that the clips last too long. Let's take what we've learned from this chapter and assemble a movie with the four pelican video clips. We're going to begin by creating another version of this same project — this time edited differently.

Remove, Replace and Rework Clips on the Timeline

1. Delete all the clips that are on the Timeline. This doesn't remove them from the bin — it just removes then from the Timeline.

2. Drag PELICAN1.MOV, PELICAN2.MOV and PELICAN3.MOV to the Timeline window, and position them, one after the other, from the beginning of Video 1A.

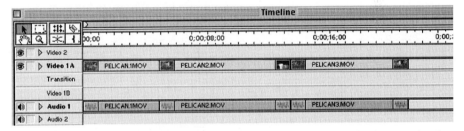

3. Save the project as "BIRDS2.PPJ" to your **Work in Progress** folder. Render the production by pressing Return/Enter, and watch a bunch of pelicans doing what pelicans like to do — eating.

4. The PELICAN1.MOV clip is too long for this production. We need to trim about one second off the front of the clip. Position the Selection tool on the Timeline at 00:00:01:02.

5. Using the Razor tool, trim the clip at the marker point. With the Selection tool active, click to highlight the first part of the PELICAN1.MOV clip. Delete this section of the clip. Notice that the audio is deleted as well.

6. Highlight the empty space that has been created. Select Timeline>Ripple Delete. PELICAN2.MOV, PELICAN3.MOV and PELICAN4.MOV move to the left to sit next to PELICAN1.MOV.

7. PELICAN2.MOV now needs to be split into three parts. Each piece will be placed in a different portion of the production. Position the Selection tool on the Timeline, and use the Razor tool to trim the video clip at 00:00:09:20 and at 00:00:11:00. The PELICAN2.MOV clip is now divided into three parts.

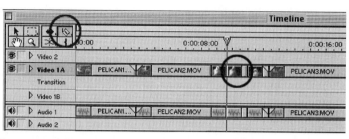

8. Using the Range Select tool, move the three pieces of PELICAN2.MOV with their audio to the end of the production, to make room for another piece of footage.

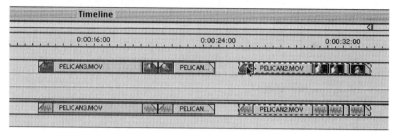

9. Use the Selection tool to secure the middle section of PELICAN2.MOV. Place that section next to PELICAN1.MOV.

10. Position PELICAN3.MOV next to the moved section of PELICAN2.MOV in the Timeline window.

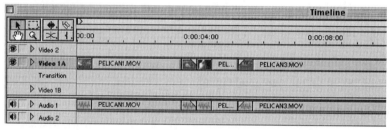

11. Position the Selection tool on the Timeline at 00:00:11:20. Use the Razor tool to trim the clip at the marker point. With the Selection tool active, click to highlight the second part of the PELICAN3.MOV clip. Delete this portion of the clip. The audio is also deleted.

12. Highlight the empty space that has been created. Select Timeline>Ripple Delete. PELICAN3.MOV and the leftover segments of PELICAN2.MOV move to the left.

13. Maneuver the first section of PELICAN2.MOV into position next to PELICAN3.MOV.

14. Place PELICAN4.MOV on the Timeline window, next to PELICAN2.MOV. Trim off about a second at the beginning of the clip, and use the ripple delete option to move it into position.

15. Pick up the final section of PELICAN2.MOV, and move it into position next to PELICAN4.MOV.

16. Save and render the production. You should see your pelican reacting to another pelican that has some food! Leave the file open for the next exercise.

Press the "C" key to access the Razor tool.

Matching Audio to Edited Footage

Making sure that the tempo, sound, volume and pan of your audio footage are correctly and appropriately set up is particularly important when you're performing complex editing. You could, for example, knock audio out of sync by editing a clip to which it was attached. You must always make sure to check your video and edit it so that your soundtracks remain synchronized to your video footage.

Add Audio to the Production

1. In the open file, drag AUDIO13.AIF to the Audio 2 track on the Timeline. Expand Audio 2 so that you can see the actual audio. Shorten AUDIO13.AIF to 00:00:14:03. Copy and paste AUDIO13.AIF so that you have two copies, side by side. Press Return/Enter to see these latest changes. Notice that the audio for the pelicans is a little loud and overwhelms the music. Let's fix this problem.

2. Expand the Audio 2 track. Select the Fade Adjustment tool, and bring up the audio level of AUDIO13.AIF. Drag the red rubberband up to add gain to the music track.

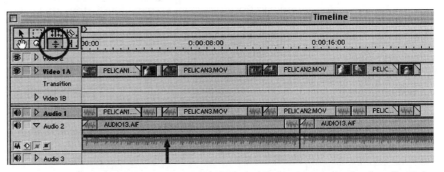

3. We need to fade the music out to end the production more professionally. Select the Selection tool again. Move the Edit Line to 00:00:21:00. Click your mouse button at that point, and a small red square (the second for that audio clip) appears. Position the Edit Line at 00:00:21:25 and click your mouse button. A third handle should appear. Drag that handle to the bottom of the audio area to fade out the music. One more square must be moved.

4. Position the Edit Line at the end of the audio clip. There should be a fourth handle already there. Drag this handle to the bottom of the audio area to match the last square. This keeps the music from fading back in.

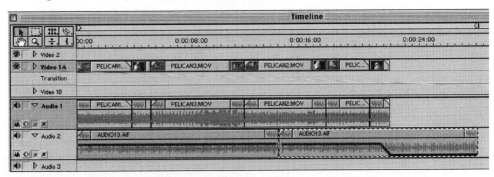

5. Collapse the Audio 2 track.

6. Leave the file open for the next exercise.

Add a Title Graphic

1. An opening title has been provided for your use in this production. In the open file, select TITLE12.PTL, and position it on Video 2 at 00:00:00:20.

2. The title lasts about five seconds. Use Clip>Duration to lengthen the title time to seven seconds.

3. Highlight the title, and choose Clip>Video Options>Motion.

4. Position the Start and Finish/End keyframes so that the title moves from bottom to top. Click OK.

5. Save and render these new changes. Watch the movie, then save it again and close it.

Planning the Types of Shots

Video production is an art form. It uses some of the same rules as painting and drawing. A picture must convey a meaningful message. In painting, this is accomplished, first, with good composition. In video production, the same rules apply.

The story is told through a series of visual sequences. Each of these sequences is made up of a group of shots. Often a variety of types of shots can help keep a narrative alive and interesting. So what, exactly, is a shot? It is a unit that is part of a larger classification of camera movements. A *shot* is the material photographed from the time the camera starts running until the camera stops running. A shot can last from a split second to several minutes.

Here are some types of shots. They are usually known as "intershot movements," because they represent the action that occurs during one shot.

Shot Definitions

- **Cover Shot**. (CS) Also called an "establishing shot." The camera sees the entire set. It covers the action or sets the scene. Frequently, the next shot to follow is an interior of the shot just established.

- **Long Shot**. (LS) The camera is at the full zoom capacity. This shot usually shows an actor, framed from head to toe.

- **Medium Shot**. (MS) This shot shows the actor cropped to include the waist, head and shoulders. This is the shot most often seen in news broadcasts. It is considered the most neutral shot in television.

- **Close-up Shot**. (CU) The camera shows the actor's face. No background is evident in the shot.

- **Extreme Close-up Shot**. (ECU) The actor's face is cropped so that only the chin and the eyes are shown. This is also known as a "reaction shot" as in, "Mary, the man is dead!" Cut to ECU of Mary's reaction!

- **Down-the-line Shot**. (DTL) The camera is set to pan or move down a row of subjects. It also makes an interesting reaction shot. Think about a shot of people looking at the bride as she walks down the aisle. The camera shows each of the happy people as they watch the bride approach.

- **Two Shot**. Two actors are framed equally in one shot.

Classes of Camera Movement

- **Pan.** Camera movement proceeds from right to left or left to right. It is created in a horizontal format.

- **Tilt.** Camera movement proceeds up or down. It is created in a vertical format.

- **Zoom.** This movement is the in or out movement of the focusing lens. The camera remains stationary.

- **Dolly.** This movement is the physical movement of the camera and the base, forward or backward, in or out of the shot.

- **Truck.** This movement is the physical movement of the camera and the base, to the right or left of the object being shot.

- **Pedestal.** This movement is the raising or lowering of the camera.

- **Crane or Boom.** This movement requires using a crane device that can move in any direction. The camera can often reach substantial height.

Test Your Knowledge

Now that you have a definition of some of the most popular types of shots, let's put them to use. Below you will see some different shot types. Let's see if you can identify them. The answers are located upside down in the Sidebar.

1. _____   2. _____

3. _____   4. _____

Test Your Knowledge:

ANSWERS

4. Close-up (CU)

3. Extreme Close-up (ECU)

2. Long Shot (LS)

1. Medium Shot (MS)

Exercise Set-up

The following exercise will help you to edit your videotapes, once you start taping and capturing video. Before you can edit, you need to log a videotape and create a shot list. Logging will save you hours of needless frustration by allowing you to quickly find any shot on your tape with the aid of the counter numbers located on your video tape recorder.

Now that you have some understanding of the types of shots, let's put this new knowledge to use. You are going to watch a half-hour television show of your choice. The best type of program to watch would be a situation comedy. If possible, videotape the show, so that you can watch the show segments again, in case you miss a shot. You will create a log of the show that you choose. Be sure to note the sample log provided in step 4.

Create a Shot List for a Television Show

1. Select a half-hour television show and viedotape it if possible.

2. Now log the television show that you selected. While sitting in front of the show, write down the types of shots that are being used as the show progresses.

   It may be difficult at first. You may find yourself wanting to actually watch the show instead of observing the technical aspects. You may find the assignment easier to do if you turn off the sound as you watch.

3. If you have taped the show:
   - Rewind the tape.
   - Set the counter to zero.
   - Start the tape.
   - Stop at each shot you wish to remember and log.

4. Use the following format to log your shots. The sample below gives you an idea of the range of shots and the notations you will probably want to make for your log.

Video Shot List

SHOT #	COUNTER	SHOT TYPE	COMMENTS
1	Pine Tree Hospital	Establishing Shot	Sets the scene
2	Interior of hospital	Two Shots of nurses	They look worried
3	Hospital room	Medium Shot	Actress is upset
4	Reverse of door opening	Long Shot	Husband enters
5	Bed	ECU	Actress in tears
6	Door to bed	Long Shot	Husband walks to wife

4. When you are finished, discuss your list with colleagues or friends, especially if any of them have done the same exercise.

   What did you discover? Does everyone see television the same way that you do? Are you starting to look at things differently?

Summary

In Chapter 9, you have learned to use some advanced editing techniques and have experimented with editing. You discovered strengths of the Range Selection tool and the Ripple Delete command.

You learned to trim a clip with In points, Out points and the Edit Line, and to use a ripple edit to move clips as a group. You became familiar with employing a rolling edit to trim clips and a ripple delete to close gaps.

You learned definitions of some of the most common types of shots and camera movements, and practiced logging shots from existing television footage.

Complete Project D: The Gold Rush

Notes:

Chapter Objective:

To learn about methods used to capture video from a camera into your computer's hard drive. To learn about preparing your computer system to be in an optimal state for capture and work with Premiere. To become familiar with some essentials for planning successful shoots. To discover how to prepare final files appropriate to the Web end-user. In Chapter 10, you will:

- Explore various format options, including analog and digital video, and issues with capturing video in these formats.

- Become familiar with Movie Capture, a discrete application built into Premiere, that provides extensive controls over incoming video footage.

- Observe how preparing for your shoots means proper planning and flexibility.

- Learn about purging your hard drive and ensuring that you have enough space for the required footage.

- Explore memory, drive space, fragmentation and other factors impacting on your ability to capture high-quality video footage.

- Become familiar with options for exporting files for the Web.

Projects to be Completed:

- The Monkey Movie (A)

- How to Make Spaghetti (B)

- How to Tame a Tiger (C)

- The Gold Rush (D)

Digitizing Your Assets

Throughout this book, you've worked with video footage and audio clips that we had already prepared. We provided these clips to keep you focused on learning the core editing and production techniques available within Premiere.

At some point, though, you're going to have to find or create your own footage. Once you do, you'll need to convert it to a digital format. You may need to put your footage on the Internet, another digitizing or conversion issue. We will discuss these issues, proper planning and attention to detail before and during the shoot, as well as a thoughtful preparation of your computer system to avoid problems during capture.

Capturing Video

There are many sources for digital video — some commercial and some public domain. For example, check out publicdomainfootage.com, a wonderful source of inexpensive clips from public domain sources.

Visit publicdomainfootage.com for an inexpensive source for video footage.

The process of capturing video from film to your computer's hard drive is known as "digitizing the video," that is converting it from analog (film) format to a digital, electronic format. In recent years, an increasing number of digital video (DV) devices have started to appear on the market. In the case of DV, no conversion is required — the footage is already in a digital format and only needs to be moved to your hard drive.

Format Considerations

The first point to consider when preparing to digitize or capture video footage for use in your own productions is the format in which you need the images. At 30 frames per second, the size of captured video can quickly overcome your computer's processing and storage capacity; a single frame of fully digitized footage is nearly 1 MB. That's roughly 30 MB for each second of film.

Playing back data at 1 MB/second is far beyond the capacity of most desktop systems. While high-end, dedicated systems might offer this sort of throughput, it's unlikely the machine you're using can handle the requirements. Fortunately, there are some solutions to the issue of storage and playback requirements. The most important, and the one most likely to impact your working environment, is compression.

Whether you're digitizing your video from conventional, analog sources or bringing in footage directly from a DV device, you'll need a special board in your computer called a "video capture board." Such boards range from inexpensive (about $75) to very expensive — it depends on what you need them to do and what your ultimate purpose is for the video. If you're producing outsource material for the silver screen, expect to spend a large amount on the board, expensive hard drives and specialized audio peripherals. If you're making training videos, or simply working on your home movies, then you can select lower-priced alternatives.

DV has some advantages over analog footage — most notably that one cable can carry the timecode (if it's available on the device), all the footage and the audio as well. If you're moving footage from an analog *deck* or camera, then you'll need three different cables. Two carry audio signals (left and right channels), and another carries the foot-age. You'll need a fourth if you want to get timecode from the device.

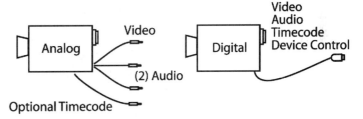

Movie Capture

Premiere provides a built-in application, Movie Capture, to help you to bring footage and audio clips into the authoring environment.

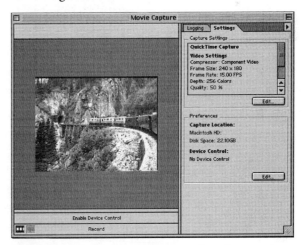

Choosing Your Settings

Once you've launched Movie Capture, you would first check the Capture settings in the Movie Capture window. This is where you can tell Premiere how to capture the video. Set key options such as screen size and frames per second. Below are some typical settings, in fact, the settings that were used to create the projects in this book.

The speed at which a computer can process and display digital video is known as the "data rate," or "throughput." If you're expecting to produce professional-quality materials, you're going to have to make a substantial investment in hardware.

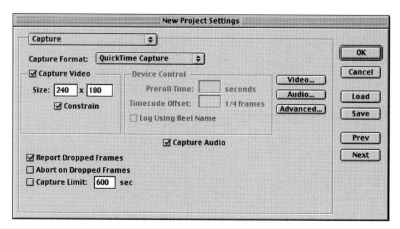

Click on Edit in the Movie Capture dialog box to display this screen.

Capture devices are hardware that converts the video signal into a digital file on your hard drive. These can include built-in or plug-in video capture boards. Check what is appropriate to and available for your system.

Next, you would make any necessary color adjustments by selecting Video, under New Project Settings. If you have a video capture device, you may be able to set brightness levels and contrast levels so that your video runs while making these adjustments. This can give you extensive control over the picture.

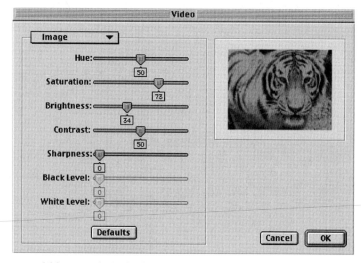

Your next step would be to select the best format for your camera or other video source.

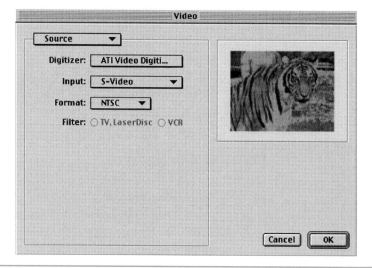

If you launch Movie Capture on a Macintosh computer, you will be prompted to deactivate AppleTalk. AppleTalk interferes with the capturing process and keeps the video from coming in properly. When you close Movie Capture, AppleTalk automatically reactivates.

New Premiere users, who didn't record any audio during the shoot, often forget a key point. Check your settings twice and don't capture audio if there is none on your tape! Remember that audio almost doubles the size of your files and can lead to dropped frames.

Planning and Setting Up the Capture

By carefully limiting the amount that you capture, and by preparing your equipment in advance, you can avoid major headaches during the capture.

- **Never bring in more video than you need.** New video producers frequently over capture video. Don't limit the number of shots in the production, just the length of each shot. Your computer is not capable of handling more than a few seconds of footage. After a point, the computer is not able to keep up with the amount of digital information streaming in and starts dropping frames. Log your raw tape so thoroughly that you know precisely which shots and what footage you will use in the final production.

- **Start your camera several seconds before you begin to capture video.** It takes a video camera or a video cassette recorder several seconds to get up to speed. While the player is starting up, it usually flashes the words "playing" or "tracking." These words record as part of the digital capture. Once this happens, there is no way to erase them. You have to start over and capture the entire project again.

- **Don't capture audio if there is none on the tape.** Audio virtually doubles the size of your files. Again the extra demand on the computer increases your chances of ending up with dropped frames. Add any soundtrack during production and editing.

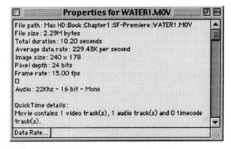

Tips on Advanced Planning and the Shoot

To obtain raw footage to later capture into your system, you must first plan and then shoot it. Some tips on how to make that process run more smoothly are listed below:

- **Start with a good idea.** When you have a story that begs to be told, script it and hire the actors. Think through the locations.

- **Plan and schedule the shoot** — the sequence of photography, the times of day and more. As you do, you may realize that certain shots should be taken as one group, while others might better be taken at a different time of day or in a different location.

- **Prepare imaginatively for possible problems.** By thinking through possible problems on the shoot, you have time to come up with alternative approaches that may work even better.

- **Shoot three to five times the actual video footage that you think you need.** By doing so, you allow for problems such as changing lighting conditions, planes flying overhead or actors' fluffed lines.

- **Log the new video clips and select the best shots.**

A good rule of thumb in shooting video is to record three to five times the footage you plan to use in the final production.

The Tiger Tamer Shoot: A Case Study

Let's consider an example of this process in action — the Tiger Tamer exercise that you completed earlier. As you recall, the fearless tiger tamer is about to tame a ferocious (well, mildly intimidating) tiger. The tamer approaches the bored, almost sleepy tiger. The tamer tries to use his whip, without results. Suddenly the tables turn, and we see the tamer running for his life as the tiger decides that a little snack might perk him up.

How was this video created? The actor, the tiger tamer, wasn't willing to stand next to a huge tiger, tame or otherwise. To resolve that problem, we decided to create an illusion. It merely had to seem that the tamer was near the tiger. First, we shot the entire feeding of the animals at the zoo, just turned on the camera and didn't stop shooting until the feeding was over. We obtained quite a variety of shots.

Once off location, we logged the shots. (Remember, you logged a series of shots similarly in an earlier chapter.) In reviewing the video we had shot, we formulated a plan. Next, we shot the tamer at a local park, which had greenery that looked similar to the greenery at the zoo. The trick was to play with the camera's light settings so that this location would look very similar to the zoo location. By selecting the zoo shots ahead of time, we were able to plan precisely what the actor would do to make the new shots most closely correspond with the existing footage. For each video clip needed, we shot the same scene four or five times.

When the shoot was complete, the new video clips logged, and the best shots chosen, we were ready to capture the video into the computer and your project was born.

Tips on Preparing Your Computer

Before you can begin to capture, your computer must be properly prepared to accept the signal. Video streams from a camera into the computer. If the computer is in a less than optimal state, it cannot accept the video at that rate. This can cause a phenomenon known as "dropped frames." A *dropped frame* is a portion of a video clip in which some of the data has not been captured successfully. The result is bad jumps in the video. So prepare your computer now.

If you're in a classroom or network environment, check with your instructor or network administrator before you do anything. Unless your instructor agrees, do not defragment your drive.

Purging Your Drive

How do you prepare your computer properly to accept video? First, clean your hard drive — you need ample free space. Digitized video can eat up huge amounts of space. The video clip WATER1.MOV, from Chapter 1, is a good example. This clip plays for 10.03 seconds and is set at a Frame Size of 240 × 178, a Frame Rate of 15 frames per second, and Cinepak compression. It uses 2.3 MB of hard drive space, and that's just one video clip. So remove any unused programs or files from your computer. The more hard drive space you have, the better.

Defragmenting Your Hard Drive

Keep your hard drive defragmented for best performance. Your computer gets a lot of use. You constantly save files, delete files and add new programs. As you delete items, they leave small spaces into which your computer saves new files. If the files don't fit in a given place, the computer saves a little in one space and a little in another. To read one file, your computer must read a number of sections of the drive, causing it to work much harder and take longer to get the information it needs. Ever have a friend come to visit at the last moment? You run through the house, grabbing clutter and throwing it into any available drawer. How do you find those items afterward? Think of a fragmented computer as several desk drawers that desperately need to be cleaned after such a visit.

If you're working on a network, check with your network system administrator about defragmentation. This may be done for you or may not be permitted on your network.

There are several methods for defragmenting a computer's hard drive; do not attempt to defragment your hard drive, however, without clearly understanding what to do and preparing properly. Consult your manual and ask for help from a knowledgeable person. Before beginning, back up your data. If this is your personal machine, be sure to back up your data frequently and consider backing the entire drive. You should do both of these processes regularly, in any case. If you are working on a computer in a classroom environment or on a network, ask your instructor or network system administrator whether it is acceptable for you to defragment the drive and whether a current backup of the drive exists. Do not proceed until you know that the data is backed and that defragmenting will not cause any problems for others.

Once the data is backed, defragmenting or optimizing your drive may require specific software intended for that purpose. For the Macintosh, there is third-party software that can optimize your drive. For a Windows-based system, there is a Windows component, Disk Defragmenter, which is included as part of the operating system. There is also third-party software available which will do the job. Whichever you use, the defragmenting software gradually searches your drive and reassembles the components of files, programs, fonts and so on, so that contiguous space is used for each. Now the computer only has to look in one place to find a particular item. This can cause your machine to run more efficiently. On a sluggish computer, it may actually increase the performance as much as 30% or more.

If you're working on your own personal computer, be certain that you understand the process fully before proceeding. Back up your data. Read the defragmentation software manual. Think out the process in advance. A little time now will save many problems later.

A second process that can improve your machine's functionality is rebuilding the desktop, suitable only if you're working on a Macintosh. The desktop file is a hidden file, which keeps track of the location of the data, applications, fonts and more on your hard drive. It can become corrupted or bloated over time, especially if you have had crashes on your system. It is recommended that you rebuild your desktop to deal with this problem. Consult your Macintosh manual for details on how to do so. For Windows-based machines, the desktop is similar but not identical. There are several hidden files that together serve the same purpose, including the Registry. These files can also become bloated with time. While there is third-party software that is intended to make the Registry run more efficiently, the process is not the same as on the Macintosh and is not part of the routine maintenance in the same fashion. Do not attempt this on a Windows-based machine unless you know what you are doing.

Closing Other Programs

Don't run any other programs while using Premiere. Premiere needs all of your processing power. Anything that interferes with the capturing process will spell disaster for your video clips.

Obtaining as Much RAM as You Can Afford

You can never have enough RAM. Adobe recommends a minimum of 48 MB. to run Premiere. This is technically correct, but not really practical. Even with 128 MB. of RAM, the program often runs slowly. Premiere will run with less memory, but it will take a very long time to capture clips and you will have to restart your computer frequently. So invest wisely — buy and install as much RAM as you can. It will pay you back.

Tips on Preventing or Resolving Problems

Murphy's Law: if something can go wrong, it will. This is especially true of video production. Batteries die on remote shoots. The company owner who insisted on being allowed to speak on camera may become so nervous that he or she cannot remember those memorized lines. A few tips are listed below to help you plan:

Planning Ahead

- **Take the time to locate good talent, suitable music and ideal venues.** The smallest details can ruin a great production. Your production is only as good as the worst item in it. Many components make a great video production and many can ruin it.
- **Watch the Weather Channel.** Don't plan an outdoor shoot without checking the weather first. There is no use traveling to a remote location only to discover that you can't even get out of the car.
- **Don't wait until the last minute.** Things always go wrong when you're in a hurry. Waiting too late in the day to begin shooting, for example, and having your client decide suddenly that an outdoor building shot is crucial can be expensive.

Watching the Details

- **Get permission to shoot in a public place.** Some of our students were almost arrested in a mall while conducting "man-on-the-street interviews." Mall security accused them of casing the place in order to rob some stores at a later date. The student IDs saved them, but they were held and questioned nonetheless. The same advice goes for airports, hospitals and nightclubs.
- **Make certain that the date/time stamp on the camera is turned off.** Many a student has returned from a video shoot to discover that the date/time stamp had not been disabled. When in doubt, tape a small segment and play it back early in the shoot.

Saving and Backing Up Frequently

- **Keep backups.** If you spill coffee on your only copy or have the unpleasant experience of seeing your original fail, you'll remember this point easily. It only has to happen to you once.
- **Save frequently.** Premiere, like most computer programs, sometimes crashes. If the worst happens, you will be grateful to have that last-saved version.

Investing in RAM will pay you back many times over. While Premiere can run slowly with lower amounts, the more RAM you have, the more easily you can work in this program.

It's always worth your time to get permission to shoot in public places. Being turned away with the whole crew and cast standing by can be expensive and embarrassing. Being accused of trespassing can be even worse.

Exporting Video to the Web

Now that you have your QuickTime movie, you may want to upload it to your personal Web site for the entire world to see. As it turns out, exporting a QuickTime movie is easy. Choosing the correct settings, however, is the hard part. When it comes to compressing movies, you have many important choices to make. These choices have a profound impact on the quality of your final compressed movie, so it is important that you understand the parameters and tradeoffs involved.

Adobe Premiere ships with a compression program — Terran Interactive's Cleaner 5 EZ. This is a "light version" of Media Cleaner Pro. Media Cleaner Pro is the current industry standard for compressing video and audio. Before we export our movie to the Web, let's examine some export options.

Save your file and back up your data frequently. It's easy to save and expensive and difficult to redo the project.

Some of the more important movie options are the Codec, Data Rate, Frame Rate (fps), Image Size and Keyframe Frequency. Here is an overview of the factors limiting your options, and general guidelines for choosing your settings.

Choosing the Codec

To choose the best Codec for your movies, you must determine the minimum system requirements of your viewers. Are they PowerMac or Pentium users? If so, then Sorenson Video is generally the best video codec choice. For a video that features music, the QDesign Music codec is a good choice for most material. If you have speech-only material, the Qualcomm PureVoice codec may be a better fit.

There is no perfect formula for all movies. Achieving the best results requires experimentation and testing, and often depends on your (or your clients') personal preferences.

If your potential Web users have 68k Macintosh or 486 Windows machines, your best option is generally to use Cinepak and IMA audio. (The newest QuickTime codecs — such as Sorenson Video, QDesign Music and Qualcomm PureVoice — don't run on 68k Macintoshes and are too CPU-intensive for 486 Windows computers.)

Determining the Data Rate

One of the most important choices you must make when preparing movies is the Data Rate. More than any other factor, the data rate affects the final image and sound quality of your movie. It also affects how big the final file will be, as well as what playback methods will be able to effectively deliver the movie. The problem is that there are many different connections to the Web: 28.8k and 56.6k modems, ISDN lines, cable lines, DSL lines and T1 lines.

Generally, if you want viewers to be able to watch your video in real time, the following numbers are reasonable starting points. Let's take a look at the file you created in Chapter 9, BIRDS2.PPJ. This file was created at 240 × 180, 15 frames per second, and after compression, the final file size was 416k for a 22-second video. The average times to download this file are listed below:

28.8 modems — 2.5k per second	2 minutes, 26 seconds
56.6 modems — 5k per second 1 minute,	23 seconds
ISDN — 12k per second	35 seconds
T1 — 20k per second	21 seconds

Making Your Web Video Look as Good as Possible

As you can see, there is a wide range of connections to the Web, and the volume of Web traffic at any given time significantly affects the possible throughput.

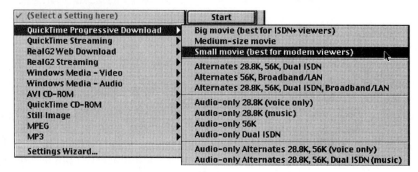

As a result, there is no way to guarantee the data rate your viewers will be able to see when they download your file. Take these key steps to ensure that your files work well for your viewers:

- **Target your files to your audience.** Most home users have either a 28.8k or 56.6k modem, although a growing number of home users have a Direct Subscriber Line (DSL). Big business use T1 or ISDN lines. The size and complexity of your final compression should be based on the client who will view it.

- **Don't create files that take too long to download.** Home users get bored quickly. If your file takes too long to download, users simply click to another site. Files created for the home market are generally created at 160 × 120. Files for the corporate market may be created at 160 × 120, but feature a higher frame rate.

- **Remember: the better the quality, the better the output.** Start a project by using good video and good audio. The compression process degrades the overall video and audio output, so you want the project to be as good as possible from the beginning.

- **Don't use a lot of type or motion.** Compressed video tends to make type look fuzzy on the screen. If you must use type, keep it simple and fairly large. Don't place a lot of type on a single screen. Consider using the full version of Media Cleaner Pro.

- **Consider offering alternative download choices.** QuickTime allows you to create alternate movies so that users get an appropriate data rate for their connection. When you create a Web site, offer your users an opportunity to select the most appropriate file size to download. Some people would rather wait a little longer to see a higher-quality video.

Export Final Project to the Web

1. Open the **Work in Progress>BIRDS2.PPJ** file. When the project opens, all related files appear on the Timeline.

2. Select File>Export Timeline>Save For Web. The Cleaner 5 EZ window appears.

3. In the Settings box, select QuickTime Progressive Download>Small Movie (best for modem viewers). Double-check that the Export: Entire Project option is selected. Click the Start button.

4. A new window appears, showing the Cleaner 5 EZ splash screen. When prompted, save your file as "BIRDSWEB.MOV" to your **Work in Progress** folder.

5. The Output window appears. Cleaner 5 EZ locates and compresses your file, taking about four minutes. When finished, Cleaner 5 EZ signals with a high-pitched sound.

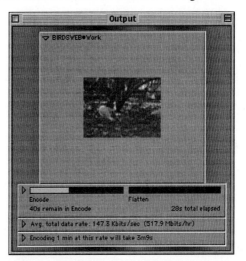

Notice that the BIRDSWEB.MOV compressed movie is now in your Work in Progress folder. Open your Web browser. Drag and drop a copy of BIRDSWEB.MOV onto your open browser window. Your video begins to play.

6. You may wish to try exporting again at a higher resolution. Select File>Export Timeline>Save For Web. The Cleaner 5 EZ window appears again. In the Settings box, select QuickTime Progressive Download>Medium-size Movie. Double-check that Export: Entire Project is already selected. Click the Start button.

7. A new window appears, showing the Cleaner 5 EZ splash screen. When prompted, save your file as "BIRDS2WEB.MOV" to your **Work in Progress** folder.

8. The Output window appears. Cleaner 5 EZ locates and compresses your file, taking roughly four minutes, depending on your machine. When finished, Cleaner 5 EZ signals with a high-pitched sound.

   Drag and drop a copy of BIRDS2WEB.MOV onto your open browser window. Your video begins to play.

9. When you are satisfied with the results, close your file and the browser.

Summary

In this final chapter, you learned about capturing video, and the difference between using an analog device and a new digital video or DV device. You became familiar with Movie Capture, a specialized application built into Premiere and designed to convert analog and DV input into a compatible format. You explored the various requirements for capturing video and how they affect final quality. You learned about settings and using the Capture window. You reviewed some key steps for planning effective shoots and preparing your system for the capture process. Finally, you learned how to take your captured footage and convert it into a format compatible with the Internet, which provides an inexpensive way to distribute your productions.

Free-Form Project #2

Assignment

It's your Grandparents' 50th wedding anniversary. As the recognized cinematic genius of the family, you've been recruited to create a video for the surprise party. Since it was your folks that decided that you were going to be the Stephen Spielberg of your clan, the production had better be good.

You should consider building the production from a combination of stills, old footage and interviews with various family members. Don't forget to use appropriate background music.

Applying Your Skills

You will create the training video by:

- Thinking of questions to ask
- Creating a storyboard
- Scanning the still images
- Shooting the interviews
- Capturing the video
- Assembling the video clips
- Adding music and voice, as necessary
- Preparing the production to play at the party as a QuickTime movie

Specifications

- Finished length: varies
- Transitions placed on all clips
- Titles — both rolling credits and static titles identifying the people being interviewed
- Transitions, where appropriate
- Split screens, where appropriate
- Filters to enhance the older footage

Included Files:

Since this is a video about your family, you have to shoot it yourself.

Publisher's Comments

This is a challenging assignment, since it requires that you use contemporary footage combined with stills and archive video to create a feeling of tradition. Humor is another consideration — people love to laugh at parties.

You might also watch some documentary productions, from the History Channel or A&E, for example, so that you can get a feel for good interviewing. It's one of the hardest things in the world to get right. You have to be objective, asking questions while keeping your own personality out of the equation. Prepare your questions beforehand, and be prepared to edit the footage to arrive at the perfect look and feel.

Review #2

Chapters 6 through 10

In Chapters 6 through 10, you learned to create titles and graphic elements, drawing basic shapes and controlling font selections, colors, illusion of motion and more. You've added and adjusted audio, combined live-action and created footage, and become familiar with the capture process. After completing the second half of this course and exploring some of the more advanced capabilities of Premiere, you should:

- Know how to use the Title window to create titles and graphic elements. You should be comfortable drawing basic shapes such as circles, ovals, squares, rectangles and polygons. You should be able to place lines on your footage and control their width. You should know how to apply colors to objects and type, how to select fonts, and how to alter font sizes and spacing. You should also be able to create gradients, and control their start and end colors.

- Be comfortable working with audio clips — importing them, listening to them in the Monitor window and using waveforms. You understand how to use the Audio Mixer to adjust levels, for mono and stereo audio clips. You should be able to control gain, fade and other aspects of audio clips. You know how to place audio on the Timeline, and how to synchronize it to video footage.

- Understand and have practiced working with still images and the pan/zoom controls to create the illusion of movement where none exists. You should know how to use alpha channels and the Title window to create stills and animations. You should have learned how to apply transparency and gradients to still images, and how to combine stills with live footage.

- Be familiar with advanced editing techniques and be able to edit more than one clip at a time. You should know the difference between rolling and rippling edits, and be able to select the appropriate method based on the requirements of specific productions. You should be familiar with common types of shots and camera movements, and the role of logging in the postproduction process.

- Understand how to use the Movie Capture program to digitize video. You should understand the difference between analog and digital video devices, and how they're connected to your workstation. You should know how to maximize your system to optimize the video production process. You should also be familiar with some tips about efficient planning and management of shooting raw footage. You should know how to prepare files appropriately sized for Web distribution.

Project A: The Monkey Movie

Every production begins with the basics. Your company's client, a zoo beginning a fund-raising campaign, wants to illustrate some of its crowd-pleasers in the midst of the antics that endear them to the public. You are part of a team producing the first part of the movie. As the newest member of the team, you are setting up the basic production that you will hand off to another member of the department to add more specialized effects. The client wants to review the basics before the special effects are added, so you will make a QuickTime movie that the client can approve the footage choices before the expensive effects are added.

You're going to use what you've learned to assemble the initial movie. The subject of the production is a group of monkeys at play. You will combine several clips, apply transitions and generate a QuickTime movie for the client's review.

Getting Started

1. Open Premiere and accept the default settings. Make sure that 240 × 180 is the screen size. Select File>Import>Folder. When the dialog box appears, locate the **RF-Premiere>Project A** folder, and select Choose.

2. In the Project window, open the Project A folder, and double-click FINAL_MONKEY.MOV. Click the Play button to preview the final project. Close the FINAL_MONKEY.MOV clip window, but leave the Project and Monitor windows open, as well as the Timeline, to begin the project.

Assemble and Place the Clips

1. In the Project A folder in the Project window, look through the files with which you will work in this project. Notice that AUDIO_A.AIF, a music selection, has already been placed on the Audio 1 track to enhance your production. You will place these shots alternately, as usual, on the Video 1A and 1B tracks of the Timeline.

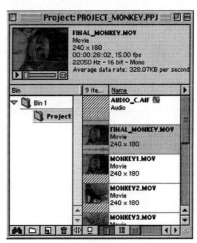

2. Drag the shots individually to the Timeline window, positioning them as indicated in the list below. Note carefully on which track they should be placed and the exact position on the Timeline:

MONKEY1.MOV on Video 1A

MONKEY2.MOV on Video 1B at 00:00:02:13

MONKEY3.MOV on Video 1A at 00:00:05:23

MONKEY4.MOV on Video 1B at 00:00:09:16

MONKEY5.MOV on Video 1A at 00:00:13:15

MONKEY6.MOV on Video 1B at 00:00:17:26

MONKEY7.MOV on Video 1A at 00:00:22:26

3. Double-check that the Work Area bar extends to the end of the production. Render the project, and watch the entire production play. Now you should see our special guest star monkey happily playing as music plays in the background.

4. Save your project as "MONKEYS.PPJ" to your **Work in Progress** folder.

Add Transitions

1. Add the first two transitions from the appropriate folders in the Transitions palette, and position them in the overlaps of the shots as indicated below. Transitions should snap into position at the overlaps:

Iris folder>Iris Diamond transition to MONKEY1.MOV and MONKEY2.MOV
Wipe folder>Clock Wipe transition to MONKEY2.MOV and MONKEY3.MOV

2. Press the Return/Enter key to render the production. You should see our monkey playing as transitions occur from shot to shot. Save your production again.

3. Now add the remaining transitions, as indicated in the list below:

Wipe folder>Barn Doors transition to MONKEY3.MOV and MONKEY4.MOV
3D Motion folder>Cube Spin transition to MONKEY4.MOV and MONKEY5.MOV
Iris folder>Iris Cross transition to MONKEY5.MOV and MONKEY6.MOV overlap
Iris folder>Iris Round transition to MONKEY6.MOV and MONKEY7.MOV overlap. Save your changes.

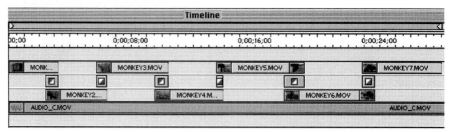

Add Color Borders to the Transitions

1. Double-click on the first transition on the Timeline — the Iris Diamond. In the dialog box, check Show Actual Sources. Notice the preview of your two video clips. Drag the Color Border slider bar slightly to the right.

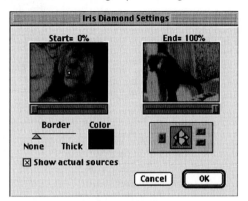

2. Click on the black rectangle. When the Color Picker appears, set Red: 0, Green: 0, Blue: 255, and click OK.

3. When you see a thin blue border appear on the animated preview, click OK. Double-click on the second transition on the Timeline — the Clock Wipe. When the dialog box appears, check Show Actual Sources. Notice a preview of your two video clips appears with the wipe beginning at the 12:00 mark.

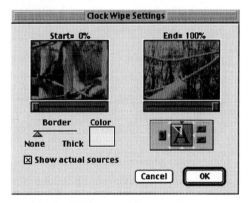

4. Click on the black rectangle. When the Color Picker appears, set Red: 249, Green: 255, Blue: 77, and click OK.

5. Move the Color Border slider from None to the right a little. A thin yellow border appears in the animated preview. Click OK.

6. Double-click on the third transition on the Timeline — the Barn Doors. In the dialog box, check Show Actual Sources. Notice the preview of your two video clips.

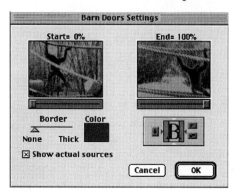

7. Again click on the black rectangle. In the Color Picker, set Red: 0, Green: 0, Blue: 255, and click OK.

8. Move the Color Border slider slightly to the right. You will see a thin blue border appear in the animated preview. Click OK.

9. Skip the fourth transition, the Cube Spin transition, and double-click the fifth transition, the Iris Cross transition. In the dialog box, click on the black rectangle. When the Color Picker appears, set Red: 0, Green: 239, Blue: 232, and click OK.

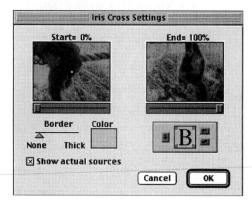

10. Move the Color Border slider to the right. When a light blue border appears around the preview in the dialog box, click OK.

11. Now modify the last transition, the Iris Round transition. Double-click on the black rectangle. When the Color Picker appears, set Red: 0, Green: 0, Blue: 255. Click OK, and click OK again to exit this dialog box.

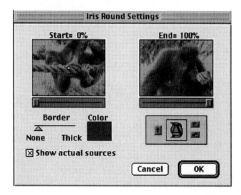

12. Render the production and watch our monkey in action with transitions between shots. Save your production again.

Export as a QuickTime Movie

1. Select File>Export Timeline>Movie. Name the project "MonkeyFinal.MOV", and click the Settings button. Make sure that the Export Audio box is selected, and then click the Next button.

2. Double-check the following settings and adjust any that are not correct — Frame Size: 240 × 180, Compressor: Cinepak, Frame Rate: 15, Quality: 100%.

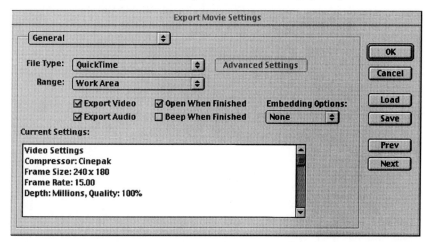

3. Click the Next button. In the Audio Settings area, select 22050kHz, 16-bit Mono, and Uncompressed.

4. Click OK to return to the main area of the Export dialog box. Double-check where your file will be saved, and click OK. It will take several minutes to complete the rendering process.

You've created the basic production that will enable your team to confirm the fancier movie production with the client. Through this QuickTime production, the client can actually see the footage under discussion, instead of just guessing at what is being described. Your client can relax, and your team can proceed with this fund-raising project.

Notes:

Project B: How to Make Spaghetti

A major software distributor has retained your agency to create a multimedia cookbook for beginning cooks. This cookbook will be marketed to college students away from home for the first time and to new brides just learning how to cook. In addition to recipes, this interactive cookbook will include a series of QuickTime movies illustrating techniques for preparing tasty dishes. You will produce the movie that demonstrates the art of making spaghetti. This segment will be incorporated into the chapter on main dishes.

For this project, you will import a series of short video clips, position them appropriately and add transitions, music and credits. You will create the titles that explain the key points of the video. When you are finished, fledgling cooks will see a friendly face in the kitchen, helping them successfully make a spaghetti dinner.

Getting Started

1. Open Premiere and accept the default settings. Double-check that your screen size is set to 240 • 180. Select File>Import>Folder. A dialog box will appear. Locate the **RF-Premiere>Project B** folder, and select Choose.

2. Open the Project B folder in Bin 1, and double-click FINAL_B.MOV to open the file as a clip window. Click the Play button to preview what your project will look like once completed. Close the FINAL_B.MOV clip window, but leave everything else open to begin the project.

Assemble and Place the Clips

1. Notice that there are 15 different shots (SHOT1.MOV through SHOT15.MOV) and the audio track AUDIO_B.AIF in the Project B folder. You will place the shots alternately on Videos 1A and 1B.

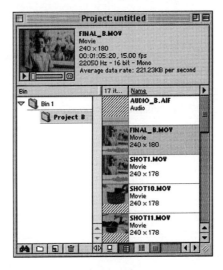

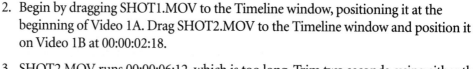

2. Begin by dragging SHOT1.MOV to the Timeline window, positioning it at the beginning of Video 1A. Drag SHOT2.MOV to the Timeline window and position it on Video 1B at 00:00:02:18.

3. SHOT2.MOV runs 00:00:06:12, which is too long. Trim two seconds, using either the Duration option in the Clip menu or the Razor tool from the Timeline.

4. Now drag the remaining shots individually to the Timeline window and position them as indicated in the list below. Note carefully on which track they should be placed and the exact position.

   SHOT3.MOV on Video 1B at 00:00:06:29
   SHOT4.MOV on Video 1B at 00:00:9:24
   SHOT5.MOV on Video 1A at 00:00:11:12
   SHOT6.MOV on Video 1B at 00:00:14:18
   SHOT7.MOV on Video 1A at 00:00:16:25
   SHOT8.MOV on Video 1B at 00:00:19:21
   SHOT9.MOV on Video 1A at 00:00:24:17
   SHOT10.MOV on Video 1B at 00:00:25:28
   SHOT11.MOV on Video 1A at 00:00:30:07
   SHOT12.MOV on Video 1B at 00:00:32:11
   SHOT13.MOV on Video 1A at 00:00:38:18
   SHOT14.MOV on Video 1A, directly after SHOT13.MOV
   SHOT15.MOV on Video 1A, directly after SHOT14.MOV

5. Drag AUDIO_B.AIF to the Timeline window, and position it on Audio 2 so that it falls at the beginning of the production directly under SHOT1.MOV. (You will need to scroll to the left in order to move to the beginning of the production.)

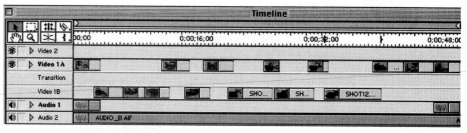

6. The Work Area bar should extend to the end of the production. If it does not, extend the bar to about the one-minute mark so you can view all of the production with visible transitions.

7. Save your project as "FINAL-B.PPJ" to your Work in Progress folder.

8. Render the production so that you can see how it looks so far. You should see chef Kathi, making spaghetti as music plays.

Add and Preview Transitions

1. From the Page Peel folder in the Transitions palette, drag the Page Peel transition to the Transition track. It should snap into position in the overlap of SHOT1.MOV and SHOT2.MOV. To access the Transitions palette, select Window>Show Transitions.

This production music is placed on Audio 2 since our chef dialog will be on the Audio 1 track.

2. From the 3D Motion folder, drag the Cube Spin transition to the Transition track. It should snap into position in the overlap of SHOT4.MOV and SHOT5.MOV.

3. Render the production and watch our chef slice veggies, with transitions between the first few video clips. Don't forget to save your production again — although the production plays, the file must be saved in its latest version.

4. Now add the remaining transitions, positioned in the overlaps of shots as indicated in the list below.

   3D Motion folder>Cube Spin transition to SHOT5.MOV and SHOT6.MOV
   3D Motion folder>Spin Away transition to SHOT6.MOV and SHOT7.MOV
   Wipe folder>Barn Doors transition to SHOT7.MOV and SHOT8.MOV
   Dissolve folder>Additive Dissolve transition to SHOT8.MOV and SHOT9.MOV
   3D Motion folder>Cube Spin transition to SHOT9.MOV and SHOT10.MOV
   Slide folder>Push transition SHOT10.MOV and SHOT11.MOV
   Iris folder>Iris Round transition to SHOT11.MOV and SHOT12.MOV
   Wipe folder>Clock Wipe transition to SHOT12.MOV and SHOT13.MOV

You may notice that there are not transitions between all of the clips. Too many splashy transitions can be overkill — too much of a good thing.

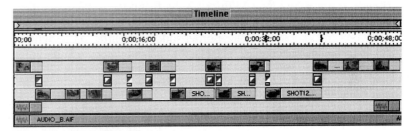

Add Color Borders to the Transitions

1. Double-click on the second transition on the Timeline — the Cube Spin. When the dialog box appears, click on the Show Actual Sources button. You will see a preview of your two video clips. Drag the Border Color slider bar slightly to the right.

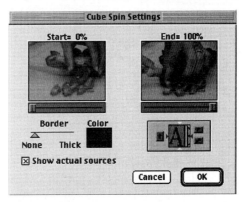

Press the Tab key to scroll quickly through the color choices.

2. At the moment, no colored borders separate the video clips. A colored border helps to define the individual sections. Click on the black rectangle. In the Color Picker, set Red: 160, Green: 251, Blue: 255, and click OK. A thin light blue border appears that separates the images. Click OK to return to the Timeline.

3. Double-click on the third transition, another Cube Spin transition. Click on the black rectangle. In the Color Picker, set Red: 250, Green: 255, Blue: 108, and click OK. Pull the Border Color slider a little to the right. A thin yellow border appears. Click OK.

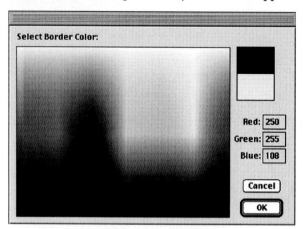

4. Double-click on the fourth transition, a Spin Away transition. Click on the black rectangle. In the Color Picker, set Red: 255, Green: 12, Blue: 48, and click OK. Pull the Color Border slider bar a little to the right. When a thin red border appears, click OK.

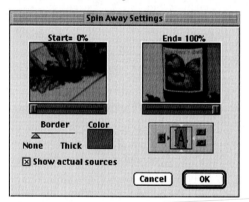

5. Double-click on the fifth transition on the Timeline — the Barn Doors transition. When the dialog box appears, click Show Actual Sources. You will see a preview of your two video clips.

6. Click on the black rectangle. In the Color Picker, set Red: 0, Green: 0, Blue: 255, and click OK. Move the Color Border bar slightly to the right. When a thin blue border appears, click OK.

7. Skip the next transition, which is the Additive Dissolve transition. Double-click on the seventh transition — a Cube Spin transition — then click on the black rectangle. In the Color Picker, set Red: 160, Green: 255, Blue: 188, and click OK. Pull the Border Color slider bar a little to the right. When a thin light green border appears, click OK.

8. Modify the rest of the transitions. Continue to move down the Timeline and select each of the remaining transitions. Apply different border colors to each in turn.

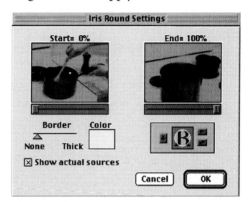

9. Save and render the production. You should see our chef cooking as transitions occur from shot to shot.

Fade the Audio Clips

You probably have noticed that he music stops abruptly at the end of this production. We need to fade the music out in order to end the production in a more professional way.

1. Click the triangle on the left side of the Audio 2 track. The audio box opens to show the music.

2. Move the Edit Line to 00:00:48:10, and click your cursor at that point. A small red square (handle) appears.

3. Position the Edit Line at 00:00:49:25, and click your cursor at that point. A second handle appears. Drag that red square to the bottom of the audio area. (This is the fade-out of the music.)

4. Position the Edit Line at 00:00:52:00, and click to place a third handle. Drag that square to the bottom of the audio area, matching where you placed the previous handle. This keeps the music from fading back in.

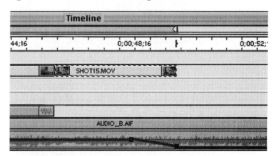

5. Click on the left-side Audio 2 track triangle to collapse the box.

Using a fade-in and fade-out gives your production a more professional look.

Create a Title

1. Select File>New>Title to display the Title Generator dialog box.

2. We need to ensure that the Title Generator is the same size as the rest of the production. Click on the untitled titled window to activate it. Select Window>Title Window Options>Title, and set Size H: 240 and V: 180, and NTSC-safe Colors: checked. Set Background: white, and click OK.

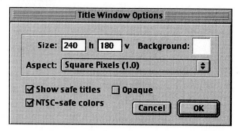

3. Click on the Text tool. Select a font from the Title menu, and click on the Drawing surface. When you see a blinking I-beam, indicating that you are ready to type some text. Type the following (each on a separate line, pressing Return/Enter at the end of each line):

   How
   To
   Make
   Spaghetti

   With the Selection tool, drag the text by its handles into position on the page.

4. Let's replace any leftover color with a new color. Click on the center of the main color palette at the left — the Object Color palette. The Color Picker appears.

5. Set Red: 214, Green: 28, Blue: 0, and click OK. Your title now has a bright red color. Click OK.

6. The words will not fit correctly unless we resize them. From the Title menu, select a point size that will enlarge the type until it fills the screen (try 36 points), and click OK to apply this.

7. The type also needs to move to the right side of the screen. Choose Title>Justify>Right, and click OK.

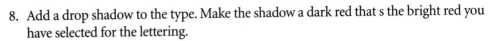

8. Add a drop shadow to the type. Make the shadow a dark red that s the bright red you have selected for the lettering.

9. When you have completed typing and enhancing the text, save the title and add it to the Timeline. Save your title as "OPENING.PTL" to the **Work in Progress** folder.

10. Once it is saved, your title automatically transfers to the Project menu. (You may need to drag it from the main project area into the same folder as your other files.) Close the Title window. You should now have OPENING.PTL in the Project A folder in Bin 1. Save the file.

Use Alpha Channels to Generate Special Effects

1. Drag OPENING.PTL to the Timeline window at the beginning of the Video 2 track. Click to highlight it. Select Clip>Video Options>Transparency.

2. When the Transparency Settings dialog box appears, OPENING.PTL is displayed in the Samples box. Double-check that Key Type is set to White Alpha Matte. Click OK to close the dialog box.

3. Click to select OPENING.PTL on the Timeline. Select Clip>Duration, and set Duration: 00:00:02:00, and click OK. Your credit contracts to two seconds.

Set the Title Opacity

As you see, the title graphic of the video starts rather abruptly at the beginning and it just drops out just as rapidly at the end. What we actually want is to have the graphic fade-in and fade-out. Premiere has the built-in controls to direct the opacity of the graphic.

1. Click on the small gray triangle to the left of Video 2 on the Timeline. The track expands to show the opacity levels for OPENING.PTL.

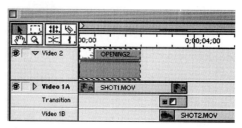

2. Notice the thin red line at the top of this window. This shows the title at 100% opacity. At the far left of the red line, notice a red handle. Move the cursor slightly to the right and click again on the red line. A second handle appears.

3. Position your cursor over the far-left handle, and drag the handle to the bottom of the window. This will be the fade-in for the title. At the far right of the red line, click once. A third red handle appears. Move the cursor slightly to the left and click again on the red line. A fourth handle appears.

4. Position the cursor over the far-right handle, and drag it to the bottom of the window. This will be the fade-out for the title. Collapse the box.

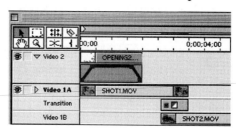

5. Save and render this production. Your title fades in and fades out as our chef prepares to cook.

Create Additional Titles

Now you'll create the four remaining titles that outline the steps necessary to make spaghetti. We'll show you how to create the first one; you'll create the other titles on your own.

1. Select File>New>Title to display the Title Generator dialog box. Double-check that the page size is set to 240h × 180v. Click on the Text tool. Select a font from the Title menu. When you see a blinking I-beam, type the following, pressing Return/Enter after each line:

   Step 1:
   Slice the
   Ingredients

The keyboard shortcut to display the Transparency Settings dialog box is Command/Control-G.

Title generator files created in Premiere automatically come with an alpha channel to work with.

2. Now you'll replace any leftover color with a new color. Click on the center of the main color palette at the left. The Color Picker appears.

3. Set Red: 0, Green: 9, Blue: 181, and click OK. Your title now has a bright blue color.

4. The words may not be correctly sized for this section of the project. From the Title menu, choose a point size that will enlarge the type until it fills the screen. (Try 36 points.) Click OK.

5. Arrange the type by choosing Title>Justify>Center, then Title>Center Vertically, and finally Title>Center Horizontally.

6. Place a drop shadow on the type. Make the shadow a dark blue that complements the bright blue you selected for the lettering.

7. You must save the title and add it to the Timeline. Save your title as "STEP1.PTL" to the Work in Progress folder.

   Once saved, your title automatically transfers to the Project menu. Drag it into the Project Bin and close the Title window.

8. You should now have STEP1.PTL and OPENING.PTL in the Work in Progress folder along with your other title and video clips. Save this file.

9. Place STEP1.PTL on the Timeline on Video 2 at 00:00:03:18. Make certain the text is highlighted, and click the Duration command located in the clip window. Set the duration to 00:00:2:15.

10. As you did with the title graphic, use the Opacity handles to make the text fade in and fade out.

11. Continue to create the titles for the rest of your production. They should look like the preview, FINAL_A.MOV, which you viewed earlier. View this movie again if you wish. Create the following titles:

   Step 2: Add the Sauce

   Step 3: Cook the Noodles

   The Final Results

Export as a QuickTime Movie

Now that you have all of the elements in place, let's review how to compress your work into a final movie. As you recall, a QuickTime movie compresses all elements into one complete movie. It flattens all of the project tracks into one track.

1. Select File>Export Timeline>Movie. Type "SPAGHETTI.MOV" as the movie name, and click the Settings button. Check Export Audio as there is audio in this project.

2. Double-check that the Frame Size is 240 × 180, and Compressor is set to Video. (You will only need to change this if you need the project to be cross-platform. If the project will be running on both Windows and Macintosh systems, select Cinepak instead. Set Frame Rate: 15. Pull the Quality bar from 100% to 80% to reduce the file size.

Cinepak takes longer to render, but it's the only way to create a truly cross platform project.

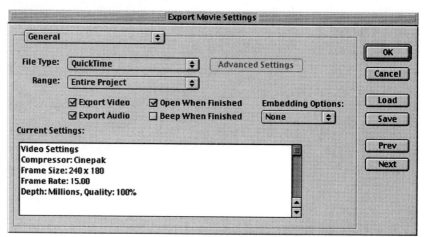

3. Click the Next button. In the Audio Settings area, select 22050kHz, 16-bit Mono and Uncompressed. These settings help to keep your file size small.

4. Click OK to return to the main area of the Export dialog box. Double-check where your file is about to be saved. Click Save. It will take several minutes to complete the rendering process.

   Now your project is a self-contained piece. You can delete all other files related to this project if you do not want to edit again.

Congratulations. Your movie will help fledgling cooks find their way preparing spaghetti and gain confidence with cooking.

Project C: How to Tame a Tiger

Your company, CyberDeluxe, provides a variety of Internet services for clients, including Web design. One client, the Community Advisory Council to the Mayor's Office, has commissioned CyberDeluxe to prepare an interactive Web site for children. This Web site will teach children about safety issues, but it will do it in a humorous way. Kids visiting this site will learn about fire safety, poisons, drugs and other hazards that concern parents. It will also have a learning section on field trips in the local area. One such field trip is a trip to the zoo. In this section of the Web site, children will learn the proper way to behave when visiting the zoo. They will learn about not teasing or feeding the animals, but in a light-hearted way to which children can relate.

As you build this production that tells a story, you will again import short video clips, trim and arrange them, and then enhance them with transitions, credits and music. You will also create titles that will explain the video and stagger the credits so that they appear on the screen at different times. When finished, your movie will teach the viewer "How to Tame a Tiger."

Getting Started

1. Open Premiere and accept the default settings. Double-check that the size is 240 ∞ 180. Select File>Import>Folder. In the dialog box, select the **RF-Premiere>Project C** folder, and click Choose.

2. Open the Project C folder in Bin 1, and double-click **FINAL_C.MOV** to open the file as a clip window. Click the Play button to preview the final project. Close the FINAL_C.MOV clip window, leaving everything else open to begin the project.

Place and Trim Clips

1. Notice the clips in the Project C folder in Bin 1 — these are the files with which you will work on this project.

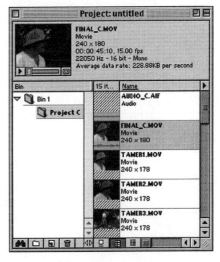

2. Drag TAMER1.MOV to the Timeline window at the beginning of Video 1A. Drag TIGER5.MOV to the Timeline and position it on Video 1B at 00:00:03:15.

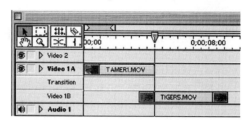

3. As you can see, TAMER1.MOV is too long for this production and must be trimmed. Drag the Edit Line to 00:00:04:15. Position the cursor at the end of TAMER1.MOV. The pointer changes to a two-sided marker. Drag the end of TAMER1.MOV until it snaps to the Edit Line.

4. Drag TAMER2.MOV to Video 1A of the Timeline window at 00:00:07:03. Drag TIGER1.MOV to Video 1B of the Timeline window at 00:00:9:08.

5. TIGER5.MOV also needs to be trimmed. Drag the Edit Line to 00:00:07:20, positioning the cursor at the end of TIGER5.MOV. When the pointer changes to a two-sided marker, drag the end of TIGER5.MOV until it snaps to the Edit Line.

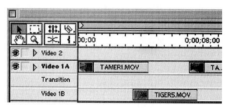

6. Position the next clips as follows in the Timeline window. Note carefully on which track they should be placed and the exact position.

   TAMER3.MOV on Video 1A at 00:00:14:27
   TIGER3.MOV on Video 1B at 00:00:17:10
   TAMER4.MOV on Video 1A at 00:00:20:17
   TIGER6.MOV on Video 1B at 00:00:22:16
   TAMER6.MOV on Video 1A at 00:00:26:00
   TIGER7.MOV on Video 1B at 00:00:28:11

7. TIGER7.MOV needs trimming. Position the Edit Line at 00:00:33:06. Drag the right corner of TIGER7.MOV until it snaps to the Edit Line. Drag TAMER5.MOV on Video 1A of the Timeline window at 00:00:32:07, and TIGER4.MOV on Video 1B at 00:00:35:13. Trim about one second off the end of TIGER4.MOV.

8. Position AUDIO_B.AIF on Audio 1 of the Timeline window it at the beginning of the production, directly under TAMER1.MOV.

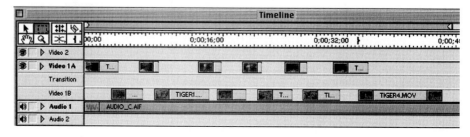

9. Make sure the Work Area bar is extended to the end of the production. Save your project as "THETIGER.PPJ" to your **Work in Progress** folder.

10. Render the production so that you can see how it looks so far. You should see our fearless animal trainer attempting to tame a tiger, as music plays in the background.

Add and Preview Transitions

1. From the Dissolve folder, drag the Cross Dissolve transition to the Transition track. It snaps into position in the overlap of TAMER1.MOV and TIGER5.MOV.

2. Select and drag another copy of the Cross Dissolve transition to the Transition track. It snaps into position in the overlap of TIGER5.MOV and TAMER2.MOV.

3. Render the production and watch our fearless tiger tamer, squaring off against the beast as transitions occur for the first couple of video clips.

4. Drag the Cross Dissolve transition to the overlap of TAMER2.MOV and TIGER1.MOV, and save your production again. (Although the production plays, the file has not been saved in its latest version.)

5. Now add the remaining transitions, positioned in the overlaps of shots as indicated in the list below:

   Dissolve folder>Cross Dissolve transition to TIGER1.MOV and TAMER3.MOV
   Stretch folder>Funnel transition to TAMER3.MOV and TIGER3.MOV
   Dissolve folder>Cross Dissolve transition to TIGER3.MOV and TAMER4.MOV
   Dissolve folder>Cross Dissolve transition to TAMER4.MOV and TIGER6.MOV
   Dissolve folder>Cross Dissolve transition to TAMER6.MOV and TIGER6.MOV
   Dissolve folder>Additive Dissolve transition to TAMER5.MOV and TIGER7.MOV
   Zoom folder>Cross Zoom transition to the TAMER6.MOV and TIGER7.MOV
   Dissolve folder>Cross Dissolve transition to TAMER5.MOV and TIGER4.MOV

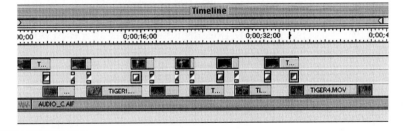

Fade the Audio Clips

1. Expand the audio box by clicking the triangle to the left of the Audio 1 track. The audio box expands to show the music.

2. Move the Edit Line to 00:00:44:10 and click. A small red handle appears.

3. Position the Edit Line at 00:00:45:07, and click at that point. A second handle appears. Drag that handle to the bottom of the audio area.

4. Position the Edit Line at 00:00:47:00. Click to place a third handle. Drag this handle to the bottom of the audio area to match the placement of the last handle. Trim off the additional music.

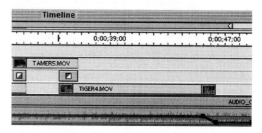

5. Collapse the audio box by clicking on the triangle to the left of Audio 1.

Create the First Titles

1. Select File>New>Title to display the Title Generator dialog box.

2. We need to ensure that the Title Generator is the same size as the rest of the production. Click on the Untitled title window to make it active. Select Window>Window Options>Title Window Options. Set the Drawing size to 240 ∞ 180, and check the NTSC-Safe Colors box. The Background should be set to white. If the options on your computer are different, make any necessary changes, and then click OK.

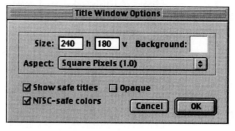

3. With the Type tool active, select a font from the Title menu. Click on the page. The blinking I-beam appears, indicating that you are ready to enter text. Type the following, pressing Return/Enter after each word:

How
To
[Leave this line blank]
A
Tiger

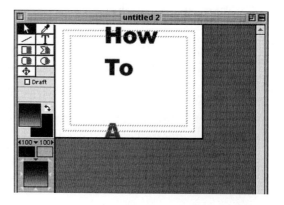

\Fade-ins and fade-outs give a more professional presentation to your production.

4. The words do not fit properly on the page. Choose Title>Leading>Less Leading, and watch the words move a little closer together. Repeat the process, selecting Less Leading as many times as necessary until the type sits comfortably on the page.

5. Let's replace any leftover color with a new color created for this project. Click on the center of the Object Color palette (the main color palette at the left). The Color Picker box appears.

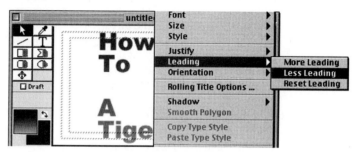

6. Set Red: 189, Green: 0, Blue: 7, and click OK. Your title now is bright red.

7. The words, however, still don't fit correctly. From the Title menu, select a point size that will increase the type size to fill the screen (try 36 points), and click OK.

8. Move the type to the right side of the screen by selecting Type>Justify>Right. Add a dark red drop shadow on the type. Create a dark red that complements the bright red you selected for the lettering above.

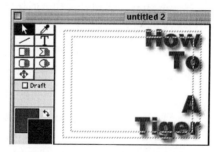

9. When you have completed working with the text, save the title as "TITLE1C.PTL" to your **Work in Progress** folder. Close the Title Generator window.

10. TITLE1C.PTL is now in the Project C folder (with your video clips) in the Project window. Save the project again.

11. Create the second part of this title by selecting File>New>New Title. With the Type tool selected, click on the screen in the approximate area of the blank line you created in the first title. Select the same font as in step #3. You will again see a blinking I-beam. Type the word "Tame".

12. The same red color should be available to you. You may still have the shadow color as the active color. Click on the Object Color box to make it active. (If your color has changed, click on the center of the main color palette at the left. When the Color Picker appears, set Red: 189, Green: 0, Blue: 7, and click OK.)

13. The words should already be the correct size. If not, select 36 points, and click OK.

14. Move the type to the right side of the screen by choosing Title>Justify>Right.

15. The type should already have a drop shadow. If not, place a drop shadow on it. Make the shadow the same dark red as the rest of the type.

16. When you have completed working the text, as before save the title as "TITLE2C.PTL" to your **Work in Progress** folder. Close the Title window.

17. TITLE2C.PTL should now be in the **Project C** folder in the Project window.

Save this project again.

Apply Transparency Settings to the Titles

Now you'll create the special effect that you observed when you previewed the project. The main part of the title appears first, followed slightly later by the second part.

1. Drag TITLE1C.PTL to the Timeline window, position it at the beginning of Video 2 and click on the title to highlight it. Select Clip>Video Option>Transparency.

2. The Transparency Settings dialog box appears with TITLE1C.PTL in the Samples box. Double-check that Key Type is set to White Alpha Matte. Click OK.

3. Click on TITLE1C.PTL on the Timeline. Choose Clip>Duration. Type 00:00:02:00, and click OK. Your credit expands to fill two seconds.

4. You need an additional video track to complete the effect. Hold down the mouse button with your cursor over the top, right triangle on the Timeline, bringing up the Timeline window Options menu. Select Track Options. In the Track Options dialog box, click the Add button to add one video track. Click OK to return to the Main menu, and click OK again. A new video track, Video 3, is available on the Timeline above Video 2.

5. Drag TITLE2C.PTL to the Timeline window, and position it on Video 3 at 00:00:01:10. Click to highlight it, and choose Clip>Video Options>Transparency.

6. The Transparency Settings dialog box appears with TITLE2C.PTL in the Samples box. Double-check that Key Type is set to White Alpha Matte. If it is not, change it, and click OK to close the dialog box.

7. Click to select TITLE2C.PTL on the Timeline. Select Clip>Duration, and type 00:00:02:05. Click OK, and your credit expands to fill just over two seconds.

Use the Motion Controls to Complete the Special Effect

1. With TITLE1C.PTL highlighted, choose Clip>Video Options>Motion. The Motion Settings dialog box appears.

2. Your title begins to move in from the left. You will make the title pause on the screen when it hits the center mark. Click on the move line at about the center point and watch a tiny white square appear.

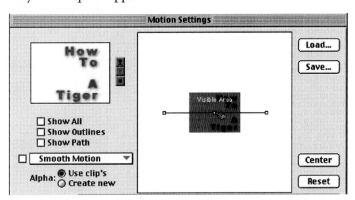

3. Type 30 in the Delay box, at the bottom of the dialog box. Click on the tiny white box you just created. The type will move onto the screen and then pause for a moment before traveling off to the right. Click OK to leave this dialog box.

4. Highlight TITLE1C.PTL. Choose Clip>Video Options>Motion. The Motion Settings dialog box appears.

5. Your title again begins to move in from the left. You will make the title pause on the screen when it hits the center mark.

   Click on the move line at about the center point; a tiny white square appears.

6. Type 30 in the Delay box. Click on the tiny white box you just created. The type now moves onto the screen and then pauses for a moment before traveling off to the right. Click OK to leave this dialog box.

7. Save and render the file to look at the results.

Create the Remaining Titles

Now you will create four additional titles that inform the viewer of the proper way to tame the beast.

1. Select File>New>Title to display the Title Generator dialog box. With the Type tool, select a font from the Title menu. When you see a blinking I-beam, type the following text with a Return/Enter after each word:

   Step 1:
   [Leave a blank line here]
   Show Him Who's Boss!

2. Replace any leftover color with a new color for this project by clicking on the center of the Object Color palette. (This is the.)

3. In the Color Picket, set Red: 187, Green: 0, Blue: 21. Click OK and notice that your title is now a new bright red color.

4. To resize the type to fit the available space, select a point size that enlarges it enough to fill the screen, and click OK.

5. Center the type, and then choose Type>Center>Vertically followed by Type>Center>Horizontally.

6. Place a drop shadow on the type. Make the shadow a dark red that complements the bright red you have used on the lettering. It can be the same red that you used previously, if you like.

7. When you have finished working with the text, save the title as "TITLE3C.PTL" to your **Work in Progress** folder. Once it is saved, your title should transfer to the Project menu. Close the Title window.

8. TITLE1C.PTL, TITLE2C.PTL and TITLE3C.PTL are now all in the Project C folder in the Project window along with your other title and video clips. Update your project by saving the file once again.

9. Place TITLE2B.PTL on the Timeline at 00:00:04:16. With the text highlighted, choose Clip>Duration, and set the duration to 00:00:01:26.

10. Continue to create the titles for the rest of your production. (Go back and preview the completed project from Getting Started, if you need to remind yourself about how they will appear.)

    Show No Fear

    Step 2: When All Else Fails...

    RUN...

Finalize Effects & Tighten Up the Production

1. We want our frightened tamer to run back and forth. Click on TAMER5.MOV. Select Window>Show Video Effects.

2. Select Windows>Show Video Effects. Open the Transform folder, and drag a copy of Horizontal Flip onto TAMER5.MOV.

3. Save and render the file to see the latest results.

4. Double-check the final results. You will probably notice a couple of spots where the video needs to be trimmed a bit more. Move through the production, and continue to tighten it up until you are satisfied with the results. Save the file again.

Export as a QuickTime Movie

1. Select File>Export Timeline>Movie. Type "TIGERFIN.MOV" as the project name, and click the Settings button. Double-check that the Export Audio box is selected, and then click the Next button.

2. Check that the Frame Size is set to 240 ∞ 180 and the Compressor is set to Video. You will only need to change the compressor if you need the project to be cross-platform. If the project will be running on both Windows and Macintosh, select Cinepak instead. Set Frame Rate: 15, and Quality: 100 %.

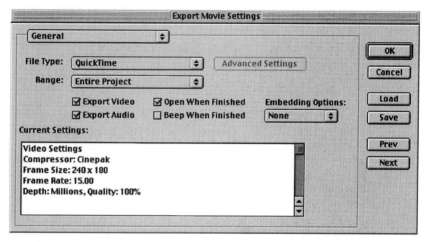

3. Click the Next button. In the Audio Settings area, select 22050kHz, 16-bit Mono, and Uncompressed.

4. Click OK to return to the General area of the Export dialog box. Double-check where your file is about to be saved. Click OK. It will take several minutes to complete the full rendering process.

   Your project is now a self-contained piece. Delete all of the other files related to this project, as you no longer require them.

Your company has succeeded. Local school children now can learn about how to handle hazards safely, a message that will please both parents and civic leaders while entertaining the children as they learn.

Notes:

Project D: The Gold Rush

A long-term client, the ATAA (Associated Travel Agents of America), has retained your company to create a series of multimedia CDs for member travel agencies to use to promote desirable summer vacation destinations. Customers can use terminals in the travel agent's waiting room to explore vacation possibilities that the agent can then book. Your team is developing a CD about vacation possibilities in California and Alaska, including a cruise to Alaska with a stop at Skagway, Alaska. To promote this scenic area and generate interest in the cruise, you are creating a movie that tells a little about the history of the Gold Rush, with the look of an "authentic" old movie, and takes you on a train journey along the Yukon Trail.

You will create a title that explains the video and incorporate a variety of shots that show the magnificent countryside.

Getting Started

1. Open Premiere and accept the default settings. Be certain that you have selected 240 × 180. Select File>Import>Folder. When the dialog box appears, select the **RF-Premiere>Project D** folder, and press Choose. Double-click **FINAL_D.MOV** to open the file.

2. Click the Play button to preview your finished project. Close the FINAL_D.MOV clip window, but leave everything else open to begin the project.

Place, Stretch and Trim Clips

1. Open Folder D in Bin 1 of the Project window. You will place the shots contained in this folder alternately on tracks Video 1A and 1B.

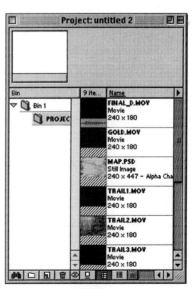

2. Drag GOLD.MOV to the Timeline window at the beginning of Video 1B. Drag MAP.PSD to the Timeline window on Video 1A at 00:00:02:13.

3. MAP.PSD runs five seconds on the Timeline, too short for this production. Drag the right edge of the still image, stretching it out to 00:00:31:18.

4. Drag TRAIN.AIF to Audio 1. It is longer than MAP.PSD. Fade the music at 00:00:31:00.

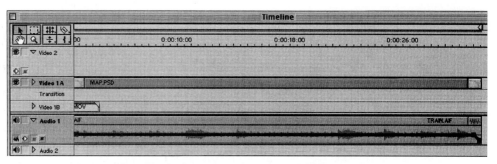

5. Drag TRAIL1.MOV to the Timeline window on Video 2 at 00:00:06:25. Drag TRAIL2.MOV to the Timeline window on Video 2 next to TRAIL1.MOV at 00:00:13:08. It stretches out to 14.10 seconds, which is too long for this production.

6. Double-click to open the TRAIL2.MOV clip window. Drag the left Set location shuttle to the right until it reads 00:00:03:04. Click the Mark Out icon. Click the Apply button. The clip shortens on the Timeline. Move it back to 00:00:13:08. Close the clip window.

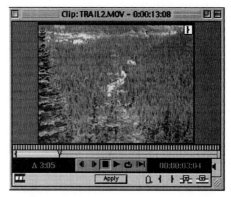

7. Drag TRAIL3.MOV to the Timeline window on Video 2 at 00:00:18:01. Drag TRAIL4.MOV to the Timeline window on Video 2 at 00:00:22:12.

8. Drag TRAIL5.MOV to the Timeline window on Video 2 at 00:00:27:17.

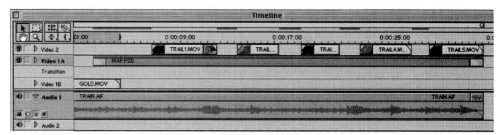

9. Save your project as "FINAL-D.PPJ" to your **Work in Progress** folder.

10. Render the production so that you can see how it looks so far. You should see some folks panning for gold, a map and train shots as music plays in the background. Now let's create some special effects.

Create the Effect of an Old Movie

1. GOLD.MOV is on the Timeline at the beginning of Video 1B. If it is not already visible, open the Video Effects palette. From the QuickTime folder, drag QuickTime Effects onto GOLD.MOV. The Select Effects dialog box appears.

2. Select Film Noise, accept the defaults as they appear in the program, and click OK.

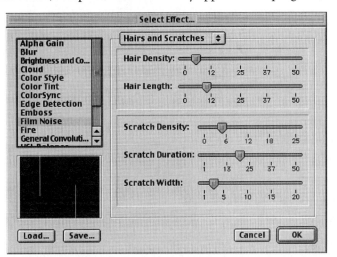

3. Close the QuickTime folder. From the Image Control folder, drag Tint onto GOLD.MOV. The Effect Controls palette appears. Notice that it shows that the QuickTime and Tint effects have both been placed on GOLD.MOV.

4. Click the Map Black Color Picker, and set Red: 255, Green: 120, Blue: 25, and click OK. Click the Map White Color Picker, and set Red: 255, Green: 262, Blue: 210, and again click OK. In the Edit Amount to Tint dialog box, set Value: 30%, and click OK.

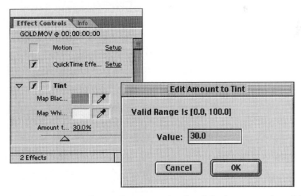

5. Render the production, and watch a seemingly old-time movie of folks panning for gold. Save your production again.

Use Transparency to Create Superimposition Effect

1. Click on TRAIL1.MOV. Expand the Video 2 track on the Timeline. Select Clip>Video Options>Transparency. A dialog box appears. Change the Key Type from None to Multiply, and click OK.

2. We want this clip to fade in and fade out. Click and create a set of two red rubberband handles. Pull the handles to create the fade in and fade out for TRAIL1.MOV. Render the production, and watch the train fade in, play and fade out, superimposed on the map.

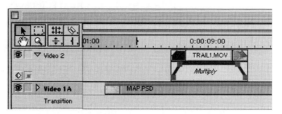

3. Add the Multiply Transparency effect to TRAIL2.MOV, TRAIL3.MOV and TRAIL4.MOV. Fade in TRAIL5.MOV, but don't fade the clip out. (Do not apply the Transparency filter to this clip.) Render these new additions to the production. Each of the video clips will fade in over the map and fade out, except the last clip.

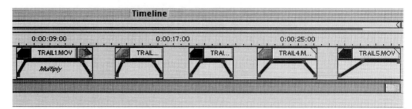

4. Save and render these newest changes.

Simulate Movement on a Still Image by an Image Pan

1. Expand the Timeline. From the Video Effects palette Transform folder, drag Image Pan onto MAP.PSD. The Effect Controls palette appears. Click Enable Keyframing. Select the first keyframe on the Timeline under MAP.PSD. Click Set-up in the Effect Controls palette. The Image Pan Settings dialog box appears.

2. Let's select a starting point for the pan. We want the pan to move from bottom to top. Hold the Option/Alt key and pull the top-right handle downward. The bounding box around the image snaps into place to keep the 3 × 4-aspect ratio of the project. Click OK.

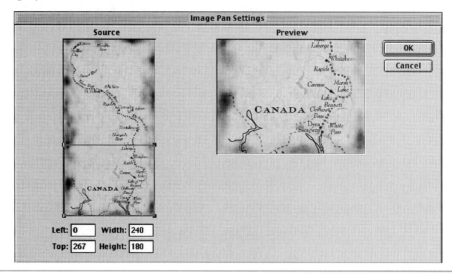

3. Let's complete the second half of the effect. Select the second keyframe, on the Timeline under MAP.PSD at the end of the clip. Click Set-up in the Effect Controls palette. The Image Pan Settings dialog box will appear once again. Let's select an ending point for the pan. Hold the Option/Alt key, and pull the bottom-right handle upward. The bounding box around the image snaps into place to keep the 3 × 4-aspect ratio of the project. Click OK.

4. Save and render these newest changes. It will take a couple of minutes for the render to take place, but you will be well rewarded for your patience!

Create the Opening Title

Now we'll create the opening title.

1. Select File>New>Title to display the Title Generator dialog box.

2. Click on the untitled titled window to activate it. Select Window>Window Options>Title Window Options. Set Size H: 240 V: 180, NTSC-safe Colors: checked, Background: white, and click OK.

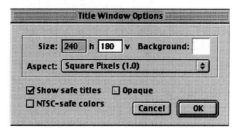

3. Select the Type tool. Choose a font from the Title menu, and click on the drawing surface. When you see a blinking I-beam, indicating that you are ready to enter in some text, type the following (pressing Return/Enter following each):

The
Gold Rush

With the Selection tool, drag the handles to pull the text into a proper position on the page.

4. Now we'll replace the current color with a new gradient color. Click on the Gradient Start color. The Color Picker appears.

5. Set Red: 162, Green: 36, Blue: 0, and click OK. Your title is now orange.

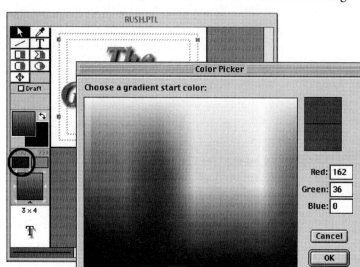

6. Click on the Gradient End color. The Color Picker again appears. Set Red: 255, Green: 145, Blue: 62, and click OK. Your title now has a light-to-dark orange gradient. Change the direction of the gradient by clicking the bottom Transparency Gradient Direction triangle (located at about 6 o'clock).

7. The words will not fit correctly unless we alter them. From the Title menu, select a point size that will enlarge the type enough to fill the screen.

8. Add a drop shadow to the type. Make the shadow a dark orange that will complement the gradient you have selected for the lettering. When you have finished working with the text, save the title as "RUSH.PTL" to your **Work in Progress** folder.

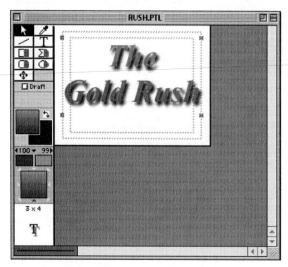

9. Once it is saved, the file should automatically appear in the Project window. (If not, choose File>Import>File.) Close the RUSH.PTL Title window.

10. Save this file again.

Use Alpha Channels and Opacity to Generate Fades

The title graphic starts abruptly and drops out just as rapidly at the end. We actually want the graphic to fade in and fade out more subtly. We also want to ensure that the title is superimposed on the video of the people panning for gold. We'll use Premiere's built-in controls to direct the opacity and effect of the graphic.

1. Drag RUSH.PTL to the Timeline window at the beginning of Video 2, and click to highlight it. Select Clip>Video Options>Transparency.

2. When the Transparency Settings dialog box appears, RUSH.PTL is displayed in the Samples box. Double-check that Key Type is set to White Alpha Matte.) If it is not, change the option from None to White Alpha Matte.) Click OK to close the Transparency Settings dialog box.

It generally takes three to five seconds for viewers to read a credit.

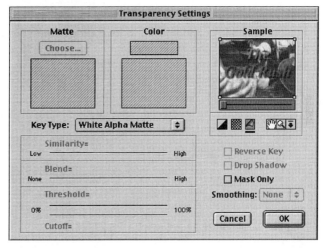

3. Your credit currently runs five seconds. If it does not, expand the clip until it does.

4. Expand the Video 2 track on the Timeline to show the opacity levels for RUSH.PTL.

5. You should see a thin red line at the top of this window, indicating that the title at 100% opacity. At the far left of the line, notice a red handle. Move the cursor slightly to the right, and click again on the red line. A second handle appears.

6. Position the cursor over the far-left handle and drag it down to the bottom of the window. This will be the fade-in for the title. At the far right of the red line, click once. A third handle appears. Move the cursor slightly to the left, and click again on the red line. A fourth handle appears.

The keyboard shortcut to display the Transparency Settings dialog box is Command/Control-G.

7. Position the cursor over the far-right handle, and drag it to the bottom of the window. This will be the fade-out for the title. Collapse this box.

8. Save and render the production. Your title fades in and fades out as the video plays.

Add a Transition

As you may have noticed, this "old-time" movie needs an "old-time" transition. Let's add one now.

1. From the Transitions palette Page Peel folder, drag Page Peel onto the Transitions track on the Timeline. It should snap into place between GOLD.MOV and MAP.PSD.

2. On the Timeline, double-click the Page Peel transition. A dialog box appears. Let's make the page peel upward diagonally, from lower right to upper left. Click the directional red arrow at the lower-right corner (about 5 o'clock). Check to ensure that Forward ("F") is selected. Click OK.

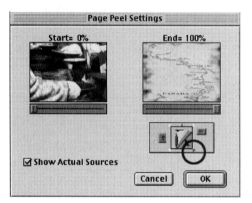

3. Save and render this file.

Export as a QuickTime Movie

1. Select File>Export Timeline>Movie. Name the movie "GOLDRUSH.MOV", and click Settings. Set Export Audio: checked as there is audio in this project.

2. The Frame Size should be set to 240 × 180. If necessary, correct those numbers. The Compressor is set to Video. Change this if you need the project to be cross-platform. If the project will be running on both Windows and Macintosh, select Cinepak. Set Frame Rate: 15, and Quality: 80%.

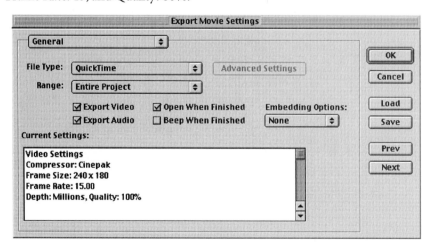

Cinepak takes longer to render, but it's the only way to create a truly cross-platform project.

3. Click the Next button. In the Audio settings area, select 22050kHz, 16-bit Mono, and Uncompressed to keep your file size small.

4. Click OK to return to the main area of the Export dialog box. Double-check where your file is about to be saved, and click Save. It will take several minutes to complete the rendering process. Now that your project is a self-contained piece, you can delete all of the other files related to this project if you do not wish to further edit the project.

The client, the ATAA, and your team will be very pleased with your production. Now customers can get a taste of the past, prompting them to book future vacations to the spot you featured in your new travel video.

Notes:

Achromatic

By definition, having no color, therefore, completely black, white or some shade of gray.

Acrobat

This program, by Adobe Systems, Inc., allows the conversion of any document from any Macintosh or Windows application to PDF format, which retains the graphics, color and typography of the original document. It is widely used for distributing documents online.

Actor

A person who performs or plays a role, typically in a dramatic presentation or commercial production.

Adaptive Palette

A sampling of colors taken from an image and used in a special compression process, usually to prepare images for the World Wide Web.

Additive Color Process

The process of mixing red, green and blue light to achieve a wide range of colors, as on a color-television screen.

Adjacent Color

An adjoining color. Since the eye responds to strong adjoining color, its perception of a particular color is affected by any nearby colors. This means that a color with adjacent colors may look different than it does in isolation.

Algorithm

A specific sequence of mathematical steps to process data. A portion of a computer program that calculates a specific result.

Alpha Channel

A fourth channel in an RGB image that defines what parts of the image are transparent or semitransparent. Programs, such as Adobe Illustrator, Photoshop and Premiere, use alpha channels to specify transparent regions in an image. If a Photoshop file uses an alpha channel for transparency, Premiere finds and reads it.

Analog

A signal that fluctuates exactly like the original, both in audio and video.

Archival storage

The process of storing data in a totally secure and safe manner. Archiving differs from backup in that it's meant to be used to restore entire systems or networks, rather than providing quick and easy access to specific files or folders.

Art

Illustrations and photographs in general. All matter other than text that appears in a mechanical.

Artifact

By definition, something that is artificial or not meant to be there. An artifact can be a blemish or dust spot on a piece of film, or unsightly pixels in a digital image.

Aspect Ratio

1. In video, the width-to-height proportions of an image. 2. For the television screen and all television pictures: four units wide by three units high.

ATM (Adobe Type Manager)

A utility program which causes fonts to appear smooth on screen at any point size. It's also used to manage font libraries.

Back Light

Lighting from behind the subject and opposite the camera.

Backing Up

The process of making copies of current work or work in progress as a safety measure against file corruption, drive or system failure, or accidental deletion. Backing up work in progress differs from creating an archive (see Archiving) for long-term storage or system restoration.

Audio

The electronic reproduction of audible sound.

Bin

Similar to folders on a hard drive. A bin is used for organizing files within a project.

Bit (Binary Digit)

A computer's smallest unit of information. Bits can have only two values: 0 or 1. This number can represent the black-and-white (1-bit) pixel values in a line-art image. In combination with other bits, it can represent 16 tones or colors (4-bit), 256 tones or colors (8-bit), 16.8 million colors (24-bit), or a billion colors (30-bit). These numbers derive from counting all the possible combinations (permutations) of 0 or 1 settings of each bit: $2 \times 2 \times 2 = 16$ colors; $2 \times 2 \times 2 \times 2 \times 2 \times 2 \times 2 \times 2 = 256$ colors; $2 \times 2 = 16.8$ million colors.

Bitmap image

An image constructed from individual dots or pixels set to a grid-like mosaic. Each pixel can be represented by more than one bit. A 1-bit image is black and white because each bit can have only two values (for example, 0 for white and 1 for black). For 256 colors, each pixel needs eight bits (2^8). A 24-bit image refers to an image with 24 bits per pixel (2^{24}), so it may contain as many as 16,777,216 colors. Because the file must contain information about the color and position of each pixel, the disk space needed for bitmap images is usually quite significant.

Bitmapped

Forming an image by a grid of pixels whose curved edges have discrete steps because of the approximation of the curve by a finite number of pixels.

Black

The absence of color; an ink that absorbs all wavelengths of light.

Bleeding

1. A key whose edges are not sharp and which let the background show through.

Blocking

Carefully worked-out movement and actions by the talent and for all mobile television equipment.

Boom

1. A type of microphone or video support. 2. To move the camera via the boom of the camera crane.

Brightness

1. A measure of the amount of light reflected from a surface. 2. A paper property, defined as the percentage reflection of 457-nanometer (nm) radiation. 3. The intensity of a light source. 4. The overall percentage of lightness in an image.

Byte

A unit of measure equal to eight bits (decimal 256) of digital information, sufficient to represent one text character. The standard unit measure of file size. (See also Megabyte, Kilobyte, and Gigabyte).

Cable Television

Distribution device for broadcast signals via coaxial or fiber-optic cable.

Calibration

Making adjustments to a color monitor and other hardware and software to make the monitor represent as closely as possible the colors of the final production.

Camcorder

A small portable camera with a built in video tape recorder.

Camera

1. A lighttight photographic device that records the image of an object formed when light rays pass through an aperture and fall on a flat, photosensitive surface. 2. The overall name for the camera head, which is made up of the lens, the main imaging device, electronic accessories and the viewfinder.

Camera Graphics

Graphics specifically designed for the television camera.

Cassette

A video or audiotape recording or playback device that uses tape cassettes.

Cause-to-effect Model

The concept of moving an idea from a production to the effect it has on the viewer.

CD-ROM

A device used to store approximately 600 MB of data. Files are permanently stored on the device and can be copied to a disk but not altered directly. ROM stands for Read-Only Memory. Equipment is now available on the consumer market for copying computer files to blank CD-ROMs..

Chroma Keying

Special key effect that uses color (usually blue or green) for the background. This color is replaced by another picture during the key. (See Color Key.)

Clip

A small piece of video footage.

Cloning

Duplication of pixels from one part of an image to another.

Close-up (CU)

The overall name for viewing an object at close range, framed tightly.

Color Bars

A color standard used by the television industry for the alignment of camera and videotape recordings.

Color Temperature

Relative to light, the red or blue cast, as measured in Kelvin degrees. The norm for TV lighting is 3,200°K, and for outdoors is 5,600°K.

Color Balance

The combination of yellow, magenta and cyan needed to produce a neutral gray. Determined through a gray balance analysis.

Color Cast

The modification of a hue by the addition of a trace of another hue, such as yellowish green, pinkish blue, etc. Normally, an unwanted effect that can be corrected.

Color Correction

The process of removing casts or unwanted tints in a scanned image, in an effort to improve the appearance of the scan or to correct obvious deficiencies, such as green skies or yellowish skin tones.

Color Gamut

The range of colors that can be formed by all possible combinations of the colorants of a given reproduction system, such as colors that can be displayed on television.

Color Key

The process of electronically replacing a color, such as green or blue, with a graphic or live video. This allows one piece of video to be keyed or superimposed upon another.

Color Model

A system for describing color, such as RGB, HLS, CIELAB or CMYK.

Color Picker

A function within a graphics application that assists in selecting or setting a color.

Color Space

Because a color must be represented by three basic characteristics, depending on the color model, the color space is a three-dimensional coordinate system in which any color can be represented as a point.

Color Temperature

The temperature, in degrees Kelvin, to which a blackbody would have to be heated to produce a certain color radiation. (A *blackbody* is an ideal body or surface that completely absorbs or radiates energy.) The graphic arts viewing standard is 5,000 K. (The degree symbol is not used in the Kelvin scale.) The higher the color temperature, the bluer the light.

Colorimeter

An optical measuring instrument designed to measure and quantify color. It is often used to match digital image values to those of cloth and other physical samples.

Compression

A digital technique used to reduce the size of a file by analyzing occurrences of similar data. Compressed files occupy less physical space, and their use improves digital transmission speeds. Compression can sometimes result in a loss of image quality and/or resolution.

Compression Utility

A software program that reduces a file's size for storage on a disk. If a compressed file is too large to fit onto a single disk, the compression utility copies it onto multiple disks.

Continuity Editing

The preserving of visual continuity from one shot to the next.

Contrast

The relationship and degree of difference between the dark and light areas of an image.

Control Track

The area of a videotape used for recording the synchronization information. It provides a reference point for the editor by giving frame counts.

Copyright

Ownership of a work by the originator, such as an author, publisher, artist or photographer. The right of copyright permits the originator of material to prevent its use without express permission or acknowledgment of the originator. Copyright may be sold, transferred or given up contractually.

Cropping

The elimination of parts of a photograph or other original that are not required to be printed.

CPU

Stands for Central Processing Unit, the main part of a computer that routes all of the system information.

Crane

A camera dolly that resembles an actual crane in appearance and operation. The crane can lift the camera from just off the video floor to more than 10 feet above.

Cue

Signal for various production activities or to select a section of a videotape.

Cue Card

A large hand-lettered card that contains copy. It is usually held next to the camera lens to ensure easy reading.

Cursor

A small symbol that can be moved around a video screen. Used to indicate position where data will be entered or an action taken.

Default

A specification for a mode of computer operation that occurs if no other is selected. The default font size might be 12 point, or a default color for an object might be white with a black border.

Demographics

Audience research factors concerned with such items as age, sex, marital status and income.

Depth of Field

The area in which all objects located a different distances from the camera all appear in focus. Depth of field depends heavily on the lens type selected.

Densitometer

An electronic instrument used to measure optical density. Reflective (for paper) and transmissive (for film).

Desktop

1. The area on a monitor screen on which the icons appear, before an application is launched. 2. A reference to the size of computer equipment (system unit, monitor, printer) that can fit on a normal desk, thus, desktop publishing.

Diffused Light

Light that illuminates a relatively large area and creates soft shadows without the use of a key light.

Digital

The use of a series of discrete electronic pulses to represent data. In digital imaging systems, 256 steps (8 bits, or 1 byte) are normally used to characterize the gray scale or the properties of one color. For text, see ASCII.

Digital Camera

A camera which produces images directly into an electronic file format for transfer to a computer.

Dimmer

A device that controls the intensity of light.

Dingbat

1. A font character that displays a picture instead of a letter, number or punctuation mark. There are entire font families of pictographic dingbats. Dingbats exist for everything from the airplanes that represent airports on a map, to telephones, stars, balloons and more. 2. Also, a printer's typographical ornament.

Directional Light

Light that illuminates a relatively small area with a strong light beam. Creates harsh, well defined light areas.

Dissolve

A gradual transition from shot to shot, in which the two images overlap.

Dolly

1. Camera movement that using both the camera and the base of the camera, cause the entire unit to move in or out of a shot. 2. The portable platform which supports the camera equipment and permits such movement.

DPI (Dots Per Inch)

The measurement of resolution for page printers, phototypesetting machines and graphics screens. Currently graphics screens use resolutions of 72 to 96 dpi, standard desktop laser printers work at 600 dpi.

Drop

Large, painted piece of canvas used for scenery backing.

Drop Shadow

A duplicate of a graphic element or type placed behind and slightly offset from it, giving the effect of a shadow.

Draw-type pictures

Pictures created from a series of instructions that tell the computer to draw lines, curves, rectangles and other objects. Also called "object-oriented images" or "vector graphics." See Bitmap Image.

Dry Run

Rehearsal without equipment during which the basic actions of the talent are worked out.

Dub

A duplication of a videotape. Digital dubbing produces copies almost identical to that of the original.

Editing

The selection and assembly of shots in a logical sequence.

Element

The smallest unit of a graphic, or a component of a page layout or design. Any object, text block, or graphic might be referred to as an element of the design.

ENG

Stands for electronic news gathering. The use of portable cameras to cover stories that are not planned.

EPS

Acronym for encapsulated PostScript, a single-page PostScript file that contains grayscale or color information and can be imported into many electronic layout and design applications.

Essential Area

The section of the television picture that contains the most needed information. It is based on the average consumer television.

Establishing Shot

Extreme long shot. Used to establish location or place.

Export

To save a file generated in one application into a format that is readable in another.

Extension

1. A modular software program that extends or expands the functions of a larger program. A folder of Extensions is found in the Macintosh System Folder. 2. A suffix used on a file name to indicate the application in which the file was created.

Fade

The gradual appearance (or disappearance) of a picture to or from black.

Feed

Signal transmission from one program source to another, such as a network feed or a remote feed.

Field Log

A record of each take during the videotaping session.

File

A specific collection of information stored on the computer disk separately from all other information. Can be randomly accessed by the computer.

Fill Light

Additional light on the opposite side of the camera from the key light to illuminate shadow areas and thereby reduce hard shadows.

Filter

In image-editing applications, a small program that creates a special effect or performs some other function within an image.

Flat Color

Color that lacks contrast or tonal variation. Also, flat tint.

Flatbed Scanner

A scanner on which the original is mounted on a flat scanning glass. See Scanner.

Floor Plan

A plan of the studio floor, showing the walls, the main doors and the location of the control room, with the lighting grid superimposed over it.

Flow Chart

A block diagram representing the major steps of an event. It is used by computer programmers to translate events into computer logic.

Folder

The digital equivalent of a paper file folder, used to organize files in the Macintosh and Windows operating systems. The icon of a folder looks like a paper file folder. Double-clicking it opens it to reveal the files stored inside.

Font

A font is the complete collection of all the characters (numbers, uppercase and lowercase letters and, in some cases, small caps and symbols) of a given typeface in a specific style; for example, Helvetica Bold.

Font Substitution

A process in which Windows or your printer uses a font similar to the one you used in your publication to display or print your publication. Although the substitute font may be similar to the original font, your publication will not look exactly as you intended; line breaks, column breaks or page breaks may fall differently, which can affect the entire look and feel of the publication.

Format

Type of television script indicating the major programming steps. Generally contains a fully scripted show opening and closing. Example: the nightly news.

Frame

In desktop publishing — 1. An area or block into which text or graphics can be placed. 2. A border on such an area.

Freeze-Frame

Continuous replaying of a single frame, which is perceived as a still shot.

f-stop

The calibration on the lens indicating the aperture or diaphragm opening. Controls the amount of light that can pass through the lens.

Gain

1. In audio, level of amplification for audio signals. 2. In video, electronic amplification of the video signal. 3. To ride the gain means to keep the levels at a proper level.

Gamma

A measure of the contrast, or range of tonal variation of the midtones in a photographic image.

Gamma Correction

1. Adjusting the contrast of the midtones in an image. 2. Calibrating a monitor so that midtones are correctly displayed on screen.

Gang

Refers to changes made to multiple tracks simultaneously. For example, if you want to change the audio volume levels in tracks 1, 3 and 4 simultaneously, gang those three together.

GCR (Gray component replacement)

A technique for adding detail by reducing the amount of cyan, magenta and yellow in chromatic or colored areas, replacing them with black.

Generated Graphics

Graphic material that is generated and/or manipulated by a computer and used directly on the air or stored for use at a later time.

GIF (Graphics Interchange Format)

A popular graphics format for online clip art and drawn graphics. Graphics in this format look good at low resolution. See JPEG.

GIF, Animated

A series of GIF graphics that functions like a film loop, giving the appearance of animation. See GIF.

Gigabyte

One billion (1,073,741,824) bytes (230) or 1,048,576 kilobytes.

Global Preferences

Preference settings which affect all newly created files within an application.

Gradient fill

See Graduated fill.

Graduated Fill

An area in which two colors (or shades of gray or the same color) are blended to create a gradual change from one to the other. Graduated fills are also known as blends, gradations, gradient fills and vignettes.

Graphics

All visuals specially prepared for the television screen, such as title cards, charts and graphs.

Gray Balance

The values for the yellow, magenta and cyan inks that are needed to produce a neutral gray when printed at a normal density.

Gray Component Replacement

See GCR

Grayscale

1. An image composed in grays ranging from black to white, usually using 256 different tones of gray. 2. A tint ramp used to measure and control the accuracy of screen percentages on press. 3. An accessory used to define neutral density in a photographic image.

Grid

A division of a page by horizontal and vertical guides into areas into which text or graphics may be placed accurately.

Group

To collect graphic elements together so that an operation may be applied to all of them simultaneously.

GUI

Acronym for Graphical User Interface, the basis of the Macintosh and Windows operating systems.

Hardware

The physical components of a computer and its auxiliary equipment.

Hard Drive

A rigid disk sealed inside an airtight transport mechanism that is the basic storage device in a computer. Information stored may be accessed more rapidly than on floppy disks and far greater amounts of data may be stored.

Headroom

The space left between the top of the head and the upper edge of the screen.

High-Definition Television (HDTV)

The use of special cameras and recording equipment for the production of high-quality pictures. The pictures have a higher resolution than regular television pictures. The aspect ratio of HDTV is 16 by 9.

Highlights

The lightest areas in a photograph or illustration.

HSL (Hue, Saturation, Luminosity)

A color model that defines color as it is displayed on a video or computer screen. See HSV.

HSV (Hue, Saturation, Value)

A color model based on three coordinates: hue, saturation and value (or luminance).

Hue

The wavelength of light of a color in its purest state (without adding white or black).

Icon

A small graphic symbol used on the screen to indicate files, folders or applications, and activated by clicking with the mouse or pointing device.

Insert Editing

Inserting shots in an existing recording without affecting shots on either side.

In the Can

A term borrowed from film, which referred to when the finished film was finally completed and stored in a storage can. Now means a finished television recording; the show is preserved and can be used any time.

Import

To bring a file generated within one application into another application.

Indexed Color Image

An image which uses a limited, predetermined number of colors; often used in Web images. See also GIF.

Intensity

Synonym for degree of color saturation.

Internet

An international network of computer networks, which links millions of commercial, educational, governmental and personal computers. See World Wide Web.

Internet Service Provider (ISP)

An organization that provides access to the Internet for such things as electronic mail, bulletin boards, chat rooms or use of the World Wide Web.

Intershot Movement

The movement that occurs during one shot regardless of length. Examples: a pan or tilt.

Jaggies

Visible steps in the curved edge of a graphic or text character that results from enlarging a bitmapped image.

JPG or JPEG (Joint Photographers Experts Group)

A compression algorithm that reduces the file size of bitmapped images, named for the Joint Photographic Experts Group, an industry organization that created the standard. JPEG is a "lossy" compression method, and image quality is reduced in direct proportion to the amount of compression. JPEG graphics produce better resolution for color photographics other than those in GIF format.

Jump Cut

Cutting between shots that are identical in subject yet slightly different in screen location. The subject seems to jump from one screen location to another for no apparent reason.

Justified Alignment

Straight left and right alignment of text — not ragged. Every line of text is the same width, creating even left and right margins.

Kelvin (K)

Unit of temperature measurement based on Celsius degrees, starting from absolute zero, which is equivalent to -273 Celsius (centigrade); used to indicate the color temperature of a light source.

Kerning

Moving a pair of letters closer together or farther apart, to achieve a better fit or appearance.

Key

1. Principal source of illumination. High- or low-key lighting. 2. Also an electronic effect; example: chroma key.

Kilobyte (K, KB)

1,024 (210) bytes, the nearest binary equivalent to decimal 1,000 bytes. Abbreviated and referred to as K.

Laser printer

A high-quality image printing system, using a laser beam to produce an image on a photosensitive drum. The image is transferred to paper by a conventional xerographic printing process. Current laser printers used for desktop publishing have a resolution of 600 dpi. Imagesetters are also laser printers, but with higher resolution and tight mechanical controls to produce final film separations for commercial printing.

Layout

The arrangement of text and graphics on a page, usually produced in the preliminary design stage.

Leading ("ledding")

Space added between lines of type. Usually measured in points or fractions of points. Named after the strips of lead which used to be inserted between lines of metal type. In specifying type, lines of 12-pt. type separated by a 14-pt. space is abbreviated "12/14," or "twelve over fourteen."

Left Alignment

Straight edge of text with a ragged or uneven right edge.

Lens

Optical device, essential for projecting an optical (light) image of a scene in front of the surface of the camera. Lenses comes in various fixed focal lengths or in variable focal lengths and with various aperture (iris) openings.

Letterspacing

The insertion or addition of white space between the letters of words.

Level

1. Audio: sound volume. 2. Video: signal strength measured in volts.

Library

In the computer world, a collection of files having a similar purpose or function.

Lightness

The property that distinguishes white from gray or black, and light from dark color tones on a surface.

Linear Editing

Nonrandom editing that uses tape-based systems.

Line Art

A drawing or piece of black-and-white artwork with no screens. Line art can be represented by a graphic file having only one-bit resolution.

Linking

An association, through software, of a graphic or text file on disk with its location in a document. That location may be represented by a placeholder rectangle, or a low-resolution copy of the graphic

Lip-sync

Synchronization of sound and lip movement.

Location Survey

Written assessment, usually in the form of a checklist, of the production requirements for a remote.

Log

The daily diary that tracks shots taken during a video shoot. Records the usefulness of the material.

Long Shot (LS)

Object seen from far away or framed very loosely.

Lossy

A data compression method characterized by the loss of some data.

Luminosity

The amount of light or brightness in an image. Part of the HLS color model.

Lux

European standard unit for measuring light intensity: 1 lux is the amount of 1 lumen (one candlepower of light).

M, MB (Megabyte)

One million (1,048,576) bytes (220) or 1,024 Kilobytes.

Macro

A set of keystrokes that is saved as a named computer file. Macros are used to perform repetitive tasks efficiently.

Medium

1. A physical carrier of data, such as a CD-ROM, video cassette or floppy disk. 2. A carrier of electronic data, such as fiber optic cable or electric wires.

Medium Shot

Object seen from a medium distance. Covers any framing between a long shot and a close-up.

Megabyte (MB)

A unit of measure of stored data equaling 1,024 kilobytes, or 1,048,576 bytes (1020).

Megahertz

An analog signal frequency of one million cycles per second, or a data rate of one million bits per second. Used in specifying computer CPU speed.

Menu

A list of choices of functions or items, such as fonts. In contemporary software design, there is often a fixed menu of basic functions at the top of the page that have pull-down menus associated with each fixed choice.

Midtones or Middletones

The tonal range between highlights and shadows.

Memory

The storage device in a computer. Its capacity is given in numbers of bytes. See RAM and Rom.

Microphone

A small, portable assembly for the pickup and conversion of sound into electric energy.

MIDI

Stands for musical instrument digital interface: a standardization device that allows various digital audio equipment and computers to interface.

Modem

An electronic device for converting digital data into analog audio signals and back again (MOdulator-DEModulator.) Primarily used for transmitting data between computers over analog (audio frequency) telephone lines.

Moiré

An interference pattern caused by the out-of-register overlap of two or more regular patterns such as dots or lines. In process-color printing, screen angles are selected to minimize this pattern.

Monochrome

An image or computer monitor in which all information is represented in black and white, or with a range of grays.

Montage

A single image formed by assembling or compositing several images.

Morphing

Short for metamorphosis. Using a computer to animate the gradual transformation of one image into another.

Multimedia

The combination of sound, video images and text to create a moving presentation.

Network

Two or more computers that are linked to exchange data or share resources. The Internet is a network of networks.

NAB

Acronym for the National Association of Broadcasters

Neutral

Any color that has no hue, such as white, gray or black.

Neutral Density

A measurement of the lightness or darkness of a color. A neutral density of zero (0.00) is the lightest value possible and is equivalent to pure white; 3.294 is roughly equivalent to 100% of each of the CMYK components.

Noise

Unwanted signals or data that may reduce the quality of output. On television it looks like snow.

Normal Key

A description of an image in which the main interest area is in the middle range of the tone scale or distributed throughout the entire tonal range.

Nonlinear Editing

Using a computer for instant random access to and easy rearrangements of shots. The video and audio information is stored in digital form on high-capacity computer hard drives or read/write laser videodiscs.

NTSC

Stands for National Television System Committee. Normally designates the composite television signal, using RGB.

Nudge

To move a graphic or text element in small, preset increments, usually with the arrow keys.

Object-oriented art

Vector-based artwork composed of separate elements or shapes described mathematically rather than by specifying the color and position of every point. This is in contrast to bitmap images, which are composed of individual pixels.

Oblique

A slanted character (sometimes backwards, or to the left), often used when referring to italic versions of sans-serif typefaces.

Offline Editing

Produces an EDL (edit decision list) or a videotape not intended for broadcast.

Omnidirectional

Pickup pattern in which the microphone can pick up sounds equally well from all directions.

Online Editing

Produces the final high-quality edit master tape for broadcast or program duplication.

Opacity

1. The degree to which paper will show print through it. 2. The degree to which images or text below one object, whose opacity has been adjusted, are able to show through.

Optical Disks

Video disks that store large amounts of data used primarily for reference works, such as dictionaries and encyclopedias.

Output device

Any hardware equipment, such as a monitor, laser printer, or imagesetter, that depicts text or graphics created on a computer.

Over-the-shoulder Shot (O/S)

Camera looks over one person's shoulder at what that individual would see.

Palette

1. As derived from the term in the traditional art world, a collection of selectable colors. 2. Another name for a dialog box or menu of choices.

Pan

Horizontal turning of the camera during shooting. The base remains stationary.

Pasteboard

In a page-layout program, the desktop area outside of the printing-page area, on which elements can be placed for later positioning on any page.

PCX

Bitmap image format produced by paint programs.

PDF (Portable Document Format)

Developed by Adobe Systems, Inc. (read by Acrobat Reader), this format has become a de facto standard for document transfer across platforms.

Pedestal

Camera dolly that permits raising and lowering the camera while shooting.

Performer

A person who appears on-camera in nondramatic shows. The performer plays him or herself and does not assume any other role. Example: a gameshow host.

Perspective

The effect of distance in an image, achieved by aligning the edges of elements with imaginary lines directed toward one to three "vanishing points" on the horizon.

PICT/PICT2

A common format for defining bitmapped images on the Macintosh. The more recent PICT2 format supports 24-bit color.

Pixel

Abbreviation for picture element. One of the tiny rectangular areas or dots generated by a computer or output device to constitute images. If a pixel is "turned on," it has color or shading. If it is "turned off," it looks like a blank space. Pixels can vary in size from one type of monitor or printer to another. A greater number of pixels per inch results in higher resolution on screen or in print.

Plot

1. The sequence of events in a story. 2. To plan out such a sequence.

Point

A unit of measurement used to specify type size and rule weight, equal to (approximately, in traditional typesetting) 1/72 inch. Note: font sizes are measured differently from leading, even though they're both specified in points. The only way you can verify font size on your hard copy is by measuring it against the designated sizes you'll find on an E-scale.

Point of View (POV)

The perspective of an individual.

Polygon

A geometric figure, consisting of three or more straight lines enclosing an area. The triangle, square, rectangle and star are all polygons.

Posterize, Posterization

1. Deliberate constraint of a gradient or image into visible steps as a special effect. 2. Unintentional creation of steps in an image due to a high LPI value used with a low printer DPI.

Postproduction

Any production activity that occurs after the production. Usually refers to either videotape editing or audio sweetening.

Postproduction Editing

The assembly of recorded material after the actual production.

PostScript

1. A page-description language, developed by Adobe Systems, Inc., that describes type and/or images and their positional relationships upon the page. 2. An interpreter or RIP (see Raster Image Processor) that can process the PostScript page description into a format for laser printer or imagesetter output. 3. A computer-programming language.

PostScript Printer Description file

(PPD) Acronym for PostScript Printer Description, a file format developed by Adobe Systems, Inc., that contains device-specific information enabling software to produce the best results possible for each type of designated printer.

Pot

Short for potentiometer, a sound-volume control.

Preferences

A set of modifiable defaults for an application program.

Preproduction

Preparation of all production details.

Preroll

To start a videotape and let it roll for a few seconds before it is put in the playback or record mode so that the electronic system has time to stabilize.

Primary Colors

Colors that can be used to generate secondary colors. For the additive system (i.e., a computer monitor), these colors are red, green and blue. For the subtractive system (i.e., the printing process), these colors are yellow, magenta and cyan.

Printer driver

The device that communicates between your software program and your printer. When you're using an application, the printer driver tells the application what the printer can do, and also tells the printer how to print the publication.

Producer

Creator and organizer of films or television shows .

Production Schedule

A plan that shows the time periods of various activities during the production day. Also called a "timeline."

Program

1. A specific television show. 2. A sequence of instructions, encoded in a specific computer language, for performing predetermined tasks.

Program Proposal

Written document that outlines the process message and the major aspects of a television presentation.

Project

A single Premiere file that describes a video work. It stores references to all clips in that file as well as information about how they are arranged. It also includes details of any transitions or effects applied.

Props

Short for properties. Furniture and objects employed for set decoration. Used by actors or performers.

Que

A set of files input to the printer, printed in the order received unless otherwise instructed.

RAM

Random Access Memory, the "work-ing" memory of a computer that holds files in process. Files in RAM are lost when the computer is turned off, whereas files stored on the hard drive or floppy disks remain available.

Raster

A bitmapped representation of graphic data.

Raster Graphics

A class of graphics created and organized in a rectangular array of bitmaps. Often created by paint software, fax machines or scanners for display and printing.

Rasterize

The process of converting digital information into pixels at the resolu-tion of the output device. For example, the process used by an imagesetter to translate PostScript files before they are imaged to film or paper.

Remote

A large television production shot outside the studio.

Render

A real-time preview of clips and all effects as your production plays.

Resolution

The density of graphic information expressed in dots per inch (dpi) or pixels per inch (ppi).

Reverberation

Technically, reflections of a sound wave after the sound source has ceased vibrating. Perceived as audio echo.

RGB

1. Acronym for red, green, blue — the colors of projected light from a computer monitor that, when combined, simulate a subset of the visual spectrum. When a color image is scanned, RGB data is collected by the scanner and then converted to CMYK data at a later step in the process. 2. Also refers to the color model of most digital artwork. See also CMYK.

Right Alignment

Text having a straight right edge and a ragged or uneven left edge.

Ripple Edit

Trims a specific clip, keeping all of the other clips intact. The additional clips are pushed or pulled into position.

Roll

1. Graphics (usually credit copy) that move slowly up the screen, often called crawl. 2. The command to start a videotape.

ROM

Read Only Memory, a semiconductor chip in the computer that retains startup information for use the next time the computer is turned on.

Rotation

Turning an object at some angle to its original axis.

Rough Cut

The first tentative arrangement of shots and shot sequences in the approximate order and length. Done in offline editing.

RTF

Rich Text Format, a text format that retains formatting information lost in pure ASCII text.

Rules

Straight lines, often stretching horizontally across the top of a page to separate text from running heads.

Running Time

The duration of a program or a program segment.

Run-through

Rehearsal before a shoot.

Safe Title Area

See Essential Area.

Sans Serif

Fonts that do not have serifs. See Serif.

Saturation

The intensity or purity of a color; a color with no saturation is gray.

Scaling

The means within a program to reduce or enlarge the amount of space an image will occupy by multiplying the data by a factor. Scaling can be proportional, or in one dimension only.

Scanner

A device that electronically digitizes images point by point through circuits that can correct color, manipulate tones and enhance detail. Color scanners usually produce a minimum of 24 bits for each pixel, and 8 bits each for red, green and blue.

Scene

Event details that form an organic unit, usually in a single place and time. A series of organically related shots that depict these event details.

Scenery

Background flats and other pieces (windows, doors, pillars) that simulate a specific environment.

Schedule Time

Shows the clock time at the beginning or the end of a program or program segment.

Scoop

A scooplike television floodlight.

Screen Shot

A printed output or saved file that represents data from a computer monitor.

Scrim

1. Lighting: a spun-glass material that is put in front of a light to diffuse the brightness. 2. Scenery: a soft material placed behind the actors to give a uniform background.

Script

Written document that tells what the program is about, who is in it, what is supposed to happen, and how the audience will view the event. The text of a production.

Scrub

Advancing or reversing a clip manually. Enables you to identify and mark events precisely.

Select

Place the cursor on an object and click the mouse button to make the object active.

Sequencing

The control and structuring of a shot sequence during editing.

Serif

A line or curve projecting from the end of a letterform. Typefaces designed with such projections are called serif faces.

Set

Arrangement of scenery and properties to indicate the locale and/or mood of a show.

Shade

A color mixed with black. A 10% shade is one part of the original color and nine parts black. See Tint.

Sharpness

The subjective impression of the density difference between two tones at their boundary, interpreted as fineness of detail.

Shortcut

1. A quick method for accessing a menu item or command, usually through a series of keystrokes. 2. The icon that can be created in Windows95 to open an application without having to penetrate layers of various folders. The equivalent in the Macintosh is the "alias."

Shotgun Microphone

A highly directional microphone for picking up sounds over great distances.

Shot Sheet

List of every shot a particular camera has to obtain. It is attached to the camera to help the camera operator remember a shot sequence.

Show Format

Lists the show segments in order of appearance. Used in routine shows, such as daily game or interview shows.

Silhouette

To remove part of the background of a photograph or illustration, leaving only the desired portion.

Skew

A transformation command that slants an object at an angle to the side from its initial fixed base.

Slate

1. Visual and/or verbal identification of each videotaped segment. 2. A little blackboard upon which essential information is written, such as the show title or take number. It is recorded at the beginning of each take.

Slow Motion

A scene in which the objects appear to be moving more slowly than normal. In television, slow motion is achieved by slowing down the playback speed of the tape, which results in multiple scanning of each television frame.

Small caps

A type style in which lowercase letters are replaced by uppercase letters set in a smaller point size.

SMPTE/EBU Timecode

An electronic signal recorded on the cue or address track of the videotape or on an audio track of a multitrack audiotape through a timecode generator. It provides a time address for each frame in hours, minutes, seconds and frame numbers in elapsed time.

Sound Bite

Brief portion of someone's on-camera statement.

Source Videotape

The tape with the original footage in an editing operation.

Special-effects Controls

Buttons on a switcher that regulate special effects. They include buttons for specific functions, such as wipes and key effects.

Split Screen

Multiple image effect caused by stopping a directional wipe before its completion. Both shots are on the screen for a period of time.

Spotlight

A lighting instrument that produces directional, relatively undiffused light with a fairly well defined beam.

Stand-by

A warning cue for any kind of action in television production.

Stock Shot

A shot of a common occurrence: clouds, crowds, cars, etc. They are generally generic and are usually available for rental or purchase from agencies.

Storyboard

A series of sketches of the key visualization points of an event along with audio information. Often includes camera angles, any camera movement and key phrases from script.

Style

A set of formatting instructions for font, paragraphing, tabs and other properties of text.

Subscript

Small-size characters set below the normal letters or figures, usually to convey technical information.

Subtractive Color

Color which is observed when light strikes pigments or dyes which absorb certain wavelengths of light. The light that is reflected back is perceived as a color.

Super

Short for superimposition. The simultaneous showing of two pictures on the same screen.

System Folder

The location of the operating system files on a Macintosh.

S-VHS

Stands for supervideo home system. A high quality 1/2 inch VHS system that meets broadcast standards.

Sweetening

Variety of quality adjustments of recorded sound in postproduction.

Switcher

1. Technical crew member working the video switcher (usually the technical director). 2. A panel with rows of buttons that allow the selection and assembly of various video sources through a variety of transition devices, and the creation of electronic special effects.

Switching

A change from one video source to another during a show or show segment with the aid of a switcher. Also called instantaneous editing.

Sync

Electronic pulses that synchronize the scanning between the origination source (live cameras, videotape) and the reproduction sources (monitor or television receiver), and other vital electronic functions between electronic equipment, such as video tape recorders.

Tagged Image File Format (TIFF)

A common format for used for scanned or computer-generated bitmapped images.

Take

1. Signal for a cut from one video source to another. 2. Any one of similar and repeated shots taken during videotaping and filming. 3. Sometimes take is used synonymously with shot. A good take is the successful completion of a shot, a show segment or the videotaping of the whole show. A bad take is an unsuccessful recording, requiring another recording.

Talent

Collective name for all performers and actors who appear regularly on television or in a production.

Target Audience

The audience selected or desired to receive a specific message.

Telephoto Lens

An optical device that gives a narrow, close-up view of an event relatively far away from the camera. Also called long focal length lens or narrow angle lens.

Teleprompter

A prompting device that projects the moving (usually computer generated) copy over the lens so that the talent can read it without losing eye contact with the viewer.

Text

The characters and words that form the main body of a publication.

Texture

1. A property of the surface of the substrate, such as the smoothness of paper. 2. Graphically, variation in tonal values to form image detail. 3. A class of fills in a graphics application that give various appearances, such as bricks, grass, etc.

Thumbnails

1. The preliminary sketches of a design. 2. Small images used to indicate the content of a computer file.

Theme

1. What the story is all about; its essential idea. 2. The opening and closing music in a show.

Three Shot

Framing of three people.

Tilt

The up and down movement of the camera, the base remains stationary.

TIFF
(Tagged Image File Format)

A popular graphics format. See Tagged Image File Format.

Tile

1. A type of repeating fill pattern. 2. Reproduce a number of pages of a document on one sheet. 3. Printing a large document overlapping on several smaller sheets of paper.

Timecode

Electronic signal that provides a specific and unique address for each electronic frame.

Time Cues

Cues to the talent about time remaining in the show.

Tint

1. A halftone area that contains dots of uniform size, that is, no modeling or texture. 2. The mixture of a color with white: a 10% tint is one part of the original color and nine parts black.

Toggle

A command that switches between either of two states at each application. Switching between Hide and Show is a toggle.

Tracking

Adjusting the spacing of letters in a line of text to achieve proper justification or general appearance. You may want to squeeze letters closer together to fit into a frame, or spread them apart for a special effect.

Transition

The change from one video clip to another. Premiere provides an extensive assortment of transitions, including cuts, dissolves, blurs, blends, wipes, zooms and many more.

Treatment

Brief narrative description of a television program or other production.

Trim

To refine or make adjustments to the in and out points of a clip.

Tripod

Three-legged camera mount, usually connected to a dolly for easy movement of the camera.

Truck

To move the camera laterally by means of a mobile camera mount.

TrueType

An outline font format, on both Macintosh and Windows systems, that can be used both on the screen and on a printer.

Two Shot

Framing two people in a shot.

Type 1 Fonts

PostScript fonts, based on Bézier curves and encrypted for compactness, that are compatible with Adobe Type Manager.

Type Family

A set of typefaces created from the same basic design but in different weights, such as bold, light, italic, book and heavy.

Typo

An abbreviation for typographical error. A keystroke error in the typeset copy.

Uppercase

The capital letters of a typeface as opposed to the lowercase, or small, letters. When type was hand composited, the capital letters resided in the upper part of the type case.

Utility

Software that performs ancillary tasks, such as counting words, defragmenting a hard drive or restoring a deleted file.

Vector Graphics

Graphics defined using coordinate points, and mathematically drawn lines and curves, which may be freely scaled and rotated without image degradation in the final output. Fonts (such as PostScript and TrueType), and illustrations from drawing applications are common examples of vector objects. Two commonly used vector drawing programs are Adobe Illustrator and Macromedia FreeHand. A class of graphics that overcomes the resolution limitation of bitmapped graphics.

Vertical Justification

The ability to automatically adjust the interline spacing (leading) to make columns and pages end at the same point on a page.

VHS

Stands for video home system. A consumer-oriented 1/2-in. VCR system. Now used extensively in all phases of television production for previewing and off line editing.

Video

1. Picture portion of a television program. 2. Non-broadcast production activities.

Videocassette

A plastic container in which a videotape moves from supply to take-up reel, recording and playing back program segments through a videotape recorder.

Videotape

A plastic, iron-oxide coated tape of various widths for recording video and audio signals as well as additional technical code information.

Videotape Recorder (VTR)

Electronic recording device that records video and audio signals on videotape for later playback or postproduction editing.

Video Tracks

Most videotape formats have a video track, two or more audio tracks and a separate timecode track.

Viewfinder

An electronic device at the back of a camera that gives a representation of the shot being taken.

Visible Spectrum

The wavelengths of light between about 380 nm (violet) and 700 nm (red) that are visible to the human eye.

Visualization

Mentally converting a scene into a number of key images. The mental image of a shot. The images do not need to be sequenced at that time.

Volume

The relative loudness or softness of a sound.

Walk Through

A rehearsal without taping. The director explains to both the talent and the camera operators what will take place during the actual shoot.

White Light

Light containing all wavelengths of the visible spectrum. Also known as 5000°K lighting.

White Space

Areas on the page which contain no images or type. Proper use of white space is critical to a well balanced design.

Wipe

Transition in which a second image, framed in some geometrical shape, gradually replaces all or part of the first one.

WYSIWYG

An acronym for "What You See Is What You Get." (Pronounced "wizzywig.") Means that what you see on your computer screen bears a strong resemblance to what the job will look like when it is printed.

Zooming

The process of electronically enlarging or reducing an image on a monitor to facilitate detailed design or editing and navigation.

INDEX